Money, Elections, and Democracy

Money, Elections, and Democracy

Reforming Congressional Campaign Finance

EDITED BY
Margaret Latus Nugent and
John R. Johannes

The Bradley Institute for Democracy and Public Values, Marquette University

Westview Press
BOULDER, SAN FRANCISCO, & OXFORD

JK
1991
.M75
1990

This Westview softcover edition is printed on acid-free paper and bound in library-quality, coated covers that carry the highest rating of the National Association of State Textbook Administrators, in consultation with the Association of American Publishers and the Book Manufacturers' Institute.

All rights reserved. No part of this publication may be reproduced or transmitted in any form or by any means, electronic or mechanical, including photocopy, recording, or any information storage and retrieval system, without permission in writing from the publisher.

Copyright © 1990 by Westview Press, Inc.

Published in 1990 in the United States of America by Westview Press, Inc., 5500 Central Avenue, Boulder, Colorado 80301, and in the United Kingdom by Westview Press, Inc., 36 Lonsdale Road, Summertown, Oxford OX2 7EW

Library of Congress Cataloging-in-Publication Data
Money, elections, and democracy : reforming congressional campaign finance / edited by Margaret Latus Nugent and John R. Johannes.
p. cm.
ISBN 0-8133-7891-5
1. Campaign funds—United States. I. Nugent, Margaret Latus, 1958- . II. Johannes, John R., 1943-
JK1991.M75 1990
324.7'8'0973—dc20 90-30294
CIP

Printed and bound in the United States of America

The paper used in this publication meets the requirements of the American National Standard for Permanence of Paper for Printed Library Materials Z39.48-1984.

10 9 8 7 6 5 4 3 2 1

Contents

Acknowledgments

We are deeply indebted to the Bradley Institute for Democracy and Public Values of Marquette University for its support of this book. The insights of Leon D. Epstein, Linda Fowler, Benjamin Ginsberg, Stephen E. Gottlieb, Brooks Jackson, Gary Jacobson, Michael J. Malbin, Susan Manes, Ellen S. Miller, Daniel J. Swillinger, and John C. Wright were invaluable in formulating our conclusions. The Institute's Director, Thomas E. Hachey, and our spouses, Frances S. Johannes and James A. Nugent, provided technical and personal support for this project. Finally, Dawn Crowley, Catherine Mitchell, and Audra Schmidkonz assisted with many details. John C. Horgan masterfully prepared the manuscript for publication, and Susan Spoerk and Norman N. Gill assisted with proofreading.

Margaret Latus Nugent
John R. Johannes

1

Introduction: What Is at Stake?

Margaret Latus Nugent and John R. Johannes

"Too much money is being given by special interest PACs. Too much money is being spent by candidates. Too much influence is being exercised through political money. The scandalous way in which congressional campaigns are financed is threatening our representative system of government—a government of, by and for the people." [1]

"Free and fair elections, it seems, are prescriptions the U.S. urges upon others. In this country, however, the system is deliberately rigged to favor those already in power. And glaring campaign-finance loopholes are further stretched enough to accommodate even Boss Tweed." [2]

"When politicians start to see a dollar sign behind every vote, every phone call, every solicitation, those other factors sometimes weighed during governance, like the public good and equal access to government, become less and less important." [3]

"When 99.2 percent of all incumbents get re-elected, many of them without opposition, there is more than the PAC issue at stake. Democracy is at stake." [4]

The ink on the post-Watergate campaign finance reforms was barely dry when challenges to the new laws arose, loopholes opened, and calls for new and better reforms sounded. Lacking a campaign finance scandal of the scope of Teapot Dome or Watergate, the Eighties might well be characterized as a pre-malignant era with hints of corruption, widening loopholes, and compounding criticisms of common campaign finance practices. Reform proposals multiplied in response to concern that a scandal was threatening and needed to be averted.

Even a very brief survey of criticisms of congressional campaign finance in the 1980s highlights these concerns among journalists, political activists, and legislators. Elizabeth Drew claims that politicians are being driven to new forms of corruption, are being hampered in their ability to govern, are circumventing the spirit of campaign finance laws through numerous loopholes, and are no longer the safeguards of our representative democracy.[5] Philip Stern has summarized the gist of his criticism in the title of his book: *The Best Congress Money Can Buy*.[6] "Honest graft" is Brooks Jackson's characterization of congressional campaign financing.[7]

Throughout the 1980s, books, newspaper articles, and popular news magazines increasingly have been charging that current practices in financing congressional elections: (a) reduce competition, guaranteeing the re-election of incumbents; (b) nationalize political influence, undermining the local ties of representatives; (c) weaken the political parties, contributing to the "Balkanization" and polarization of Congress; (d) promote legislative corruption and fundraising fraud; and (e) perpetuate numerous other abuses and loopholes that violate the spirit of the Federal Election Campaign Act. For example, a single issue of *U.S. News and World Report* contained articles on campaign financing entitled: "A Case of Legal Corruption," "What Dollars Can Buy," and "The Dirty Big Secret of Campaign Finance."[8]

The media are not alone in their concerns. For over twenty years, Common Cause, the self-styled citizens' lobby, has pushed for campaign finance reform. More recently, it has been joined in its efforts by other think tanks and interest groups such as Democracy Project, The Center for Responsive Politics, and Citizens Against PACs. Members of Congress have joined the attack. A survey of members of Congress in 1987 indicated that almost half admitted that fundraising duties cut into the time they devote to legislative work. Forty-three percent said that PACs have had a negative or somewhat negative effect on the operations of Congress. At least one-third were concerned that the current campaign finance system makes representatives less inclined to compromise on legislative issues. One Member claimed that incumbents are responsible for extorting money from PACs. Another complained that "PACs and interest group contributions have led to the 'Balkanization' into separate little power fiefdoms."[9] Not surprisingly, Congress has responded with reams of legislation on campaign financing.

Campaign Finance Reforms in the Progressive Tradition

Concerns about campaign financing are not new in American

politics, often giving rise to reform movements. Since 1907, the "persistent populist Progressive predispositions of Americans"[10] have led to changes in our campaign finance system that were designed to achieve a series of goals: (1) Oppose the influence of money on the behavior of those elected; (2) assure that "narrow interests" do not prevail over the "public good;" (3) prohibit money from distorting the integrity of elections; (4) prevent the unequal distribution of wealth from undermining political equality; and (5) require "open government" that precludes secrecy in raising and spending campaign funds.

The first federal laws of this century focused on the potential for campaign funds to corrupt the activities of government. The Tillman Act of 1907 was passed in response to allegations that contributions to Teddy Roosevelt's 1904 presidential campaign were given in exchange for protection from "trust busting."[11] The Tillman Act's restriction on corporations' contributions to federal elections was extended to labor unions in the 1943 Smith-Connally Act, which was followed by the 1947 Taft-Hartley permanent ban on such contributions. A second approach to preventing *quid pro quos* has been to place limits on the size of contributions from individuals to candidates. Such limits were enacted as part of the Federal Corrupt Practices Act of 1925 and the 1940 Hatch Act, although loopholes were commonplace and enforcement rare.

Contribution limits actually became a potentially effective protection against the corruption of government after the Federal Election Campaign Act Amendments of 1974, which included the creation of the Federal Election Commission to oversee enforcement. The FECA limited individual contributions to $1,000 per candidate per election (with a total limit of $25,000 per year), and PAC contributions to $5,000 per candidate per election (with no aggregate limit). The 1974 Act also restricted independent spending on behalf of or against candidates to $1,000 for individuals, a limitation subsequently struck down by *Buckley v. Valeo.*[12] Finally, in response to abuses in the 1972 election (such as large contributions from the dairy industry in exchange for price supports), the 1974 Act established a method for public funding of presidential elections.

The same concern about corruption undergirded the Supreme Court's decision in *Buckley* to uphold most of the 1974 Amendments. According to the Court, the only appropriate legislative goal justifying restricting political liberty in campaign spending is to prevent corruption or the appearance of corruption. Corruption itself was narrowly understood as contributions "given to secure a political *quid pro quo* from current and potential office holders...."[13]

A Progressive populist corollary to concerns over special favors has run through reform debates: the fear that "narrow interests" could distort the legislative and regulatory agenda against the interests of the "public good." James Madison's classic articulation in *Federalist 10* shows the enduring nature of this issue: "By faction I understand a number of citizens, whether amounting to a majority or minority of the whole, who are united and actuated by some common impulse of passion, or of interest, adverse to the rights of other citizens or to the permanent and aggregate interests of the community."[14] The fear of special control has led to limits on campaign contributions, and, in 1940, to the Hatch Act, which forbade individuals or businesses working for the government to contribute to federal elections. Recent critics insist that more needs to be done to protect the public from plundering by the special interests.

Reformers have feared that the corruptive danger of money extends beyond its potential for altering public policy. They worry that spending in elections might distort the integrity of the electoral process itself, ultimately determining the outcome of elections. Naturally, legislators have opposed blatant violations such as vote buying, as with the 1918 prohibition against bribery in federal elections.[15] Reforms from 1911 to 1974 have also tried to protect the fairness of elections by placing spending limits on the campaigns themselves. The Federal Election Campaign Act of 1971 also imposed a limit on what candidates could spend on their own behalf, and the 1974 Amendments retained this limit.

The Supreme Court's view of the importance of maintaining the integrity of elections has been mixed, however. On one hand, the decision upholding the Federal Corrupt Practices Act of 1925 stated, "To say that Congress is without power to pass appropriate legislation to safeguard such an election from the improper use of money to influence the result is to deny the nation in a vital particular the power of self protection."[16] On the other hand, in striking down the 1974 FECA's limits on campaign expenditures and limits on what candidates can spend on their own behalf, the Court stepped away from the concerns of *Burroughs*. In fact, a later decision that corporations are not precluded from spending public funds on referenda and ballot issues rests on the

logic that such expenditures represent free speech and cannot be corruptive even though they may influence the outcome of such campaigns.[17]

Enhancing political equality has been a fourth concern of the Progressive tradition, as many of the campaign finance reforms discussed above also illustrate. The general objection is that the unequal distribution of wealth can undermine political equality because the "haves" use their resources to gain more political clout than the "have nots." Such clout then becomes the means to guarantee even more economic advantages to the wealthy. Egalitarianism has stood behind movements for public financing of elections, limits on contributions as well as total campaign spending, and restrictions on how much candidates can spend on their own behalf.[18] Recently, however, the Supreme Court has rejected the legislative goal of "equalizing the relative ability of individuals and groups to influence the outcomes of elections,"[19] suggesting that, in the eyes of the Court, the value of political equality is secondary to that of political liberty.

The last Progressive value that has found expression in campaign finance laws throughout the century is the distrust of secrecy, expressed in requirements to make public the sources and uses of campaign funds. Disclosure of the financing of congressional elections was first required in 1910 and 1911.[20] The reporting of sources of campaign funds in federal elections was strengthened by the Federal Corrupt Practices Act of 1925 and extended to primary elections by the Hatch Act of 1940. As with other aspects of these laws, however, disclosure was inadequate because of the lack of an enforcement process and the prevalence of loopholes. Replacing the Federal Corrupt Practices Act, the Federal Election Campaign Act of 1971 placed more stringent requirements for reporting and disclosure on all candidates for federal office. More importantly, the creation of the Federal Election Commission in the 1974 Amendments actually provided for an agency to help publicize these reports as well as to enforce the laws requiring disclosure.

Despite the wealth of data made available by the FEC, some current critics charge that problems with secrecy remain. The most obvious case is the use of "soft money" contributions from corporations, labor unions, and individuals used for party building activities in the states.[21]

Articulating Values

As this brief historical sketch shows, campaign finance is important because of its effect on our electoral system and on our representative democracy in general. Elections institutionalize social conflict; select governmental officials and hold them accountable to the public; express citizen preferences about policies and candidates; educate citizens; provide legitimacy to the government, and preserve for the ruled the final control over their rulers.[22] Thus, whatever affects elections also influences core democratic values. This book, therefore, is concerned with how the existing system of congressional campaign financing and proposals for its reform affect key values.

Which values matter? Since, above all, governments must govern, systemic *effectiveness* is essential. So is *legitimacy*, defined as the public's acceptance of the government. In democratic systems, other values become important: *representation, accountability, political liberty, political equality*, and *participation.* Obviously, these values are required for all governmental institutions and practices, but they are essential in the electoral system. That system best incorporates these values when it is *competitive*—when voters, with equal and free votes participate in an act of choosing among those candidates who, in their judgments, best represent their policy preferences.

Governmental Effectiveness

Governments need to be able to act. Thus, obstacles to governmental effectiveness should be viewed critically. Can elections and campaign finance hinder effectiveness? Yes, argues David R. Mayhew. The end (government) has been manipulated into serving the means toward that end (election). Much of Congress, he claims, has been structured to promote the goal of re-election, to the detriment of the institution's ability to govern.[23] Add to Mayhew's argument Jacobson's claim that campaign financing operates as a "natural selection" process to alter the type of candidates who predominate: those who play the pork barrel game, cultivate constituents, serve local interests, and rely extensively on PAC money, all at the expense of effective national policymaking.[24] What we may be faced with is Walter Dean Burnham's "governability crisis," the lack of governmental capacity to act.[25]

What we need instead is a Congress in which members accept not only their obligations to constituents, but their responsibility to the legislature. Such responsibility includes doing one's

share of the legislative work, accepting responsibility for the output of Congress, disciplining the improper acts of colleagues, and correcting the structural defects of the system that inhibit effectiveness.[26] Presumably, these defects include obstacles to the congressional capacity to govern effectively.

Despite the importance of effectiveness, an efficient tyranny would not promote the values of democracy. Legitimacy is also crucial. The historical concern of campaign finance legislation to prevent corruption, coupled with increasing public cynicism about the credibility of campaign finance laws and the disruption of the electoral and representative process, suggests that preserving the legitimacy of government is a fundamental goal for a campaign financing system. Some evidence indicates that citizens are growing wary. For example, a 1980 poll showed 71 percent agreeing that "PACs are pouring too much money into the whole political process." In 1982, 84 percent of those queried agreed that "those who contribute large sums of money have too much influence over the government," and 62 percent believed "the excessive campaign spending in national elections" was a "very serious problem."[27] If elections legitimize the authority of government,[28] certainly our system of financing elections must not undercut that legitimacy.

Governmental effectiveness and legitimacy have a symbiotic relationship. The more Congress is perceived to be legitimate, the more likely its laws are to be respected and obeyed—hence, effective. Conversely, the more effective Congress is in acting, the more respect citizens have for its legitimacy as an institution.

Representation and Accountability

The closely interrelated values of representation and accountability protect the democratic features of Congress. Representation requires a correspondence between the characteristics, interests, political attitudes (ideological and partisan), and policy preferences of representatives and their constituencies.[29] Accountability means that the ruled have channels of control over their rulers—not necessarily to dictate every action, but to provide a means of influence and evaluation of their actions overall. Though most discussions of representation and accountability intermingle the two terms, we distinguish them for several reasons: It is possible to have a government that is highly representative of its citizens (such as one drawn by lot) that has no channels for accountability, such as free elections. One can also have a government or organization that has many mechanisms of accountability but fails adequately to represent or consider the needs of minority interests or—owing to poor information, even majority concerns. Finally, the promotion of each of these values places different demands upon our electoral and campaign finance system.

Accountability and representation are systemic values that should characterize our democratic government, but the following discussion explores how elections and election finances should exemplify these values in addition to fostering them generally.

In an electoral system, representation requires a correspondence between the candidates and those who fund and elect them. Thus, an ideal system for financing campaigns should select and fund candidates who represent the policy preferences, interests, partisanship, and ideologies of their geographic constituency. But what of the views of minorities who are unable to elect appropriate candidates in their own districts? Virtual representation might be provided by allowing contributors to fund candidates in other districts who reflect their interests and concerns.[30] For example, Republicans in the previously solidly Democratic South, or liberals in conservative Orange County, or any minority in a district where the opposing majority routinely dominates the elections could contribute to PACs or to candidates in other districts who are more akin to their political philosophy, leading to the representation of viewpoints that might otherwise be overlooked. Precisely for such reasons, advocates of stronger political parties often argue the virtue of national representation via parties. Regardless of the district election results, national divisions of ideology and party loyalty should be reflected in the aggregate make-up of Congress. Some consideration also should be given to funding candidates who can represent the interests of various ethnic, racial, gender, socio-economic, and religious groups, even if these candidates do not share these characteristics themselves. Finally, a campaign finance system that truly promotes representation would not select and fund candidates whose views corresponded only with those of contributors, but also with those of the bulk of the citizenry. If contributors and non-contributors are essentially alike, no problem should arise. If they differ, some concerns about representation may be in order.

Accountability refers to the channels of control that constituents have over those who claim to represent them.[31] It is not only the elected official who must be accountable. Those orga-

nizations which serve as mediators in campaign funding—PACs and political parties—must also accurately and accountably reflect the views and wishes of those they claim to represent. Members need mechanisms by which they can evaluate the actions and actors of their leaders and express their satisfaction or dissatisfaction. Implementing the following kinds of accountability will differ for Members of Congress as opposed to the leaders of PACs and party organizations, but the ideals apply to all: First, supporters/constituents should have opportunities to express their policy preferences.[32] Another type of accountability provides a forum for interaction between supporters/constituents and their leadership or representatives.[33] A third conception of accountability involves evaluating the actions of the institution as a whole (Congress or the political organization) rather than individual actors. This sort of accountability is fostered by a responsible party system that allows the electorate to vote the "ins" out, or by diversity among political organizations that provides alternative groups for one to join if one is dissatisfied with the actions of the one currently supported. The most basic way to assure the accountability of representatives—elected or not—is that of withholding crucial resources: votes, contributions, voluntary services, and membership itself.[34] Hirshman calls this method of accountability the right of "exit"—expressing dissatisfaction with an organization by refusing to continue to support it.[35]

An important requirement for accountability is accurate information about the activities of the leaders or representatives. Undistorted knowledge of the actions and policy preferences of those who act on one's behalf is a prerequisite for judging whether they merit continued support. Full disclosure of the sources and uses of political funds by candidates and political organizations allows contributors and the electorate at large to assess how well they think their representatives, elected or otherwise, are remaining accountable to them. Has the PAC been responsible in its allocation of resources? Does it accurately reflect the views of its supporters? Or does it generate distorted independent expenditure advertisements for which it is accountable to no one, not even its supporters? On the other hand, have campaign contributions from special interests or citizens outside the district significantly focused the attention of candidates on interests other than those of their constituents? Where PAC contributions simply reflect the industries and interests that predominate in the district, they may not alter the accountability of representatives to their most basic constituency. But, as Frank Sorauf argues, "The people who give the resources... are increasingly different from the people who vote in the election."[36] If so, accountability may be at risk.

Political Liberty

Any restrictions on campaign spending must incorporate the Supreme Court's ruling that spending is constitutionally protected free speech.[37] The protection of free speech was the central objection opponents raised to the 1974 Amendments to the Federal Election Campaign Act. In accepting the argument that "money is speech and speech is money," the Court in *Buckley* established a strong precedent against limiting contributions and expenditures in elections, although not all restrictions were struck down. Looking beyond free speech, restrictions on the organization and activities of PACs and/or political parties might similarly be considered to impinge upon the First Amendment right of political association. Although these liberties are considered essential for the preservation of democracy, they should not be deemed absolute. Rather, any restrictions ought to promote other compelling public values, such as legitimacy, effectiveness, or accountability.

Political Equality

The public value most often cited as conflicting with that of political liberty is that of equality. Robert E. Mutch notes that egalitarian concerns underlay most limits on political contributions and expenditures enacted from 1911 to 1974.[38] If one views campaign spending not purely as free speech but as speech that influences and enhances votes, then one might share Alexander Heard's conclusion "that people who give in larger sums or to more candidates than their fellow citizens are in effect voting more than once."[39]

Several difficulties arise when considering how to promote political equality. One is the tension already noted between equality and liberty. Second, one must decide between formal equality (for example, the equal right to make political contributions) and substantive equality (adjusting for the unequal distribution of economic resources that can make formal equality essentially meaningless). The rich and poor may be equally free to contribute to elections, but, as Sen. Robert Dole (R-Kansas) has said, "There aren't any poor PACs or Food Stamp

PACs...."[40] Failure to promote economic equality can actually result in decreasing political liberty in circumstances where individuals lack the resources to exercise their rights. Third is the question of whether to promote equal opportunity or equal outcomes, with the latter being impossible to maintain.[41] These theoretical dilemmas cannot be resolved here, but they must be acknowledged, for they will doubtless appear in some form in debates over the ideal system of campaign financing.

Citizen Participation

Participation in elections is generally considered of value for several reasons. It provides a mechanism for citizen control of government, decreases the likelihood that certain interests are being overlooked in the policy-making processes, and enhances the perceived legitimacy of the government.[42] Additionally, Mill argues that an extended suffrage is important because it promotes the political education of the public and increases their concern for the common welfare.[43] More widespread participation also enhances representation, if new views are heard thereby.

Extending the concept of participation to include campaign contributions, independent expenditures, or other campaign activities should serve to supplement the voice that citizens have in elections through their votes. Broadening participation in financing campaigns may reduce the likelihood of the interests of the disadvantaged being overlooked by policy-makers. More widespread involvement by citizens, coupled with limits on contributions, can promote the legitimacy of the government by reducing the appearance that representatives are beholden to wealthy contributors or special interests. Finally, financing campaigns enhances the citizen's psychological investment in the outcome of the election.

More participation is not necessarily better. First, if those who already participate adequately represent the concerns of nonparticipants as well, then more involvement will not improve matters. In fact, some have argued that political apathy also benefits democracy.[44] More importantly, any participation based on distorted information and faulty reasoning can prove disruptive, if not destructive. Thus, our ideal is for reasonably rational citizen participation; that is, actions based on undistorted information about the candidates, parties, or PACs seeking their contributions. Contributors should have accurate information on the goals of the individuals or groups to which they contribute, the activities in which these organizations will engage, and the effectiveness of their efforts.[45]

Competition in Campaigns

Unless we presume that the absence of a competent contender in a given election indicates perfect support for the unopposed candidate, genuine competition seems to be the best guarantee that citizens are actually able to control their government. In order to serve as democratic institutions, elections must provide genuine choices.[46] Competitive elections even encompass an aspect of personal liberty: "Freedom of choice has little significance, too, in a situation where actors are unaware of the possibilities,"[47] or are never presented with them in the form of opposing candidates. The value of viable competition in campaigns carries with it, however, the implicit understanding that "viable competition" requires adequate financing to offset the advantages of the opponent, such as incumbency or personal wealth.

Conclusion

Doubtless, some will disagree with the values we propose or suggest others. As Jacobson notes, "Ethical dilemmas are intrinsic to the American system of electoral politics, an inevitable consequence of the diverse values elections are supposed to promote."[48] The rest of this book also makes clear that there are significant obstacles to trying to promote all eight of these values in campaign financing. Sometimes these values conflict. Other times they are difficult to implement. Often the impulse for reform is based on questionable assumptions. Usually the quest for electoral success leads to the exploitation of loopholes. If not, reforms themselves result in unintended and undesirable consequences. Finally, even if we could conceptualize an ideal system of campaign financing, overcoming the political hurdles to passage in our real-world Congress may be overwhelming.

The brief essay that follows presents many of the concerns about campaign finance that have been popularized by Common Cause, the media, and Members of Congress. It raises many of the issues that are systematically addressed by scholars in subsequent chapters, sometimes with conclusions directly opposed to the Common Cause viewpoint. The remainder of the book focuses on specific problems with the sources of campaign funds, undesirable consequences of the campaign finance system, and difficulties with reforming the current system. Our concluding chapter presents our views of how congressional campaign financing as a whole should be reformed to promote the key values essential to representative democracy.

NOTES

1. Common Cause Magazine, January/February 1988, 46.

2. Gloria Borger, "The Dirty Big Secret of Campaign Finance," *U.S. News and World Report*, November 7, 1988, 29.

3. Amy Dockster, "Nice PAC You've Got Here... A Pity If Anything Should Happen To It: How Politicians Shake Down the Special Interests," *Washington Monthly*, January 27, 1987, 24.

4. House Minority Leader Robert H. Michel, cited in Chuck Alston, "Campaign-Finance Gridlock likely to Persist," *Congressional Quarterly Weekly Report*, December 17, 1988, 3525.

5. Elizabeth Drew. *Politics and Money: The New Road to Corruption* (New York: Macmillan, 1983).

6. Philip Stern. (New York: Pantheon Books, 1988).

7. Brooks Jackson. *Honest Graft* (New York: Alfred A. Knopf, 1988).

8. *U.S. News and World Report*, November 7, 1988, 20-24, and 29.

9. Peter Lindstrom, et. al., *Congress Speaks—A Survey of the 100th Congress* (Washington, D.C.: Center for Responsive Politics, 1988) 81, 83, 87, and 91.

10. Frank Sorauf, *Money in American Elections*, (Boston: Scott Foresman, and Company, 1988), 326.

11. Robert E. Mutch, *Campaigns, Congress, and Courts: The Making of Federal Campaign Finance Law* (New York: Praeger, 1988), 1-8.

12. *Buckley v. Valeo* 424 U.S. 1 (1976).

13. *Buckley v. Valeo*, 26-27.

14. *The Federalist Papers* (New Rochelle, N.Y.: Arlington House), 7.

15. Mutch, *Campaigns, Congress, and Courts*, 16.

16. *Burroughs v. U.S.*, 290 U.S. 534 (1934), 545.

17. *First National Bank of Boston v. Bellotti* 435 U.S. 765 (1978), 790.

18. Mutch, *Campaigns, Congress, and Courts*, 53.

19. *Buckley v. Valeo*, 48.

20. Mutch, *Campaigns, Congress, and Courts*, 8-15.

21. "Soft money" refers to funds from corporations, labor unions, or individuals that would not be allowed as standard contributions in federal elections because of the restrictions of the FECA.

22. Kay Lehman Schlozman, ed., *Elections in America* (Boston: Allen & Unwin, Inc., 1987), ix; Walter Dean Burnham, "Elections as Democratic Institutions," in *Elections in America*, 57; and Bruce Jennings and Daniel Callahan, eds. *Representation and Responsibility: Exploring Legislative Ethics* (New York: Plenum Press, 1985), 75-78.

23. *Congress: The Electoral Connection* (New Haven: Yale University Press), 1974.

24. "Political Action Committees, Electoral Politics, and Congressional Ethics," in Jennings and Callahan, *Representation and Responsibility*, 57.

25. "Elections as Democratic Institutions," in Schlozman, *Elections in America*, 30.

26. Amy Gutmann and Dennis Thompson, "The Theory of Legislative Ethics," in Jennings and Callahan, *Representation and Responsibility*, 174-181.

27. These data are drawn from Frank Sorauf's contribution to this volume.

28. V. O. Key, *Politics, Parties, and Pressure Groups*, 4th ed. (New York: Thomas Y. Crowell Company, 1958), 589.

29. Pitkin provides a detailed discussion of various meanings for representation. See Hanna F. Pitkin, *The Concept of Representation* (Berkeley, CA: University of California Press, 1967).

30. For example, John Stuart Mill claimed that real equality of representation is only preserved when minorities scattered throughout the nation might be able to combine in some way to elect a representative. See his *Representative Government* in *On Liberty, Representative Government, The Subjection of Women: Three Essays by John Stuart Mill* (London: Oxford University Press, The World's Classics, 1966), 254.

31. We need not get involved with consideration of whether such control reflects the trustee, delegate, responsible party, or some other model of representative accountability. As Pitkin has suggested, what matters for political representation and accountability "is not any single action by any one participant, but the over-all structure and functioning of the system, the patterns emerging from the multiple activities of many people." Pitkin,

The Concept of Representation, 221-222.

32. Andrew S. McFarland calls this "consensus democracy," and he explains how Common Cause polls its members and allows for a minority veto to assure that the only policy stands adopted by the organization represent a true consensus of supporters. See *Common Cause: Lobbying in the Public Interest*, 94.

33. McFarland argues for the ideal of face-to-face interactions, which he characterizes as "participatory democracy." McFarland, *Common Cause*, 94.

34. McFarland refers to this as the "exchange model of democracy." McFarland, *Common Cause*, 93.

35. Albert O. Hirschman, *Exit, Voice, and Loyalty* (Cambridge, MA: Harvard University Press, 1970).

36. Sorauf, *Money in American Elections*, 348.

37. *Buckley v. Valeo* 424 U.S. 1, 1976.

38. Mutch, *Campaigns, Congress, and Courts*, 53.

39. Heard, *The Costs of Democracy* (Chapel Hill: University of North Carolina Press, 1960), 48-49.

40. As quoted in Elizabeth Drew, "Politics and Money, Part I," *The New Yorker*, December 6, 1982, 147.

41. J. Roland Pennock *Democratic Political Theory* (Princeton, NJ: Princeton University Press, 1979), 42.

42. Ibid., 441-445.

43. Mill, *Representative Government*, 274-277.

44. Bernard R. Berelson, Paul F. Lazarfeld, and William McPhee. *Voting: A Study of Opinion Formation in a Presidential Campaign.* (Chicago; The University of Chicago Press, 1954), 305-323.

45. See Stanley Kelley's ideal guidelines for rational voting in *Political Campaigning: Problems in Creating an Informed Electorate* (Washington, D.C: The Brookings Institution, 1960). Kelley argues that rational voters require full information about the alternatives, full knowledge of the effects of choosing each alternative, and a system of preferences for evaluating these effects. The information should come from both sides, be free of distortion, focus on the differences between the alternatives, provide reasons for preferring one alternative over another, and clearly identify the sources of the information.

46. Burnham, "Elections as Democratic Institutions," 28. Robert Dahl has also cited the importance of "continuous political competition among individuals, parties, or both," for maintaining social control and keeping governmental leaders "so re-

sponsive to non-leaders that the distinction between democracy and dictatorship still makes sense." See his *Preface to Democratic Theory*, (Chicago, IL: Chicago University Press, 1956), 131-132.

47. Pennock, *Democratic Political Theory*, 33.

48. "Political Action Committees, Electoral Politics, and Congressional Ethics," in Jennings and Callahan, *Representation and Responsibility*, 41.

2

Up for Bid: A Common Cause View

Susan Manes

A national consensus now exists that the current congressional campaign finance system is in urgent need of comprehensive reform. In recent years, campaign spending has escalated dramatically. The massive sums being spent for campaigns increasingly are putting public office beyond the reach of those who are unable or unwilling to raise the vast amounts required or who are not personally wealthy. The explosion in campaign spending is changing the very nature of elective office itself, forcing candidates to spend more and more of their time raising campaign funds at the expense of other responsibilities. Political action committees (PACs) are playing an ever more prominent role in financing congressional campaigns, accounting for a growing proportion of candidates' war-chests. The enormous escalation in the role played by PACs in financing congressional elections is undermining public confidence in our system of electing Members of Congress and in the congressional decision-making process. As many have noted, the current campaign finance system also has diminished the appeal of public service—a factor in the decision of a number of Members of Congress to retire from public life, and a deterrent to others from seeking office. The current congressional campaign finance system is eroding the competition of the electoral process. The enormous sums of money required to mount a successful run for public office—and the sharply pro-incumbent bias of PAC contributions—have put challengers at an extreme disadvantage. Unless the congressional campaign finance system is overhauled, incumbents will find themselves increasingly immune to electoral challenge. At stake is the fairness of the electoral process itself and the ability of citizens to hold their elected representatives accountable. The most serious problems in the current system—the prominent role of special interest money in financing campaigns and the high and growing cost of running for a seat in Congress—are distorting and undermining processes fundamental to our democracy. The openness, competitiveness and fairness of the process by which American citizens elect their representatives in Congress is threatened, as is the integrity of the Congress itself.

The Case for Reform: Campaign Spending

"Our nation is facing a crisis of liberty if we do not control campaign expenditures," former Senator Barry Goldwater (R-AZ) has said. "Unlimited campaign spending eats at the heart of the democratic process."[1]

Under the current congressional campaign financing system, there are no limits on the amount of money congressional candidates may spend on their election efforts. Like the nuclear arms race, in which the superpowers compete to build up their arsenals, congressional candidates today vie to outspend one another to achieve electoral security. The result is that the congressional campaign financing system has become consumed with raising and spending money.

Spending for congressional campaigns has skyrocketed in recent years, rising from $99 million in 1976 to nearly $400 million in 1988. In just 12 years, spending in Senate races has increased five fold, from $38.1 million in 1976 to $190 million in 1988. In 1975–76, Senate winners spent an average of $610,026; in 1987–88, Senate winners averaged $3.7 million each in campaign spending.[2]

Spending in House races has also soared. In the last 12 years, spending in House races has more than tripled from $61 million in 1975–76 to $204 million in 1987–88. In 1975–76, House winners spent an average of $87,356; in 1987–88, House winners averaged $358,992 each in campaign spending.

Incumbents have far outstripped challengers in both fundraising and spending in recent elections. In the 1988 elections, Senators seeking re-election outraised and outspent their challengers by a 2.3-to-1 margin. In addition, Senate incumbents outraised their challengers in 24 of 27 races and outspent their challengers in 25 of 27 races. House incumbents in the 1988 elections outraised challengers on the average by 3.6-to-1 and outspent them by 3-to-1.

The massive sums being spent for campaigns are shutting out challengers who lack the built-in fundraising base of congressional incumbents, lack vast personal financial resources, or are unwilling or unable to raise large sums from outside sources. As former Senator Goldwater has stated, "What are we doing? Are we saying that only the rich have brains in this country? Or only the people who have influential friends who have money can be in the Senate?"[3]

The escalation in campaign spending has discouraged potential candidates. "A few years ago," Senator Max Baucus (D-MT) said, "I called various people around the country encouraging them to run for the Senate. We found a lot of very good people, highly intelligent, deeply dedicated to their States and to our country, who said yes, we are excited about running for office. But when they thought about how much it would cost, how much money they would have to raise, and as they were not millionaires in their own right, they began to back away. ...We are losing very good people because the present system shuts them out."[4]

The enormous expenditures involved in running for Congress threaten to alter the very nature of congressional office. A winning Senate race in 1988, on average, cost $3.9 million; raising this sum requires raising $12,500 every week during the six-year term. Faced with the necessity of raising large sums of money for their next race, many Members of Congress must devote substantial amounts of their time and energy to fundraising—time and energy that could be spent on activities that would better serve their constituents. As former Senate Majority Leader Robert Byrd (D-WV) has said, "To raise the money, Senators start hosting fundraisers years before they next will be in an election. They all too often become fundraisers first, and legislators second."[5] Congressional business too often takes second place to fundraising demands.

Finally, the need to raise large amounts of money to wage a competitive campaign increases candidates' dependence on special interest money.

In short, the ramifications of unlimited congressional campaign spending pervade and threaten virtually every aspect of congressional campaigns and, ultimately, the nature of representation in Washington. As Senator Jeff Bingaman (D-NM) has summed up, "Year by year, election by election, we are losing control of our political election process. Political influence in this country is shifting further toward well-financed special interest groups represented by PAC's and away from individuals. It is also clear that Members of Congress are spending ever-increasing amounts of their time raising funds for their campaigns and less time working on the crucial issues facing this country."[6]

The Case for Reform: PACs

In 1974 there were 608 PACs; today there are more than 4,200. And PAC contributions to congressional races have skyrocketed, from $12.5 million for congressional races in 1974 to nearly $150 million in 1988.

Not surprisingly, PACs are financing a growing proportion of candidates' campaign chests. On average, the 33 Senators elected in 1988 received 26.4 percent of their total 87–88 receipts from PACs; by contrast, the 33 Senators elected in 1976 received 15 percent of their funds from PACs. During the six-year election cycle, Senators elected in 1988 raised an average of $1 million each in PAC contributions for their Senate campaigns. That brings the number of PAC millionaires in the Senate to more than 30.

Almost half of the Members of the House of Representatives elected in 1988—210 of the 433 current Members—received 50 percent or more of their campaign funds from PACs.

As these figures so graphically demonstrate, the 101st Congress came into office more indebted to special interest money than any other Congress in the nation's history.

Most PACs are arms of organized lobbying efforts. Some defenders of PACs suggest that the massive influx of PAC dollars into congressional campaigns is a healthy form of citizen participation in the political process; after all, they argue, a PAC is simply a group of people joining together to express a collective political opinion.

But PAC involvement in the political process differs markedly from direct individual participation. Individuals generally approach representation on a broader basis than PACs. In deciding whether to vote for a candidate for public office, an individual usually assesses that candidate by weighing a variety of factors. An individual, for instance, may be concerned about the candidate's position on education, crime, unemployment, taxes, nuclear arms and defense issues. PACs assess candidates based on a much more narrow agenda—generally closely related to their specific legislative goals. Although contributions to PACs initially come from individuals, those contributions change their character when they go to a PAC because they then are tied to an organized lobbying campaign and take on the narrow identity of the interest group represented by the PAC.

Furthermore, the way in which PACs give is different from direct individual involvement in the political process. Common Cause found that in nine contested 1986 Senate races, there were 494 examples of PAC double giving—contributions to both the Democratic and Republican candidates in the same race. In the Oklahoma 1986 Senate race, 165 PACs made contributions to both the incumbent and the challenger. The fact that PACs regularly give to both candidates in a single race underscores the fact that PACs often don't contribute because of a candidate's philosophy, ideology or political party; they give in an effort to gain access and influence in Congress.

The fact that PACs contribute substantially more to incumbents than to challengers serves to underscore the nature of their involvement in the political process and their overriding interest in gaining access and influence in Congress. For example, PACs contributed 4.3 times more to Senate incumbents in 1988 than to their challengers; House incumbents, on average, outraised challengers in PAC receipts by a 7.3-to-1 margin in 1988.

There is a growing awareness that massive special interest giving makes a difference in the legislative process. More and more Members of Congress, from both parties and representing a wide variety of viewpoints, have commented on the influence of PAC contributions on decision-making in Congress:

> Representative Tony Coelho (D-CA) explained his view of how PACs affect congressional decision-making: "Take anything. Take housing. Take anything you want. If you are spending all your time calling up different people that you're involved with, that are friends of yours, that you have to raise $50,000, you all of a sudden, in your mind, you're in effect saying, I'm not going to go out and develop this new housing bill that may get the Realtors or may get the builders or may get the unions upset. You know, I've got to raise the $50,000; I've got to do that."[7]
>
> Senate Minority Leader Robert Dole (R-KS) has said: "When these political action committees give money, they expect something in return other than good government. It is making it much more difficult to legislate. We may reach a point where if everybody is buy-

> ing something with PAC money, we cannot get anything done."[8]
>
> As Senator William Proxmire (D-WI) has noted, the influence may take an indirect and subtle form: "It may not come in a vote. It may come in a speech not delivered. The PAC payoff may come in a colleague not influenced. It may come in a calling off of a meeting that otherwise would result in advancing legislation. It may come in a minor change in one paragraph in a 240-page bill. It may come in a witness not invited to testify before a committee. It may come in hiring a key staff member for a committee who is sympathetic to the PAC. Or it may come in laying off or transferring a staff member who is unsympathetic to a PAC."[9]
>
> Senator David Durenburger (R-MN) stated, "I can honestly say... having to raise money does influence where you put your time and effort. ...all those who are interested enough to get in the process through the fundraising are the ones you pay attention to."[10]

The growing number of PACs has enabled those PACs which share the same legislative interest to align together to exert even greater influence in the legislative process. Through their aggregate contributions, these PACs are able to exert considerably more pressure, and gain access and influence in Congress. As Representative David Obey (D-WI) has said, frequently in Washington "[a]n issue affects an entire industry and all of the companies and labor unions in that industry. When that occurs, when a large number of groups which have made substantial contributions to members are all lobbying on the same side of an issue, the pressure generated from those aggregate contributions is enormous and warps the process. It is as if they had made a single, extremely large contribution."[11]

A Common Cause study of PAC contributions to Senate Finance Committee Members in their last election underscores Representative Obey's assertion. The 1986 study found that the 20 Members of the Committee received total campaign contributions of $956,742 from energy PACs, $969,213 from insurance PACs, $1,153,857 from labor PACs and $300,120 from law PACs. Contributions of this magnitude, far in excess of the individual PAC contribution limits, lead to disproportionate influence in the legislative process.

As noted earlier, PAC contributions also skew the electoral process by heavily favoring incumbents over challengers. Disproportionate PAC giving to Members of Congress over challengers exacerbates the built-in advantages of incumbency and undermines competition in congressional races. In 1988, an all-time record of more than 98 percent of the congressional incumbents were re-elected.

Finally, the prominent role played by PACs in financing congressional campaigns has sharply undermined public confidence in the integrity of our electoral process and decision-making in Congress. Polling data from the last several years indicates that the public is concerned about the role of PACs in congressional campaigns.

Reforming the Congressional Campaign Finance System

There are a number of basic steps that must be taken to address the problems of PACs and unlimited spending. Aggregate PAC receipts must be limited in order to bring about a reduction in the substantial role that special interests now play in financing congressional campaigns. Diminishing the role of PAC contributions in congressional races—and the access and influence which such contributions often provide—would advance the integrity of the congressional decision-making process and public confidence in that process.

Overall limits on spending are needed to provide a more level field between incumbents and challengers. Spending limits also would de-escalate the current arms-race mentality that characterizes many congressional races today and promote an environment in which Members of Congress and challengers are not required to devote ever increasing amounts of their time and resources raising campaign funds.

It is important that spending limits be set high enough for a challenger to run a competitive campaign. Although a challenger does not always have to spend more than an incumbent to win, a challenger must be able to spend sufficient funds to make a case and be competitive.

Partial public financing should be made available as a means of giving challengers access to campaign resources, of giving incumbents an alternative to PAC contributions, and to fulfill the requirements set forth in the 1976 Supreme Court decision in *Buckley v. Valeo*, which upheld the constitutionality of spending limits as part of a system of providing public financing or other benefits to candidates.

Notes

This paper was prepared in large part from Common Cause materials. The author wishes to acknowledge the assistance of Common Cause staff members Jeffrey Denny and Susan Aceti of the Issues Development staff, and Karen Hobert and Kathy Mountcastle of the Campaign Finance Monitoring Project.

1. U.S. Congress, Senate Committee on Rules and Administration, "Hearings on Campaign Finance Reform Proposals of 1983," 403.
2. All campaign fundraising and spending figures cited in this paper are taken from Common Cause studies based on data compiled by the Federal Election Commission.
3. *The Washington Post*, November 4, 1986.
4. *Congressional Record*, February 18, 1988.
5. *Congressional Record*, January 6, 1987.
6. *Congressional Record*, February 18, 1988.
7. *The Wall Street Journal*, July 18, 1986.
8. *The Wall Street Journal*, July 26, 1982.
9. *Congressional Record*, August 11, 1986.
10. *Congressional Record*, February 23, 1988.
11. Statement of Representative David Obey, Democratic Study Group, Washington, D.C., July 26, 1979.

Part I: Problems with Funding

Our concerns about campaign financing begin with the sources of funding. Who gives and how they give affect values such as participation, representation, legitimacy, and accountability. This section examines several issues that arise in raising and spending funds.

Focusing on the value of participation in campaign finance, Ruth Jones considers whether reforms and technological developments that have provided more opportunities for citizens to participate politically by contributing to campaigns have really led to more donors and more donations. Her comparison of the contributor base of political parties with those of candidates and PACs suggests that each taps a contributing elite with slightly different characteristics. The new technologies for solicitation also reach slightly different potential contributors and have coincided with a rise in the number of donors. Yet the proportion of the electorate contributing has remained relatively constant; overall, the same old elite is being represented. Only the checkoff for the presidential election has attracted involvement from a broader sector of the electorate, but these donors seem to be motivated more by civic virtue than political interest, and their numbers are dwindling. These findings are sobering for reformers who seek to improve the campaign finance system by expanding its base of contributors. Jones speculates that perhaps low participation in funding elections reflects dissatisfaction with the electoral and governmental systems. If so, reforms of the problems detailed in the rest of this book may be a prerequisite to resolving the problem of participation.

Those who choose not to contribute directly can still participate in the electoral system through independent spending. Candice Nelson explores the extent of this activity, viewed as a threatening loophole by some, yet as valued political liberty by the Supreme Court. Although the amount of independent expenditures has risen dramatically in a decade, Nelson notes that only a few PACs and individuals utilize this tactic, the total spending of which pales in comparison to the direct contributions of individuals and PACs. The problems that occasionally arise from independent spending—skewed representation, decreased political equality, reinforcement of the incumbency advantage, unaccountability of independent spenders to voters or candidates, and violations of the requirement of independence—have heretofore been minimal because of the limited use of this form of spending. Because of the Court's sanction, however, a dramatic increase in independent expenditures could be an unintended consequence of reforms that constrain more traditional campaign financing activities. If so, the negative aspects of independent spending will also flourish, perhaps outweighing the benefits of reform.

Independent spending is but one of the many loopholes or abuses that, while not widespread, undermine the legitimacy and effectiveness of our campaign finance system and support public cynicism and distrust of government. Anne Bedlington examines loopholes and abuses including soft money, bundling of contributions, and the use of tax-exempt foundations for political purposes. She also examines questionable but legal practices by Members of Congress, such as the personal use of surplus campaign funds and excessive acceptance of honoraria and travel allowances. In addition to the harm these practices cause to legitimacy and effectiveness, Bedlington argues that activities that allow wealthy individuals or corporate and labor donors to regain the influence that the Federal Election Campaign Act sought to reduce further threaten political equality and accountability.

Political equality and accountability are also the focus of David Adamany's conclusion to this section. Where political equality is preserved, the principle of "one person, one vote" suggests that representatives would be equally attentive to all voters, mitigating concerns about other channels for accountability. Because of unequal resources throughout the campaign finance system, however, Adamany examines why, how, and to whom the actors raising and spending these funds should be accountable. Specific problems with accountability arise because of 1) the unaccountability of PACs to voters or donors; 2) treasury subsidies to connected PACS; 3) independent expenditures; 4) soft money; 5) out-of-district giving; and 6) the impact of political contributions aggregated by individuals, candidates, PACs, and parties. Adamany calls for improving accountability to voters and donors through the use of disclosure and disclaimers, revised limits on contributions, public financing, and methods to enhance donor control. Since absolute political equality conflicts with unfettered political liberty, Adamany's attention to the accountability of political money suggests a means of mitigating this dilemma as it applies to financing campaigns.

3

Contributing as Participation

Ruth S. Jones

Documentation of U.S. campaign financing reveals a very narrow pyramid of political contributors: historically, few people gave but many of them gave very large sums. The evolution of campaign technology, especially mass mailing techniques, easy access low-cost WATS telephone facilities, and computerized mailing addresses and phone numbers have created new avenues through which to expand appeals for campaign contributions. Campaign finance reforms of the 1970s, including contribution limits and tax check-offs, sought to broaden the base of political givers as well as reduce the dominance of the relative few who contributed very large sums.

These reforms notwithstanding, the perennial question raised by money and politics remains: Where does the money come from? In this era of opportunities for mass-based political contributions, who is asked to contribute? Who actually responds? Do new modes of solicitation tap new sources of money? Do different modes of solicitation tap new sources of money? Do different modes tap different sources? In short, how different is the campaign financing of the 1980s from the system described by Pollock and Overacker a half century ago?[1]

These questions are important because they relate directly to fundamental issues of widespread citizen participation and representation in the electoral process. Campaign finance reforms and technological advances in campaign financing have the potential to alter sharply the pattern of who gives to whom and why. Mechanisms that truly expand the contributor base of campaigns can be viewed as consistent with the tenets of an open, participatory system. Yet, new structures and processes that may appear to include more and different publics may in reality scarcely change the character of the contributing public and may actually reinforce the status quo.

Typically, no more than 10 to 12 percent of the electorate have provided financial contributions to electoral campaigns, but recent changes in campaign and electoral politics would seem to have increased the potential for a new base of campaign financing. Whereas Gallup poll data from as early as 1947 indicated that only 5 percent of all respondents said they had given to a campaign, 27 percent said they would give if asked.[2] If there is an untapped "market" of political contributors within the mass electorate, then the successful use of new solicitation technologies such as mass mailings and WATS lines may provide not only an expanded base but a potentially quite different base of contributors to political campaigns.[3]

Means of participation in federal campaign finance also have changed. The Federal Election Campaign Act of 1971 (FECA) established the income tax check-off as a new means of financing presidential elections. The FECA also meant that the 1980s would see increased electoral activities by political action groups, issue committees, and other non-party, non-candidate organizations which could institutionalize issue-based giving. The question remains: will new technologies and modes of participation result in quantitative or qualitative changes in the pool of contributors? Changes in contributing behaviors need not necessarily translate into a qualitative change: more contributors may not indicate a more diversified or representative set of contributors.

The National Election Studies data[4] include information on each of these modes of contributing and on the modes of solicitation. Unfortunately, the NES design did not integrate questions on giving with the questions on solicitation. Consequently, we cannot link the types of solicitation (mail, phone, face-to-face) to the channels of giving (party, candidate, or PAC/issue group organizations); all we can explore is the intersect of solicitation and response as reported by those who recall the solicitations.

This chapter tests four basic propositions that underlie both the general arguments for campaign finance reform and the use of modern technology in fundraising: (1) more opportunities to contribute will produce more contributors; (2) more opportunities will encourage different publics to contribute; (3) political solicitation will facilitate political contributing; and (4) differing modes of political solicitations will reach different publics.

Who Gives—and How?

Underlying political reform in this century has been the assumption that if the avenues for political participation are expanded, citizen involvement in politics will increase. Similarly, the arguments for campaign finance reform often call for expanding the contributor base of campaigns. As electoral politics shifts from party dominated campaigns to include candidate-centered organizations, PACs and public campaign financing, the expectation has been that more citizens will become involved in the funding of campaigns.

Our data provide only limited confirmation of this expectation. Despite a continuing increase in the amount of money contributed to campaigns and the use of modern technology, the proportion of contributors and the general pattern of contributing do not appear to have changed markedly over the four elections studied here. Only a minority of the electorate is engaged in financing elections. Unless those who use the tax check-off are included, the overall proportion of contributors has remained between 10 percent and 15 percent of the electorate over the 34 years of NES data collections.

Use of the income tax check-off is not considered by many critics to be a form of political contributing because it requires so little effort to give so little money. Nevertheless, we take special note because check-off moneys provide the single largest source of funds for presidential campaigns, even though only one-third of the electorate use the check-off.[5] In 1988, for example, candidates Bush and Dukakis each were eligible to use $11.5 million in matching funds from the check-off generated Presidential Election Campaign Fund to finance their primary campaigns as well as the $46.1 million flat grant from the fund for general election campaign costs.

The data suggest that, beyond the check-off, contributors to recent campaigns have chosen to contribute through all of the traditional channels for contributing, that no single channel has dominated, and that there has been only minor variation in the modes of contributing from election to election.[6] From 1980 to 1986, the only marked change in the numbers of contributors reporting gifts to the two major parties saw the parties becoming more evenly matched. Although contributions to the Republican party continue to be more numerous, by 1986 the Republican advantage (3:2) among the two party contributors was considerably less than the 3:1 advantage they enjoyed in 1980 or the 2:1 edge in 1982. By 1986 there was an actual reversal of the 1980 Republican advantage in the number of contributors giving to individual candidates, further suggesting that recent Democratic efforts to catch up in mass-based fundraising may be paying off (See Table 3.1).

Although these figures provide some evidence of greater balance in partisan fundraising efforts in terms of numbers of people involved, the data do not address the amount of money represented by the different contributions. FEC reports for 1988 election cycle, for example, reveal that the Republican national party committees raised $263 million compared to $128 million raised by their Democratic counterparts, 87 percent and 68 percent respectively contributed by individuals.

Who Gives to Whom?

A comparison of the three basic categories relevant to contributing behaviors—those who did not contribute at all (non-contributors), those whose only financial involvement was through checking the appropriate box on their federal income tax return (check-off only contributors) and those who may or may not have used the check-off but who chose to contribute through a formal organization (organizational contributors)—provides a basic overview of "contributing behaviors." Despite apparent continuity in the patterns of campaign finance, analysis reveals that these three groups are markedly different, and that contributor bases have changed rather perceptibly over the six year period.

In terms of demographic attributes, in all four years the non-contributors were less well educated and had lower incomes whereas the organizational givers were better educated and financially well off. Contributing also was related positively to union membership. In 1980 the non-contributors tended to be elderly, whereas the young and middle aged dominated the "check-off only" group and the middle aged were over represented among the organizational givers. By 1986, the young dominated the ranks of the non-contributors, the middle aged swelled the ranks of the check-off only users, and the middle aged and seniors were increasingly over represented among the organizational contributors.

Consistently, the partisan distribution among non-contributors closely paralleled the partisan distribution in the electorate. With the exception of 1984, Democratic contributors were more likely to be check-off only users but in 1984 and 1986, compared to their distribution in the electorate, Republicans decreased organizational giving but increased check-off use. Indeed, in 1984 and 1986, the numbers of Democratic organizational contributors increased to match the Republicans, despite the fact that in the overall distribution of party identifications the Democratic national plurality had been reduced.

Table 3.1

Modes of Contributing: 1980–1986
(in percentages)

	1980 N=1395	1982 N=1418	1984 N=1989	1986 N=2176
Federal tax check-off	29	30	33	30
State tax check-off [a]	30	33	NA[b]	NA
Candidate Org.	6	7	4	5
Rep.[c]	59	39	42	43
Dem.	30	55	47	48
Both	NA	NA	6	5
Other	11	6	5	4
Party Org.	4	4	4	5
Rep.	76	67	52	55
Dem.	24	33	40	38
Both	NA	NA	4	5
Other	0	0	4	2
PAC	7	8	NA	NA
Ballot Issue	NA	NA	2	NA
Other Group	NA	NA	2	3
Summary				
Non-contributor	64	63	63	66
Check-off only	23	21	24	25
Organizational giver	13	16	13	9

[a]Asked only of respondents living in the states that have a public campaign finance check-off program.
[b]NA indicates the question was not asked.
[c]Perfect comparability of partisan giving between years is impossible because the questions and response codes varied slightly; see the appropriate National Election Study codebooks for details.

The most obvious linkage between ideology and contributing was that those who could not locate themselves on the liberal/conservative scale consistently were over-represented among the non-contributors. Belying the fact that public funding is viewed as a liberal policy opposed by conservatives, check-off only users are disproportionately moderates; liberal and conservative representation among check-off users closely mirrors their distribution in the population. On the other hand, both liberals and conservatives were consistently above average in contributing to organizations.

Finally, as one would expect, those less psychologically predisposed toward government and politics were disproportionately likely to be non-contributors, whereas the ranks of the organizational contributors were filled by those with interest and involvement in campaigns.

In sum, these baseline data suggest that, using the threefold hierarchy of contributing behavior, the relationships of attributes to contributing closely parallel the patterns associated with participation more broadly defined. And the differences between the non-contributors, check-off only contributors and the organizational givers suggest that at least the new opportunity represented by the federal income tax check-off does encourage response by a different public.

Looking more closely at organizational givers does not reveal a sustained preference for one type of organization over another (See Table 3.2). Surprisingly, in contrast to rhetoric of PAC dominance and party decline, the percentage choosing to give only to parties has increased while the proportion giving to non-party, non-candidate organizations has decreased.[7] Most significant in terms of the thesis that new modes of contributing will encourage increased contributing behavior is the increase in the percentage of contributors who use more than one channel of giving. The most common pattern of multiple giving combines giving to party (the traditional mode) with giving to candidate organizations.

Moreover, the NES data indicate that donor profiles differ somewhat according to the type of organization (party, political action group or candidate) receiving the contribution. Between 1980 and 1986, party contributors included slightly higher proportions of union-affiliated supporters than did candidate contributors, but party contributors were also clearly more Republican than candidate contributors. Those who gave to either the party or candidate organizations were quite similar in terms of psychological orientations, but the party funders were somewhat less involved in visible, participatory campaign activities.

Table 3.2

Channels of Contributing: Political Organizations
1980–1986
(in percentages)

	1980 N=183	1982 N=220	1984 N=181	1986 N=203
Channel				
Party	15	11	27	24
Candidate	27	27	23	31
Issue Group	38	42	18	14
Multiple	20	20	32	31

In contrast, the organizational contributors who selected the non-party, non-candidate organizations for their donations were much more likely than party or candidate supporters to be young and less well off, perhaps reflecting the anti-party mood of many who reached their majorities in the early and mid-1970s. Political action group contributors were at least as likely as the supporters of party or candidate organizations to be from union households but considerably more likely to be Independents. Issue/PAC contributors voted; otherwise, they appeared a little less interested, less civic minded, and much less politically active than those who chose party or candidate organizations as the mode of their support. By 1986 these issue/PAC contributors were as likely as party or candidate supporters to be contacted by the parties but were more likely to have been targets for non-party contacts, suggesting perhaps the growing institutionalization of political action networks.

The "multiple contributors" who chose to give through more than one mode made up the most distinctive contributor base of all. Compared to other contributors, to say nothing of the non-contributing public, the multiple contributors were decidedly more likely to be well educated, well-to-do conservative partisans (Republicans) who were both interested in the elections and vigorously engaged in political campaign activities. In sum, there is a hierarchy of contributors in which, by 1986, party contributors occupied a middle position. At the bottom of the hierarchy, of course, are the non-contributors. They are followed by check-off only users, PAC/issue-group only supporters, party only contributors, candidate organization funders and, at the top, those who give to more than one political organization. We now know that the presence of alternative modes of funding campaigns is complemented by the presence of distinguishable sets of contributing elites that can be characterized by certain "core" attributes, some of which are subject to change within and across contributing publics election to election.

How are Contributors "Tapped"?

These differences in the characteristics and targets of contributor and non-contributor groups may reflect deliberate decisions by contributors as they sort themselves out according to their preferred modes of contributing. Alternatively, these differences and changes in contributor bases may reflect the fact that different sectors of the electorate are differentially solicited, solicited more heavily, or targeted more effectively by different fundraising organizations using different modes of solicitation. Consequently, who contributes to whom may also be a function of who is asked to contribute through which solicitation mechanism.

As Table 3.3 indicates, mail solicitations reached a very large portion (41 percent) of the electorate in 1984.[8] However, although the use of telephone banks was highly publicized as a campaign tool in the 1984 campaigns, only 5 percent of the sample of the national electorate (perhaps 7 or 8 million people) reported that the phone was used to solicit their financial support. Despite the easy potential access to contributors that the phone provides, at least as many respondents (6 percent) reported an individualized, face-to-face solicitation.[9] Nevertheless, adding mass mail and phone solicitation techniques clearly increases the stimuli to contribute.

Of those who were solicited, one in four contributed. Out of those in the population reporting no mail, phone or face to face solicitation, less than 2 percent reported contributing money.[10] Over 80 percent of the contributors were solicited by mail; about a quarter were solicited by face-to-face contact and almost as many (23 percent) were solicited by phone. All told, among the 13 percent of the population who gave to campaigns in 1984, almost 85 percent recalled some form of direct campaign solicitation. Among the 87 percent who made no contribution, only about 1 in 3 recalled having been solicited.

The effectiveness of solicitations in gaining a response varies. The mode that reaches the widest audience, mail solicitation, also produces the highest *number* of positive responses (albeit only a

4 percent response rate). The mode that reaches the smallest audience (phone) produces the lowest (1 percent) proportion of contributors.[11]

However, among those who gave who *attributed* their giving to a specific type of solicitation, telephone solicitations drew no more than a 37 percent response compared to a 35 percent response for mail. At the same time, although face-to-face contact was apparently no better targeted than were the phone calls, some 70 percent of the face-to-face contacts with contributors produced contributions attributed to the contact.

The apparent relationship between solicitation and contributing does not, however, directly address the causal question: Do solicitors target potential contributor populations or do potential contributors respond disproportionately to solicitation? We cannot resolve this issue conclusively, but an examination of the intersect between reported solicitation and reported giving suggests that phone solicitation seems better targeted than does solicitation by mail. Over half of those reporting phone solicitation eventually made a donation, compared to one-fourth of those solicited by mail. Phone and face- to- face solicitations were equally targeted on eventual contributors (52 percent), but face- to- face solicitations were more readily acknowledged as the stimulus for giving.

Table 3.3

Solicitation and Response by Mode of Solicitation
(in percentages)

	Mail	Phone	Face-to-Face
Solicited			
Total Electorate	41	5	6
Contributors	81	23	25
Non-Contributors	36	3	3
Attributed Contribution			
Total Electorate	4	1	2
Solicited Contributors	35	37	72

[a]In 1982, the percentage of respondents reporting mail solicitation was almost identical to 1984; the response rates were higher however (16% within the total population and 49% among contributors).

Contributors are not an automatic soft touch for every solicitation. One in six who received mail or personal requests to give were in fact contributors who declined to respond to the mail or personal request; one third of those who were contacted by phone similarly contributed but apparently not in response to the telephone contact. Generally, however, solicitation (as well as specific solicitation techniques) corresponds to contributing behaviors.[12]

Who is "Tapped" How?

Do different political solicitations reach different populations? Our data support the conventional wisdom that face- to-face solicitation takes place within small personal networks and is very successful. By contrast mail solicitation and, to a lesser extent, phone solicitation, depend upon the development of less personalized lists of names and addresses and are less well regarded even by those who contribute.

With the attention the Republican party has given to mass mail activities, it is not surprising that a higher proportion of Republicans than Democrats report that they are solicited by mail. Nor is it surprising that partisans, in general, are on more mailing lists than are independents. Conservatives are somewhat more likely than liberals to receive mail solicitations, and centrists are less likely than ideologues. There are, however, no sharp partisan or ideological differences associated with telephone and personal solicitation.

Any form of solicitation is clearly aimed at those who are actively involved in campaign politics. Targeting these activist populations with both telephone and face- to- face solicitation is particularly prominent. Three out of five campaign workers received mail solicitations, a rate 50 percent above the national average. Moreover, nearly a quarter received phone and face- to-face requests to give money, more than five times the national figure. Members of politically oriented groups were also exceptionally likely to receive mail solicitations, although not as likely as campaign workers. In contrast, union household respondents were not more heavily solicited, by any mode, than were non-union household members. This calls into question the assumption that unions (beyond extracting COPE dues) provide heavily used networks for political solicitation.

All modes of appeal are heavily targeted on the better aged stratum of the electorate, but selective emphasis, not surprisingly, is greatest for face- to- face solicitation among citizens where activities are likely to identify them to campaign workers and thereby get their names on lists for contacts. Mail reaches many non-voters (18 percent of them), but the efforts at telephone or personal contact seldom stray to the ranks of the non-voters.

Who Gives When Asked?

Among those Democrats and Republicans who were solicited by face- to- face requests, Democrats were more often contributors; among those solicited by phone, liberals more often than conservatives were numbered among the givers.[13] Every campaign worker in the sample who was personally asked to give was indeed a contributor. And for the campaign activists who were solicited, face- to- face and phone requests were the modes most prominently associated with contributing. While union households were not any more likely to be solicited than non-union households, once they were solicited, by any of the three modes, the likelihood of contributing was visibly higher in union than in non-union homes. Finally, face- to- face solicitation seems to be relatively more effective than phone requests with people otherwise less likely to give—the less interested, lower income, less well educated younger citizen.

In sum, political solicitation is widespread and the different modes of soliciting reach somewhat different publics. Each mode of solicitation, however, evokes a different pattern of response from selective publics although all three are most successful when appealing to those who are already politically engaged.

The subgroup of those who give to political organizations also shows differential targeting and response patterns. First, party and candidate organization supporters, as well as multiple contributors, are obviously central targets for mass mail solicitation and this is predictably most true for those who give through multiple channels. They also are heavily targeted for phone solicitation. Second, those who contribute only to ballot issue or PAC-type organizations (non-party, non-candidate) are somewhat outside the direct mail effort, and they clearly are not included on many of the lists for telephone solicitation. They are, however, clearly caught up in personal networks; face- to- face solicitation was reported more often by them than by the most active and visible of the other groups of contributors.

Finally, it appears that party supporters may be more amenable to mail solicitations whereas candidate supporters are more likely to respond to phone requests. Curiously, although party organizations have the more established institutional networks, these data suggest that the more ephemeral candidate or issue-based organizations may provide more effective personal networks for campaign financing.

Representation, Participation and Campaign Contributing

Analysis of these NES data help us assess how well the current system of campaign financing promotes broad-based representation and widespread citizen participation through political contributions. Returning to the four questions raised at the beginning of our inquiry, the findings suggest only limited success in expanding the contributor base of election campaigns.

Do more opportunities to contribute produce more contributors? The answer is mixed. The proportion of respondents reporting contributions to political organizations has not changed markedly since 1952, but the tax check-off has almost doubled the number of citizens who provide the money for campaigns. Yet, when the tax check-off is excluded, the percentage of the electorate contributing to campaigns over the past two decades has remained relatively constant, suggesting that the new techniques have merely allowed contributing to keep pace with population growth. On the other hand, given the surge in the amount of money raised for campaigns, the new techniques may be effective in eliciting larger amounts from "core" givers than they are in broadening the base of contributors.[14]

Do new opportunities to contribute enlist support from different sectors of the public? Check-off only users share so many attributes of the non-contributing publics that it may be a misnomer to define check-off use as a political contribution. But in the very differences with other participants they do provide evidence that new opportunities for involvement may elicit support from new sectors of the public. And the comparison of the contributor base of political parties, the traditional channel for campaign financing, with candidate organization or political action group supporters reveals three overlapping but analytically distinct profiles rather than a single contributing elite.

Does political solicitation facilitate political contributing? Despite their limitations, the NES data indicate that those who are asked are more likely to give. In fact, contributors attribute their contributions to having received particular solicitations. Obviously we know too little about the strategies of solicitation to begin to disentangle the cause-effect relationship between these two activities, and we remain uncertain about the availability of a primed but untapped market of political contributors. The techniques of mass mail and phone solicitation have different publics.

Finally, differing modes of political solicitation made it possible to reach more and different types of potential contributors than are reached by the personal networking upon which traditional fundraising at one time depended. On the other hand, the actual change in the characteristics of the contributing public seems to be much less dramatic than campaign finance reformers, mass mail experts, or technology-driven campaign operatives might lead us to believe.

Although the surge of mass solicitation activity, especially mail solicitation, may expand the numerical base of fundraising and may extend vertically (downward) through multiple strata of the electorate to reach here-to-fore ignored sectors of the electorate, the most likely targets for mass solicitations remain those who have traditionally made up the contributing elite.

Lessons for Future Reform

The reforms of the 1970s were aimed at altering the shape and size of the contributing elite. In effect, the intent was to cut off the top of the contributor triangle by limiting the amount any one individual could give and to expand the base by encouraging small (even single dollar) contributions from the mass electorate. The effects of the changes appear to be modest in degree rather than dramatic in kind. A contributing elite still exists. Nonetheless, the experience has taught us several lessons.

The first lesson should encourage a realistic appreciation of what the income tax check-off can be expected to accomplish. When use of the check-off is defined as a contribution, the number of citizens participating in the financing of campaigns doubles and millions of dollars suddenly are made available to fund election campaigns. However, although participation is virtually without cost to the participant, only one quarter to one-third of the population actually take part in the federal check-off program, with the proportion declining in recent years. With a few exceptions, this same pattern has been observed in states with tax check-off systems for state elections. It would be helpful to know why two-thirds of the taxpayers do not use the check-off and why tax check-offs are declining. In the meantime, those who look to the tax check-off system as a means of changing congressional campaign financing cannot ignore the relative low level and declining participation in present check-off systems.

Similarly, the appropriateness of interpreting check-off use as an indicator of political contributing or participation should be reconsidered. We do not know how our respondents themselves view the use of the check-off, but we do know that those who use only the federal tax check-off are more like non-contributors than contributors, resembling the latter only in terms of psychological orientations toward politics and civic duty. Thus, the quantitative increase in check-off "participants" has not been accompanied by the qualitative characteristics we associate with serious citizen participation. Limited state-level case studies indicate that tax check-off users most frequently cite sense of civic duty or general support for elections as the reason for using the check-off. They do not see it as another avenue for participating in the electoral system.

Interesting questions arise for reformers who seek to create a tax check-off to fund congressional campaigns. Would use of the tax check-off increase if there were a concerted effort to motivate public participation through appeals to sense of civic duty and promotions of elections as a collective good? Is the check-off actually a bridging mechanism that enables taxpayers who are predisposed toward political involvement to break ranks with the disinterested and the free riders? If so, do the tax check-off only users then form a receptive target group that, effectively motivated, could be transformed from a civic-minded but passive, uninvolved subset of the electorate into an activist cadre? In short, is check-off use the first step toward greater political involvement? Is it then a means toward a desired end or does it remain an end in itself?

A second lesson to be learned is that we should reassess the assumption that there is an unexploited "contributor market" waiting to be tapped. While it is true that more and more people are now asked, by phone and mail, to make political contributions, the response rate is generally very low. Modern technology notwithstanding, face- to- face appeals continue to be the most effective way of soliciting political contributions. There does not seem to be a large, undifferentiated electorate just waiting for an invitation to contribute to campaigns.

Experiences in several states that have enacted "add-on" legislation underscore the fact that simply providing an opportunity to contribute does not change the nature of the contributing public. Add-ons create a system for providing campaign funds which, like the tax check-offs, use the income tax form as a means of collecting contributions. Unlike check-off systems, however, add-on systems do add to tax liability, do "cost" the tax payer something. And, uniformly across all add-on programs, participation rates are extremely low—often less than one percent of all taxpayers.

Third, not everyone who is asked to give actually gives, but most contributors identify their contributions as being responses to particular solicitations. Because techniques of raising money reach somewhat different sectors of the electorate and different publics respond differently to each type of solicitation, new technologies have the potential to introduce new biases into the campaign financing process. This fact, combined with the knowledge that different publics choose different channels of contributing, should foster a greater sensitivity to the fact that who gives to whom may be determined by who has the most sophisticated techniques for targeting and reaching potential donors.

And finally, our inquiry indirectly calls into question the strategy of expanding the base of campaign contributors as a first step in altering the nature of the contributing elite. The tax check-off and new solicitation techniques are aimed at directly motivating individuals to respond within the current system. The implicit assumption is that the system will be improved when more and different contributors are involved.

But this argument may have the causal order reversed: perhaps when the system is "improved," more citizens will be willing to contribute. For example, strict ethics and conflict of interest laws accompanied by rigorous enforcement might increase public confidence in elected leaders. Stronger political parties might take on a quasi ombudsman role and provide accountability that would appeal to members of the mass electorate. The pluralism that PACs represent could be nurtured and expanded under conditions that diminish group impact on the funding of campaigns but increase opportunities for other forms of involvement in the campaign process.

During the 1980s the electorate received very mixed signals. Contribution limits on individual and PAC giving sought to reduce inequalities and special interest involvement. At the same time, truly wealthy individuals financed expensive campaigns through independent expenditures. Political parties competed with a large array of PACs and ultimately took advantage of the loopholes that permit "soft money" contributions. Although clearly within the letter of the law, the publicity surrounding heavy use of soft money raised serious questions about compliance with the spirit of the law. And finally, the public was exposed to almost weekly news reports of conflicts of interest, illegal activities or other obvious abuses of power by elected and high-level appointed political officials.

Even in this context, the actual *number* of people making political contributions during the 1980s increased. The proportion of contributors in the electorate, however, remained reasonably steady. In a democracy, the goal is to have widespread participation that is representative of the full spectrum of interests in society. Given this goal, we cannot be particularly sanguine about the impact of campaign finance reform on political participation and interest representation.

Nevertheless, some progress has been made. No longer does a small political party elite dominate the ranks of contributors and political activists. Today the most politically active contributors are those who give directly to candidate organizations or give to more than one electoral group. One quarter of the electorate has taken advantage of the federal check-off opportunity to move from being a non-contributor to joining a collective effort to fund presidential campaigns. Tapping a slightly different strata of society, PACs and issue groups have successfully motivated yet another segment of the electorate to become involved in the financing of campaigns. And finally, although they still are most successful in generating funds, personal networks and face-to-face appeals are not the only way to raise large sums of campaign money. Today, different solicitation techniques reach somewhat different publics and thus provide opportunities for widening participation and representation in the campaign funding process.

These are modest changes to be sure. They have not moved us as far or a quickly toward the goal of a more participatory, responsive and accountable political system as we would like. It will take bold action and steadfast commitment to address perceptions of political corruption, integrity of office holders, special interest influence, equity and fairness. These issues transcend the particulars of campaign financing for they are the heart and soul of a viable democratic campaign and electoral system. The data we have presented here are proof that the current system is not intractable; they suggest areas that may be amenable to further change; and they provide encouragement for those who dare to propose changes in the status quo.

NOTES

1. James K. Pollock, *Party Campaign Funds* (New York: Knopf, 1926) and Louise Overacker, *Money in Elections* (New York: Macmillan, 1931).

2. *Gallup Poll: Public Opinion 1935–1971* (New York: Random House, 1972), 742.

3. For a more detailed discussion of the methodology for analyzing contributors, see Ruth S. Jones and Warren E. Miller, "Financing Campaigns: Macro-Level Innovations and Micro-Level Response," in *Western Political Quarterly*, 38 (June, 1985), 187–210. For a state-level pilot study of this inquiry, see Ruth S. Jones and Anne H. Hopkins, "State Campaign Fund Raising: Targets and Response," in *Journal of Politics*, 47 (May, 1985), 427–449.

4. The American National Election Study data were originally collected by the Center for Political Studies of the Institute for Social Research, The University of Michigan, for the National Election Studies, and were made available through the Inter-university Consortium for Political and Social Research.

5. This figure is higher than the percentage of tax returns the Internal Revenue Service reports use the income tax check-off option (generally about 25%), and it is lower than the estimates of individual taxpayer use of the check-off by Noragon and Hill. See Jack L. Noragon, "Political Finance and Political Reform: The Experience with State Income Tax Check-offs," *American Political Science Review*, 75 (September, 1981), 667–687; and Kim Quaile Hill, "Taxpayer Support for the Presidential Election Campaign Fund," *Social Science Quarterly* 62 (December, 1981), 767–71.

6. Responses to a state-wide survey in Wisconsin and Minnesota suggest the variation in contributing behaviors that exists across the U.S. In these two Midwest states known for citizen participation in politics and the spirit of open, competitive elections, patterns of political contributing are more highly developed than in many other states. It is interesting to note that although the political parties in these two states are reasonably strong, giving to interest groups or PACs was more common than contributing to parties.

	Wisconsin	Minnesota
Gave to candidate	22	24
Gave to group or PAC	28	31
Gave to party	13	25
Federal Check-off	27	25
State Check-off	42	28

Source: St. Norbert College Survey Center, "Wisconsin-Minnesota Common Cause Survey," St. Norbert College, De Pere, WI. December 1987.

7. Because so few chose the non-party, non-candidate "other" our sample data do not provide very reliable data for a discussion of separate categories for these contributors. However, with a few exceptions, the supporters of ballot issues and the supporters of other politically active groups are remarkably alike. The most noteworthy difference distinguishing the two subsets of non-party, non-candidate organization contributors is that the supporters of the political action groups were disproportionately young and Republican, whereas ballot issue supporters were somewhat more middle aged and Democratic. By combining the "political action" group with the ballot issue supporters, it becomes possible to compare the funding base of non-party, non-candidate organizational contributors with the candidate organization supporters and the more traditional party organization contributors.

8. These data are derived from a question in the 1982 NES study on mail solicitations and a 1984 question on the frequency of recalled telephone and face-to-face requests in additional to mail solicitations. In order to make comparisons between the modes of solicitation, the discussion is limited to the 1984 data. Analysis of the patterns associated with mail solicitation and response in 1982 were remarkably similar to those of 1984.

9. This comparison may, of course, reflect differences in respondents' recall of personal contact compared to remembering an impersonal telephone request for money.

10. Pursuing the notion that some of the respondents might have considered the Presidential Campaign Fund dollar check-off as their "contribution," we found that indeed half of those reporting a contribution but no solicitation were check-off users. If one assumes the check-off was their only contribution, this would mean that less than one percent of the sample contributed to a political organization in the absence of a solicitation.

11. These national patterns of solicitation and response among contributors are quite similar to those reported by Jones and Hopkins in their study of contributors to state-level elections. However, among Arizona and Tennessee contributors in 1982, mail solicitations were more heavily targeted and more frequently responded to suggesting that within the state gubernatorial and legislative campaigns, the mailing lists are such that they more successfully tap potential contributors. The state-level rates of response to phone and personal solicitations are very similar to those found within the national sample in 1984.

12. Observation and experience suggest that there is a great deal of overlap in the targeting strategies of various campaign organizations. Respondents were therefore asked about the frequency of the solicitations they received. Predictably, just as more people reported receiving at least one solicitation by mail, over half of the contributors (57%) reported receiving a "great many" mail solicitations. However, only a quarter of the contributors reached by phone reported large numbers of phone solicitations, and just 11% of those reached in person reported large numbers of person, face-to-face solicitations. Not only do the less personal modes of solicitation reach more people, but they reach more people more often. Conversely, the more personal modes are more constrained and probably more discrete.

13. Our initial analysis strategy looked at each mode of solicitation and the direct linkage with giving in response to each mode of solicitation. This did not prove to be a useful analysis strategy because the pattern of response/no response was different only in magnitude from the solicited/not solicited pattern. The discussion that follows simply describes the proportion of contributors who were solicited by each mode.

14. The presidential primary public funding program as well as several state level public financing plans require (for certification or matching) that candidates raise money in relatively small sums from a large number of individuals. The original intent of this requirement was to reduce the influence of the wealthy and of special interests and to broaden the base of the contributing public. These reforms plus the new technologies of solicitation notwithstanding, there has been no transformation to a mass based participatory system of campaign financing.

4

Loose Cannons: Independent Expenditures

Candice J. Nelson

Independent expenditures have been called "loose cannons on deck"[1] and no doubt more, since the National Conservative Political Action Committee (NCPAC) first used independent expenditures in 1978. The Federal Election Campaign Act defines an independent expenditure as "an expenditure by a person expressly advocating the election or defeat of a clearly identified candidate which is made without cooperation or consultation with any candidate, or any authorized committee or agent of such candidate, and which is not made in concert with, or at the request or suggestion of, any candidate, or any authorized committee or agent of such candidate."[2]

When Congress passed the 1974 amendments to the FECA it established not only limits for individual, party and PAC contributions to congressional campaigns but it also established limits on what individuals and organizations could spend on independent expenditures. The 1974 amendments limited what an individual or organization could spend on behalf of a candidate to $1,000. However, when the Supreme Court reviewed the constitutionality of the 1974 amendments the Court ruled, in its decision in *Buckley v. Valeo*, that there could be no limits on independent expenditures, because independent expenditures were constitutionally protected free speech. In its decision the Supreme Court argued that "the independent advocacy restricted by the provision [the $1,000 limit] does not presently appear to pose dangers of real or apparent corruption comparable to those identified with large campaign contributions," but the limit "heavily burdens core First Amendment expression."[3] As a result of the Supreme Court's decision, independent expenditures have become an unlimited channel of expenditures for individuals and organizations wishing to influence federal elections.

Since the passage of the FECA in 1971, the majority of PAC activity has been in the form of direct campaign contributions to federal candidates, particularly congressional candidates. However, independent expenditures in federal elections also have increased over the last decade. While independent expenditures currently represent only a small proportion of expenditures in presidential and congressional elections, they are expenditures which need to be considered in any discussion of campaign finance reform, because they have the potential to increase dramatically if other forms of expenditures, particularly direct contributions by political action committees to candidates, are further limited by reform.

Independent Expenditures from 1978 to 1988

When the Supreme Court handed down its decision in *Buckley v. Valeo*, independent expenditures were a very small part of the financing of presidential and congressional elections. In 1976 $2.9 million was spent on independent expenditures, compared to the approximately $300 million spent in the 1976 presidential and congressional elections.[4] In one sense independent expenditures are still a small part of spending in federal elections; in 1988 $19.5 million was spent on independent expenditures, compared to the hundreds of millions spent in the 1988 presidential, House and Senate elections. However, independent expenditures have increased over the last ten years, and likely will continue to play a role in federal elections.

Figure 4.1 depicts the growth in independent expenditures between the 1977–1978 and 1987–1988 election cycles. Two points are worth noting. First, independent expenditures are higher in presidential election years than in off-years. Second, when independent spending in presidential year and off-year elections is compared separately, there is a steady increase in independent spending in off-years; independent spending rose from $310,000 in 1978 to $10.2 million in 1986. In presidential election years total independent spending rose from $16 million in 1980 to $23.4 million in 1984, and then declined to $19.5 million in 1988. Spending in presidential elections increased between 1980 and 1984, rising from $13.7 million in 1980 to $17.4 million in 1984; in 1988 spending in the presidential race was slightly less than spending in 1980. In congressional elections independent spending increased between 1978 and 1986, from $310,000 in 1978 to $9.3 million in 1986 and then declined to $6.1 million in 1988.

Figure 4.1

Growth in Independent Expenditures
(in $ millions)

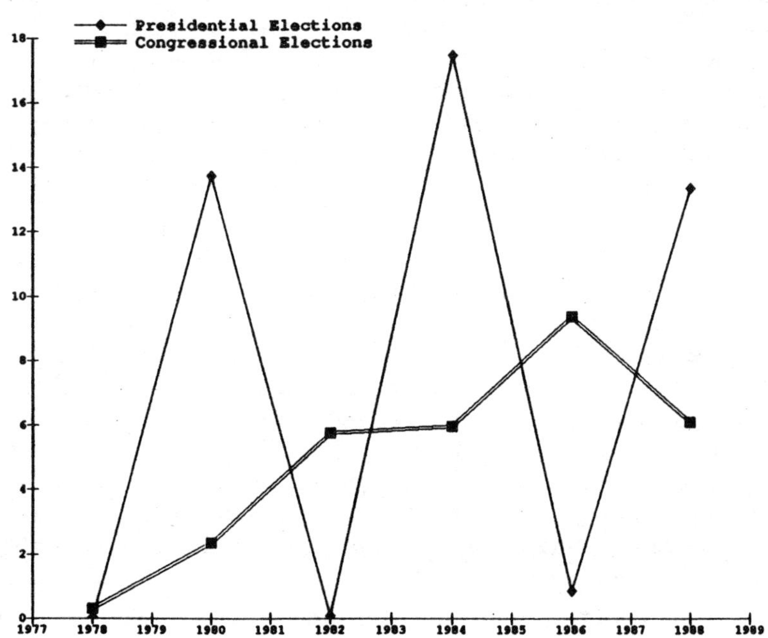

Source: FEC Press Release, October 9, 1980; 1979–86: FEC Press Release, March 31, 1988 (corrected release); 1988: FEC Post-general election reports (preliminary figures).

It is not surprising that independent spending would be higher in presidential election years than in off-years, given the visibility of the office involved in the former. Moreover, because individuals and PACs cannot contribute to presidential candidates receiving public funds in the general election, independent expenditures provide the only means, other than soft money, for individuals, and, more importantly, for political action committees, to influence financially the presidential general election.

Sources of Independent Expenditures

While independent expenditures have increased in both presidential and off-year elections, there has been no comparable increase in the numbers of individuals and political action committees making independent expenditures. The number of PACs making independent expenditures has fluctuated from a low of 87 in 1982 to a high of 185 in 1980; in 1984, 1986 and 1988 the number of PACs making independent expenditures did not vary much. Similarly, the number of individuals making independent expenditures fluctuates in presidential and off-years, but there has not been an overall increase in the number of individuals making independent expenditures. Thus, while the amount spent on independent expenditures has increased over the last decade, the number of individuals and PACs making those expenditures has not.

Most independent expenditures are made by political action committees. While individuals also have the opportunity to make independent expenditures, very few have done so. In 1988 only twenty individuals made independent expenditures; in 1986 there were only seven. Moreover, the amounts spent by individuals on independent expenditures are not large. Only 22 individuals have ever spent over $10,000, and ten of those did so in 1980. The largest individual independent expenditure in any federal election was made by Michael Goland, who spent $1,100,000 in negative advertising against Senator Charles Percy in the 1984 Illinois Senate election.[5]

More money is spent on independent expenditures in presidential election years than in off-years. However, with the exception of Goland's expenditures in 1984, independent expenditures by individuals have been declining in size since 1980. In 1980, 10 individuals spent $20,000 or more on independent expenditures, only 9 individuals in the next four elections combined spent over $20,000 on independent expenditures.

There is wide variation in the amount individuals have spent on independent expenditures; the amount spent drops off quite precipitously even among the highest spenders. The same is true for independent spending by political action committees. In 1980 the largest independent expenditure by a PAC was $4,601,069; the tenth largest independent expenditure was $119,891.[6] Six years later, in 1986, the National Committee to Preserve Social Security PAC led PAC independent expenditures, spending $1,931,600, while American Citizens for Public Action, tenth in spending on independent expenditures, spent only $147,063.[7] In 1988, the National Security PAC spent $8.3 million on independent expenditures while the Conservative Victory Committee, the tenth largest independent expenditure PAC, spent just \$318,877.[8] Similar declines in the amount spent on independent expenditures among the top ten PACs occurred in 1982 and 1984.[9] Thus, it is important to remember that 1), relatively few PACs make independent expenditures, 2), the number of PACs which do make independent expenditures has not increased very dramatically since 1980, and 3), the amount of money most PACs spend on independent expenditures is not very great. These three facts may console those who fear the potential power of independent expenditures. They also suggest, however, that independent expenditures are not enhancing representation or increasing political equality by broadening participation in campaign finance.

Forms of Independent Expenditures

Because independent expenditures can advocate either the support or the defeat of a candidate, independent expenditures fall into two categories: expenditures made on behalf of a candidate, and expenditures made against a candidate. Figures 4.2 and 4.3 compare independent expenditures for and against presidential and congressional candidates between 1978 and 1988.

In examining total independent expenditures it is clear that, with the exception of 1982, independent expenditures have been made predominantly to support candidates. However, there are substantial differences in both the types of independent expenditures used in presidential and congressional elections and changes in the use of independent expenditures over time. Independent expenditures in presidential elections overwhelmingly are made in support of presidential candidates. This is true in both presidential primary and general elections.

However, independent spending in congressional elections is not so easily generalized. While independent spending in the 1978 congressional elections was primarily in support of candidates, independent spending against congressional candidates exceeded that in support of candidates in both 1980 and 1982. In 1984 independent spending in support of congressional candidates once again exceeded spending against congressional candidates, and by 1986 independent expenditures in support of congressional candidates were six times greater than those expenditures opposing congressional candidates.

Not only are independent spending patterns different for presidential and congressional elections but there are also differences in both the amount of money spent on independent expenditures by different types of PACs and in the patterns of spending. With the exception of cooperatives, corporations are the least likely PACs to use independent expenditures. Somewhat more money is spent in presidential than in congressional elections, but the amount spent by corporations on independent expenditures has only ranged between $16,000–$33,000 and, with the exception of 1988, corporate expenditures in both presidential and congressional elections have been overwhelmingly in support of candidates. Labor unions have a pattern of independent expenditures similar to their corporate brethren, though labor PACs have spent more on independent expenditures than have corporate PACs, with a low of $24,000 in 1980 and a high of $306,000 in 1984.

Figure 4.2

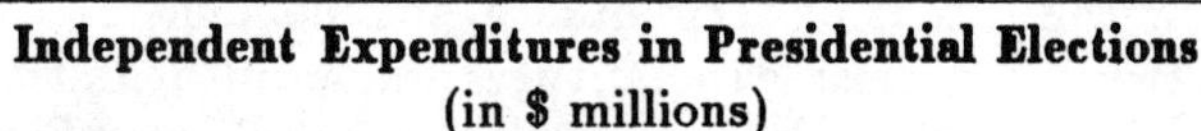

Independent Expenditures in Presidential Elections
(in $ millions)

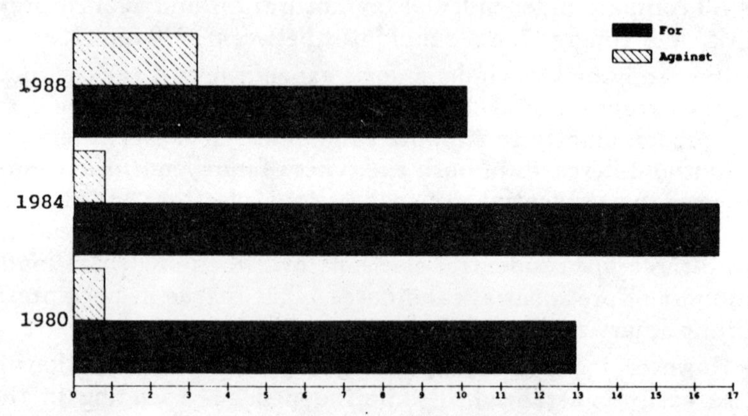

Source: FEC Press Release, October 9, 1980; 1979–86: FEC Press Release, March 31, 1988 (corrected release); 1988: FEC Post-general election reports (preliminary figures).

Trade, membership and health PACs have been more active in making independent expenditures than have corporate and labor PACs. Independent expenditures on behalf of candidates increased steadily from $108,000 in 1978 to over $4 million in 1986, and then declined to $2.2 million in 1988. These PACs have also made independent expenditures against candidates in larger amounts than corporate and labor PACs, though the amounts spent in support of candidates far exceed the amounts spent in opposition to candidates in every election except 1988.

Figure 4.3

Independent Expenditures in Congressional Elections
(in $ millions)

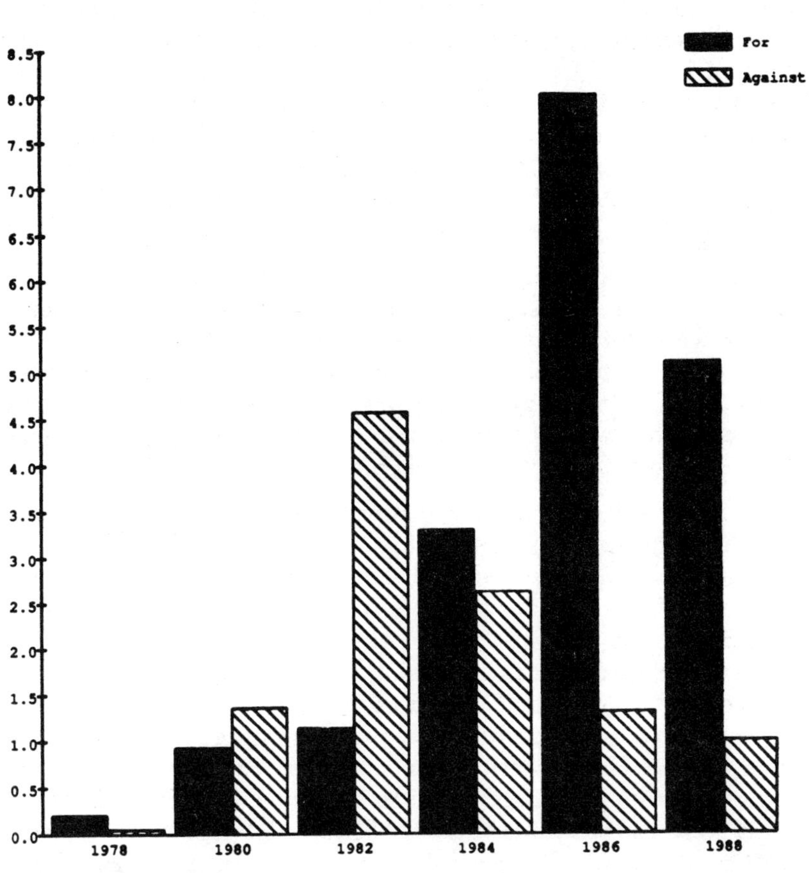

Source: FEC Press Release, October 9, 1980; 1979–86: FEC Press Release, March 31, 1988 (corrected release); 1988: FEC Post-general election reports (preliminary figures).

The largest use of independent expenditures has been by non- connected PACs. In 1980 over $16 million was spent in independent expenditures and $13.1 million, or 81%, was spent by non- connected PACs. While the percentage of independent expenditures made by non- connected PACs has declined somewhat in recent years, as other types of PACs have increased their independent expenditures, non- connected PACs still spend more money on independent expenditures than do any other type of PAC. Not only do non- connected PACs use independent expenditures more than any other type of PAC, spending over $19 million in 1984, but non- connected PACs also have spent more on independent expenditures against candidates than any other type of PAC. In 1982 $5.8 million was spent on independent expenditures, and $4.5 million of that was spent by non- connected PACs against congressional candidates. In more recent elections non- connected PACs have spent more on behalf of candidates than against them. Nevertheless, non- connected PACs continue to lead all other types of PACs in negative spending.

Most independent spending has been in support of candidates, but has this support favored challengers or incumbents? PACs who shifted away from expenditures against incumbents may tend to channel funds in support of challengers. Furthermore, PACs tend to give two-thirds to three-quarters of their direct contributions to incumbents. Does their independent spending re-inforce or correct for this bias?

Tables 4.1 and 4.2 help answer these questions by examining independent spending on behalf of incumbents and challengers in congressional elections. The little that corporate and labor PACs have spent independently has been heavily in support of incumbents in the Senate, but occasionally support for House challengers has almost equaled that of incumbents. The more interesting independent spending in congressional races occurs with non- connected and trade, membership and health association PACs. The patterns of independent expenditures for both types of groups changed considerably over the ten-year period. In 1978 House elections and 1980 Senate elections non- connected PACs spent over a million dollars in support of House and Senate challengers, while spending only thousands in support of incumbents. Spending in support of challengers also exceeded spending in support of incumbents in House elections in 1980 and Senate elections in 1978 and 1982, but not as dramatically.[10] By the 1982 House elections and 1984 Senate elections, non- connected PACs support for incumbents far exceeded their support for challengers, and that pattern continued through the 1988 elections.

The pattern of contributions for trade, health and membership PACs is particularly interesting when the 1984, 1986, and 1988 elections are compared. Through 1984 trade PACs made the majority of their independent expenditures in support of incumbents. However, these PACs made substantial expenditures in support of challengers in 1986. In House races twice as much was spent in challenger races as in incumbent races, and in Senate races spending was almost evenly divided between the two. However, in 1986 trade PACs learned the lesson non- connected PACs learned in 1982—namely, that spending against an incumbent, by supporting his or her challenger, isn't successful. By 1988 virtually all independent spending by trade, health and membership associations was in support of incumbents.

Table 4.1

Independent Expenditures on Behalf of Senate Incumbents and Challengers, by Type of PAC
(in thousands of dollars)

		'77–'78	'79–'80	'81–'82	'83–'84	'85–'86	'87–'88
Corporate							
	Incmb.	5.7	3.1	3.4	1.4	1.6	.9
	Chall.	.8	.5	2.0	0	0	0
Labor							
	Incmb.	2.0	7.1	2.7	.4	3.2	0
	Chall.	.2	2.8	.05	0	0	2.2
Non-Connected							
	Incmb.	6.1	18.8	60.5	558.1	1,776.3	1,261.3
	Chall.	8.7	119.3	100.1	108.4	144.2	274.2
Trade/Mem/Health							
	Incmb.	25.4	93.9	134.7	400.6	698.6	469.9
	Chall.	3.1	61.9	27.6	25.4	635.1	(-2.7)
Cooperative							
	Incmb.	0	0	4.0	5.0	.5	0
	Chall.	0	0	0	0	0	0
Corporations w/o Stock							
	Incmb.	.5	0	0	7.2	21.4	14.0
	Chall.	0	0	0	.9	29.3	17.7

Source: 1978–1986: FEC Reports on Financial Activity, Financial Reports, Party and Non-Party Political Committees, Vol. I, Summary Tables; 1988: FEC post general reports, preliminary figures.

Table 4.2

Independent Expenditures on Behalf of House Incumbents and Challengers, by Type of PAC
(in thousands of dollars)

		'77–'78	'79–'80	'81–'82	'83–'84	'85–'86	'87–'88
Corporate							
	Incmb.	2.8	6.7	7.1	18.5	15.9	3.5
	Chall.	3.2	6.3	7.0	3.0	3.6	3.0
Labor							
	Incmb.	10.5	4.7	15.8	23.7	33.3	2.2
	Chall.	1.5	1.6	6.6	3.5	27.3	2.8
Non-Connected							
	Incmb.	4.4	23.6	70.4	262.6	1,463.8	441.9
	Chall.	109.7	61.1	11.9	143.7	222.0	43.9
Trade/Mem/Health							
	Incmb.	45.9	236.9	457.3	362.1	225.0	1,014.9
	Chall.	15.8	172.6	95.3	264.6	581.7	.7
Cooperative							
	Incmb.	1.0	1.5	0	5.7	6.0	0
	Chall.	0	0	0	0	.05	0
Corporations w/o Stock							
	Incmb.	.4	1.3	7.4	10.9	86.8	8.4
	Chall.	.7	.1	9.7	4.7	28.7	3.7

Source: 1978–1986: FEC Reports on Financial Activity, Final Reports, Party and Non-Party Political Committees, Vol I, Summary Tables, 1988: FEC post-general reports, preliminary figures.

The Consequences of Independent Spending

When the Supreme Court struck down the limit on the amount an individual or PAC could spend on independent expenditures there was widespread concern that independent expenditures would be used by individuals and PACs, but particularly PACs, excessively to influence the outcomes of federal elections. Independent expenditures by NCPAC in the 1978 and 1980 elections fueled such a concern. In 1978 NCPAC targeted Senator Dick Clark of Iowa, and used independent expenditures to run an ad campaign attacking Clark as being too liberal to represent the interests of Iowa in Congress. Clark was defeated, and NCPAC claimed credit for his defeat. In 1980 NCPAC targeted six liberal Democratic Senators, including John Culver, Iowa's other Democratic Senator, and George McGovern, Frank Church, Alan Cranston, Birch Bayh, and Thomas Eagleton, and made independent expenditures against them. Of the six, four were defeated; only Cranston and Eagleton were re-elected. By the end of 1980 NCPAC had established both itself and independent expenditures as major forces in congressional elections.

NCPAC's early success in using independent expenditures to defeat five incumbent Senators is the example which is most often cited to illustrate the effect of independent expenditures on election outcomes. However, NCPAC's use of independent expenditures in 1978 and 1980 is the only example of unequivocal success in using independent expenditures to elect or defeat a candidate. The effect of independent expenditures on election outcomes since 1980 is much less clear. In 1982 NCPAC targeted 17 candidates for defeat; 16 of them were re-elected.[11] NCPAC's lack of success in 1982, compared to 1978 and 1980, is in part explained by the fact that the incumbents targeted—incumbents such as Edward Kennedy, Robert Byrd and Paul Sarbanes—had much safer seats and were much more ideologically attuned to their states than were the Senators defeated in 1978 and 1980. In addition, a number of liberal PACs formed following the 1980 election, and these liberal PACs were active in the 1982 election in both supporting liberal incumbents and targeting conservative incumbents. Thus, in 1982, as opposed to earlier years, the conservative PACs took on tougher candidates in a much more diversified environment of independent expenditures.

In 1986 some trade and health association PACs made major independent expenditures on behalf of challengers to House and Senate incumbents. The American Medical Association PAC (AMPAC), the National Association of Realtors PAC (RPAC) and the Auto Dealers for Free Trade PAC were among the top five PACs making independent expenditures, yet only one-half of the candidates supported by AMPAC were elected, only one of the six candidates supported by the Realtors was successful, and four of the seven Senate incumbents supported by the Auto Dealers were defeated.[12] While there are clear examples of independent expenditures by trade and health PACs making a difference in specific races in 1986, there are also examples to the contrary. One example of AMPAC's success in 1986 occurred in an open seat race in Colorado's 2nd congressional district. AMPAC spent $100,000 in independent expenditures in the last twenty days of the campaign to support Democratic candidate David Skaggs. Skaggs, who had been 20 points down in the polls in the spring, narrowly won—51.4 percent to 48.5 percent.[13] To quote Skaggs, "When you win with 51.5 percent of the vote and the AMA spent... $100,000 versus my spending of $500,000, you can draw your own conclusion."[14] While AMPAC successfully elected its candidate in the Skaggs-Norton election, it was not so successful when it took on Congressmen Fortney (Pete) Stark and Andrew Jacobs Jr. AMPAC spent $315,000 in independent expenditures in support of James Eynon, Jacobs opponent, and $252,000 in support of David Williams, Stark's opponent. Both Jacobs and Stark were re-elected by comfortable margins.[15] When the amount of money spent by trade and health associations in 1986 on independent expenditures in support of challengers is compared with the electoral success of those candidates, there is little evidence that independent expenditures consistently influenced the election outcomes.

While independent expenditures have not had the dramatic effect on election outcomes in recent years that they had in 1978 and 1980, the fact that they play a role in some elections is enough to give candidates pause. Independent expenditures, in addition to affecting the outcome of elections, can also be used to encourage incumbents to think twice before acting, or voting, against the interests of a group which has the resources to spend independently. For example, AMPAC chairman Dr. Thomas Berglund claims that AMPAC never expected to defeat Jacobs or Stark. However, because both congressmen opposed the interests of the American Medical Association and were members of the House Ways and Means Committee, AMPAC wanted to let Jacobs and Stark, and others, know that the PAC was willing to spend money independently to make its views known and to send a message to members in other less safe seats. Berglund stated, "I hope it sends a message to everyone in Congress who won by 51 percent."[16] Of course, these days, there are very few members who are re-elected by such small margins. Nevertheless, to the extent that members are concerned about antagonizing a PAC with the capacity and willingness to make independent expenditures, the very possibility of an independent expenditure campaign can have a chilling effect on legislative action, and thus decrease legislative effectiveness.

In addition to influencing election outcomes and congressional behavior, a third role which independent expenditures play in elections is to provide an alternative means of participation. For example, in 1986 the National Association of Realtors made a conscious decision to invest heavily in independent expenditures. In 1984 the Realtors spent $355,000 in independent expenditures; in 1986 they spent $1.6 million, second only to the National Committee to Preserve Social Security. Given the number of business PACs active in elections in the late 1980s, the Realtors felt that direct contributions to candidates no longer had the impact that they had a decade ago. "Not only has the PAC explosion devalued the political currency, but the value of campaign money has also been eroded by inflation. 'In that kind of environment, you're only deluding yourself if you think giving $5,000 to a candidate will have an impact in a campaign,"' said NAR Vice President Gary South.[17] The Realtors saw independent expenditures as an alternative to direct contributions, and an alternative with potentially more impact on elections.

Values Raised by Independent Expenditures

Despite the constitutional protection which independent expenditures enjoy as a result of *Buckley v. Valeo* there are still a number of concerns which are raised about their role in federal elections. Three questions raised by independent expenditures when they first became a force in federal elections are less problematic in hindsight. It was initially feared that independent expenditures would provide an avenue for wealthy individuals to use their wealth in federal elections, despite the contribution limits of the FECA.[18] As we have seen, very few individuals have used independent expenditures, and, with the exception of Michael Goland's expenditures against Senator Percy in 1984, the expenditures have not been very large. It is soft money, rather than independent expenditures, which has been the avenue by which wealthy contributors have gotten back into electoral politics.[19]

There was also a concern that the opportunity to spend unlimited amounts on independent expenditures would lead to just that—massive amounts of money being spent on independent expenditures. That too has not happened. While spending on independent expenditures has increased, it still pales in comparison to direct contributions from both individuals and PACs. Moreover, the number of individuals and groups using independent expenditures has remained fairly steady since 1980; there have been some fluctuations, but there is no decidedly upward trend.

In fact, in 1988 fewer PACs used independent expenditures than in either 1984 or 1986.

Finally, concerns were raised following the 1980 and 1982 elections about the effects of negative independent expenditures on participation in elections and attitudes towards the political system.[20] While these are still real concerns, independent expenditures are no longer the source of negative advertising. Since 1982, independent expenditures have been primarily in support of candidates; it is candidates themselves who have adopted negative advertising as a campaign mode.

Two serious concerns about independent expenditures remain: the lack of accountability on the part of those who make independent expenditures and the question of how "independent" independent expenditures actually are. When a PAC or an individual makes a direct contribution to a candidate, the candidate is free to accept the contribution, or not. The same situation does not apply to independent expenditures. Any individual or PAC who makes an independent expenditure does not have to explain that expenditure to candidates, to voters, and, in the case of PACs, very rarely to its own internal membership. The lack of accountability of independent expenditures raises problems in all three instances.

Examples of the lack of accountability of independent expenditures within PACs occurred in the 1986 election. Late in the 1986 campaign the National Association of Realtors spent $500,000 in independent expenditures to help Congressman Jim Jones in his ultimately unsuccessful effort to defeat incumbent Senator Don Nickles, despite the fact that the Oklahoma chapter of the NAR. had rated Nickles their "number one legislator."[21] Similarly, the Auto Dealers for Free Trade spent $400,000 in support of Senator Paula Hawkins re-election bid, even though the state's chapter was supporting Governor Bob Graham's effort to unseat Hawkins.[22] Because independent expenditures are uncoordinated, national groups are able to come into a state or district and spend money, even against the interests of their own local and state affiliates.

While the trend since 1982 has been to make independent expenditures in support of candidates, candidates are not always, or even necessarily often, willing recipients of such largess. One PAC manager, whose PAC does not use independent expenditures, described the problem. "Basically, with independent expenditures you're substituting your own judgment for the judgment of the candidate and his campaign managers, and I don't think that's appropriate."[23] A former campaign manager also sees independent expenditures as dangerous to the success of a campaign. "Independent expenditure scares the daylights out of me. A third party comes in that doesn't know my strategy or my budget and interjects itself. This could terribly jeopardize a campaign."[24] Thus, even independent expenditures meant to help a candidate can be potentially harmful to a campaign. The message, or tone, of the independent expenditure may be different than that of the campaign. Moreover, the independent expenditures themselves may become an issue, as they did in the 1982 Senate race in Maryland.[25] Even if the expenditures are not harmful, they are not always welcome, because they are out of the candidate's control. For example, C. Fred Bush, Deputy Finance Chair of the Bush for President Committee in 1988, was not particularly appreciative of the independent expenditures made by the Americans for Bush Committee during the 1988 presidential election.[26] If independent expenditures in support of a candidate raise such questions, negative advertising is even more disturbing to candidates. Once again, Senators McGovern, Bayh, Culver and Church are etched in the back of many candidates' minds.

Finally, those making independent expenditures have no accountability to the voters. While Americans for Bush had no connection with the Bush for President campaign, most Americans did not know that. Unless voters know who is making independent expenditures, and know that they are independent, voters have no way of evaluating the message being communicated.

The second concern remaining about independent expenditures is the extent to which they are truly independent. When candidates object to independent expenditures in support of their candidacy they assume that such expenditures are independent, and thus could upset the message the candidate is trying to convey. However, arguments are made that it is virtually impossible for an independent expenditure to be just that. As Larry Sabato states, "The network of friends and associates among campaigns and PACs is so large and so informed that anyone seriously desiring to know a candidate's campaign needs or plans has very little trouble doing so. The news media may be the best source of all for campaign information, and it is supplemented by a candidate's own literature and advertising, which often clearly reveal his underlying strategy."[27] Roger Stone, a Republican political consultant, agrees. "In Washington, everyone talks. Politics is a relatively small industry... and the world gets even smaller within a congressional district."[28] While there have been numerous allegations of collusion between campaigns and organizations making independent expenditures, there have been very few FEC findings that coordination occurred. Once such example of collusion occurred following the 1982 Senate election in New York, when Senator Moynihan charged that his opponent, Bruce Caputo, and NCPAC, which spent $73,000 against Moynihan[29] used the same campaign consultant, thus, NCPAC's independent expenditures were anything but independent. In the Moynihan case the Federal Election Commission ruled that NCPAC's expenditures were illegal,[30] but the Moynihan case has been by far the exception, rather than the rule. If independent expenditures are not just that—independent of a candidate or his or her campaign—then the legal credibility of the independent expenditure provision, and the justification for its existence, is undermined.

While some of the earlier concerns about independent expenditures appear to be unfounded, their lack of accountability, on one hand, and their potential lack of independence, on the other hand, remain. These problems will likely worsen if reforms increase the incentive for more individuals and PACs to spend independently.

Independent Expenditures Under Campaign Finance Reform

Because the Supreme Court has given privileged status to independent expenditures, no reforms can likely eliminate them. Instead, the fear is that reforms might increase the attractiveness of independent expenditures. While independent spending is an avenue for both individuals and PACs, most reform proposals suggest either raising individual contribution limits or keeping them at their current levels. In addition, given the opportunities for wealthy individuals to contribute to party-building activities through the parties' soft money accounts, there is little reason to expect an explosion of independent expenditures on the part of individuals. However, suggested reforms to reduce the contribution limits on PACs or put an aggregate limit on what candidates can receive from PACs could cause a surge in independent spending by PACs. Lowering the individual PAC contribution limit could mean that a PAC which wanted to support a candidate, but was limited to only $1,000 per election, might choose to spend the additional funds which are now contributed directly to the candidate in independent expenditures. Similarly, if a PAC was unable to contribute to a candidate it supported because the candidate had reached the aggregate limit he or she could accept from PACs, the PAC might choose to make independent expenditures on behalf of the candidate.

Not all PACs would react to further restrictions on PAC contributions by expanding their independent expenditure programs. As we have seen, the vast majority of PACs do not use independent expenditures, and that probably would not change under campaign finance reform. As a spokesman for the National Association of Realtors said, "independent expenditures are an attractive alternative [to direct contributions] for PACs that can afford to engage in the legally complicated and politically sensitive activity."[31] Most PACs have neither the sophistication nor the resources to conduct independent expenditure campaigns, and most probably would not.

However, it is the largest PACs which would be most likely to expand their independent expenditures if direct contributions to candidates were curtailed. PACs with large receipts likely would spend excess money on independent expenditures. For example, in 1986 the Auto Dealers and Drivers for Free Trade made $1.3 million in direct contributions to candidates, but still found itself with $1.6 million in additional funds. Of the $1.6 million, $1.2 million was used for independent expenditures.[32] The Auto Dealers are an example of how other large PACs might behave under campaign finance reforms which restrict PAC contributions. Increasing the tendency for only the largest PACs to have an additional outlet for political influence might further undermine the values of representation and political equality in our campaign finance system.

Other campaign finance reforms have been proposed to address the problems identified with independent expenditures. One proposal is to provide compensation to candidates who have independent expenditures run against them or on behalf of their opponents. For example, Senator Boren's bill, S. 137, introduced at the beginning of the 101st Congress, contained compensation provisions. Other reform bills have proposed providing free broadcast time to candidates to respond to independent expenditures.[33] However, one consequence of providing free broadcast time might be to discourage broadcasters from accepting independent expenditures, knowing that they would have to provide equal time to a candidate to respond to the expenditure.

While this might be one way to reduce independent expenditures, it also restricts participation through independent expenditures in elections.

A second consequence of providing compensation would probably be new machinations on the part of those making independent expenditures to get the candidates they support free air time. For example, the late Terry Dolan said NCPAC would welcome compensation for independent expenditures. Dolan said he "would simply run $100,000 in ads 'attacking' a favored candidate and urging that he be defeated for 'lowering taxes, opposing busing, and standing for a strong defense.' Besides identifying his candidate with a litany of popular positions, Dolan's independent salvo would trigger another $100,000 in free response time for his candidate."[34] Finally, providing compensation for independent expenditures raises free speech questions. If an individual or group exercises its right to participate in elections through independent expenditures, what is the constitutional justification for allowing a candidate to receive compensation to respond to the independent expenditures?

Reforms also have been proposed to assure that independent expenditures are truly independent. A bill by Senator Dole, for example, would prohibit candidates and "persons" making independent expenditures from using the same campaign consultant.[35] One reform which would at least increase the accountability of independent expenditures would be to require an independent expenditure to be clearly and largely labeled as such. Senator Boren's S. 137 would require that all television ads paid for by independent expenditures display the individual, PAC or organization that paid for the ad continually throughout the ad and state that the advertisement was not subject to campaign contribution limits.[36] Even identifying the name of the organization, and stating that the advertisement was not sponsored by either candidate would alert voters to the source of the advertisement, and perhaps better enable them to judge the message.

Finally, proposals have been made to limit independent expenditures, thus directly challenging the Supreme Court's decision in the *Buckley* case. While some reform advocates favor court review of the *Buckley* decision, arguing it was a poorly reasoned decision, others fear that to ask the Court to once again get involved in campaign finance reform may do even more harm. The easiest way to limit independent expenditures would be to pass a constitutional amendment giving Congress the authority to set spending limits in federal elections. However, amendments to do just that were introduced in the 100th Congress in both the House and the Senate, but no action was taken on them.

Under the most likely campaign finance reform scenario some further restrictions will be placed on PAC contributions, and large, well-financed PACs will compensate by increasing their independent expenditures. Because independent expenditures are seen as "loose cannons," federal candidates, particularly congressional candidates, have reason to be concerned about any escalation of independent spending. Obviously, candidates would prefer to control all spending on their behalf. However, unless the current pattern of support for incumbents changes, increased independent expenditures will not likely have the dramatic effects they did in 1978 and 1980.

Conclusions

As a protected expression of political liberty, independent expenditures provide an opportunity for individuals, PACs, and organizations to participate in the electoral process, unencumbered by contribution limitations. To date both the number of individuals and groups using independent expenditures and the effect of those expenditures have generally been marginal, with a few notable examples discussed above. If the status quo remains, independent expenditures will remain a fairly benign form of campaign activity. The problems they occasionally raise are real—skewed representation, decreased political equality, reinforcement of incumbency, unaccountability and questionable independence—but their impact is minimal because of the limited use of independent spending.

The concern, however, is that the status quo will change under campaign finance reform. Because independent expenditures are unrestricted, they remain the most obvious outlet for spending which is curtailed under various reform proposals. Further limits on PAC contributions might lead PACs to spend more on independent expenditures. Restrictions or prohibitions on private money in congressional general elections, as some public funding schemes propose, might cause both individuals and PACs to spend money independently, as they do now in presidential elections.

In addition, there are other values at risk by the use of independent expenditures. The growing tendency of independent expenditures to be in support of incumbents reinforces the existing bias of PAC contributions to incumbents, thus further reducing opportunities for competition in congressional elections. Because only a few of the wealthiest individuals and PACs use independent expenditures, representation of diverse interests is diminished, as are opportunities for political equality among competing interests. Fear of the effects of independent expenditures may reduce governmental effectiveness by causing members to avoid issues likely to spark independent expenditure campaigns.

Independent expenditures raise concerns because they have the ability to affect an election outcome, without any accountability to the candidates involved in the election, and, at least at the moment, any requirement to make their purpose known to potential voters. It is this lack of accountability that is of greatest concern. As long as independent expenditures remain only a small part of any election, participation is enhanced, with little or no adverse effects. However, if independent expenditures were to play a much larger role, and begin to seriously affect election outcomes, then their presence in elections becomes much more serious and much less positive.

Of course, viewing independent expenditures as "loose cannons" assumes that they are in fact independent. If they are not, they undermine individual and PAC contribution limits, and further disadvantage the candidate who is not the beneficiary of independent expenditures. Such coordinated activity would further undermine the opportunities for a "level playing field" in federal elections, already an illusory concept.

Notes

1. Viveca Novak and Jean Cobb, "The Kindness of Strangers," *Common Cause Magazine*, September/October 1987, 1.
2. 2 U.S.C. 431 (17).
3. *Buckley v. Valeo*, 424 U.S. 1 (1976).
4. Herbert Alexander, *Financing the 1976 Election*, (Washington, D.C.: Congressional Quarterly Press, 1979), 166.
5. "FEC Reports 1983–1984 Independent Spending Activity," FEC Press Release, October 4, 1985, (corrected version).
6. "FEC Study Shows Independent Expenditures Top $16 Million," FEC Press Release, November 29, 1981.
7. "Final FEC Report on 1985–1986 Independent Expenditures Shows Changes in Spending Patterns," FEC Press Release,

March 31, 1988 (corrected release).

8. Figures provided to the author by the Federal Election Commission.

9. "FEC Issues Final Report on 1981–1982 Independent Spending," FEC Press Release, October 14, 1983; "FEC Reports 1983–1984 Independent Spending," FEC Press Release, October 4, 1985 (corrected version).

10. Much of these spending patterns can be explained by the large expenditures of NCPAC in 1978 and 1980.

11. Herbert Alexander, *Financing Politics: Money, Elections and Political Reform*, 3rd ed., (Washington, D.C.: Congressional Quarterly Press, 1984), 147.

12. Novak and Cobb, "The Kindness of Strangers," 34.

13. Ibid., 32.

14. Ibid.

15. Ibid., 37.

16. Ibid.

17. *PACs and Lobbies*, January 7, 1987, 7.

18. Margaret Latus, "Assessing Ideological PACs: From Outrage to Understanding," in Michael J. Malbin, ed., *Money and Politics in the United States*, (Washington, D.C.: American Enterprise Institute for Public Policy Research, 1984), 150.

19. See Anne Bedlington's contribution to this volume.

20. Ibid.

21. Novak and Cobb, "The Kindness of Strangers," 36.

22. Ibid.

23. Larry Sabato, *PAC Power: Inside the World of Political Action Committees*, (New York: W.W. Norton and Co., 1984), 102.

24. Ibid.

25. NCPAC targeted Senator Paul Sarbanes and ran negative advertising early in 1982. NCPAC's advertising backfired; Sarbanes was able to raise money from liberal supporters precisely because of the NCPAC ads. Larry Boyle and John Hysom, "Independent Expenditures: Cutting Through Barriers," *District Lawyer*, May/June 1986, 41.

26. Remarks made at the Presidential Finance Officers Conference, Washington, D.C., December 9, 1988. Bush said he would like to see a prohibition on use of a candidate's name in a committee making independent expenditures.

27. Sabato, *PAC Power*, 184.

28. Novak and Cobb, "The Kindness of Strangers," 35.

29. FEC Index of Independent Expenditures, 1981–1982, September, 1983.

30. Novak and Cobb, "The Kindness of Strangers," 35.

31. *PACs and Lobbies*, January 7, 1987, 7.

32. Ibid., 8.

33. Ibid., 198.

34. The actual language in S. 7 prohibits candidates and persons making independent expenditures from both retaining the "professional services" of the same person "in connection with the candidate's pursuit of nomination for election, or election to federal office,. . . including any services relating to the candidate's decision to seek Federal office." *Congressional Record*, daily edition, January 25, 1989, Part II, S211.

35. *Congressional Record*, daily edition, January 25, 1989, Part II, S466.

5

Loopholes and Abuses

Anne H. Bedlington

This is a tale of limits and of the attempts by some to escape from them. The behavior of the escapees has consequences for representative democracy in America, especially for the legitimacy and effectiveness of the electoral and policy-making processes. Candidates, individuals, PACs and party officials have found ways to abuse the Federal Election Campaign Act or stretch its loopholes such that serious questions arise about how well the laws achieve their objectives.

The campaign finance regulatory system attempts to prevent large contributors from corrupting or appearing to corrupt elected officials. It restricts the amount of financial help an individual may give to a congressional candidate, whether acting alone or as a member of a political party or interest group. An individual may give $1,000 per election directly to a candidate, $5,000 a year to a PAC or $20,000 to a party, with an overall limit of $25,000 a year.[1] This system employs a very broad definition of support (money, goods or services, or anything of value), leaving no loopholes. It also anticipates that congressional candidates will spend campaign funds for a variety of political uses beyond electioneering. In legitimizing these uses, the FECA system holds that an individual may only give a restricted amount of financial assistance to a candidate for all of the candidate's political projects.

Incomplete evidence suggests that, in the past decade, abusive behavior has slowly increased (but is not common) and that the use of loopholes has become suddenly popular with wealthy individuals and large political interests. As a consequence, media insistence that the campaign finance system has become a scandal interacts with public cynicism to produce a consensus that a crisis exists. Among the smaller segment of the population participating in campaign finance as individual donors, party and interest group officials, and candidates, trust in the regulatory system seems to have declined. Even small increases in the number of abuses which go unpunished politically or legally demoralize the honest and embolden the dishonest. In addition, a feeling that large "smart money" interests are moving outside the regulatory system to pursue special access has reduced confidence in the ability of the FECA system to monitor political money.

Congressional Candidates and Political Money

This section focuses on questionable behavior by some congressional candidates, especially incumbents. Some newly elected incumbents, by accepting perfectly legal retroactive support to repay their personal campaign debts, offer ammunition to critics of the campaign finance system by appearing to sell influence to their "johnny come lately" benefactors. Some incumbents, by setting up their own personal political action committees to pursue their political purposes, offer individuals and PACs the opportunity to abuse the FECA's contribution limits.[2] A diminishing number of incumbents have the legal option to convert campaign funds into personal funds after retirement; those who do may erode citizens' trust in democratic institutions. Incumbents who accept speaking fees and travel for their personal and political gain offer interest groups the chance to stretch the FECA's constraints. Finally, incumbents who establish tax-exempt foundations for their personal and political use provide individuals and groups a chance to donate undisclosed and unlimited amounts through a loophole in the campaign finance regulatory system.

Campaign Debts

The FECA allows congressional candidates to spend unlimited amounts of personal funds for their campaign. Candidates may give the money to their treasuries as a contribution or lend it with the hope of repayment. They may also pledge personal assets as collateral for bank loans, provided that the loan terms are those that the bank routinely offers to others. Candidates' supporters may loan them $1,000 per election, if they have not already made contributions.[3]

Debts at the end of a campaign are a problem. A Congressional Research Service investigation of 1984 general election campaigns concluded that 89 percent of House and 78 percent of Senate candidates gave or lent their efforts $25,000 or less, but that 3 percent of House and 15 percent of Senate aspirants gave or lent more than $100,000.[4] Unsuccessful challengers and open-seat candidates face the dreary prospect of years of debt retirement. Conversely, winners face a more pleasant if thornier alternative; they become incumbents with real prospects of receiving contributions to repay the debts from erstwhile nonsupporters. Their new donors, individuals and PACs, may or may not have helped the incumbent they defeated. A Congressional Quarterly study of eleven newly elected Senators who had 1986 campaign debts found that they had raised nearly $3.1 million in the first six months of 1987 to repay their obligations completely or significantly. Fifty-two percent of their receipts came from PACs. Forty-one percent of the PAC money was from groups who had previously contributed to the defeated incumbent, while 13 percent was from groups who had supported both sides in the election.[5] PACs' post-election contributions to new incumbents whom they had not previously supported have been roundly criticized by Common Cause and the media as attempts to buy influence.[6] Yet, such gifts are only different in form and timing from pre-election gifts. The goal is the same: access.

Personal PACs

The hybrid multi-candidate committee commonly called a "personal" or a "leadership" PAC was not envisioned by the FECA. The Act allows individuals to give only $1,000 per election and PACs only $5,000 per election to the authorized campaign committee of a congressional candidate. A candidate's authorized committee wishing to give money to another federal candidate is limited to $1,000 per election. An inventive congressional incumbent who establishes a multi-candidate personal PAC for his political use, however, may accept $5,000 per year from an individual who has already given $2,000 to his campaign and $5,000 per year from a PAC which has previously donated $10,000 to his authorized committee. The personal PAC may give $5,000 per election to another federal candidate, in addition to $2,000 from his authorized committee.[7] Thus, the use of personal PACs clearly circumvents limits set by the FECA.

As Clyde Wilcox notes, these personal PACs are not a healthy development, for several reasons. First, they distort the channels of accountability between a PAC and its donors. When a PAC gives money to an incumbent's personal PAC, it abdicates its responsibility to decide which candidates to support. Second, leadership PACs could create inequality of access. Those individuals and PACs who are willing to stretch the spirit of the Act by giving to personal PACs gain potentially greater access to the PAC's sponsor—often a member of Congress in a powerful position. Third, by making such stretching of the law possible, personal PACs endanger the democratic system by undermining its legitimacy.

Personal Use of Campaign Funds

The 1979 Amendments to the FECA allow the personal use of surplus campaign funds by those persons who were a "Senator or Representative in, or Delegate or Resident Commissioner to, the Congress on January 8, 1980,"[8] once they retire. The Senate, however, prohibits both sitting Senators and former members from converting campaign funds to personal use. The House rule barring such conversion applies only to incumbents, not to former members. Slightly more than 40 percent of the House members in the 101st Congress which convened in January 1989, therefore, may elect to take advantage of this "grandfather" clause.

Ever since its enactment, this exception has been criticized by political reporters and other commentators as a vehicle for lining the pockets of willing House incumbents. Journalists report, for example, that thirty-eight House incumbents each had more than $300,000 in unspent funds after the 1986 elections,[9] including Dan Rostenkowski, Chairman of the Ways and Means Committee, who had $589,500.[10] Many of their reports state or assume that any grandfathered lawmaker who ends an election cycle with a nontrivial surplus has consciously collected more money than necessary for his campaign in order to build a retirement bonus. The reader is often left with the impression that grandfathers will take the bonus.

In fact, according to the Center for Responsive Politics, of the twenty- six eligible 1986 House retirees, only two had converted money to personal use by the end of 1987—William Carney (R-NY) took $83,700 and Eldon Rudd (R-AZ) $53,800 after donating $150,000 to a nonprofit educational organization. Three others had significant amounts of cash-on-hand as of December 31, 1987 ($191,500, $29,400 and $13,400).[11] The other twenty-one retirees either have small amounts remaining or none. In sum, depending on the behavior of the three with nontrivial funds, 81 percent to 92 percent of 1986 retirees did *not* take advantage of the grandfather clause.

Nonetheless, the grandfather clause is difficult to defend and may provide a legal avenue for bribery or for the appearance of bribery, to the detriment of public trust in Congress as an institution. Retirement and mortality may resolve the situation, or the clause could be abolished. Since all Senators and slightly under 60 percent of House members in the 101st Congress cannot use the clause, preventing the others from doing so seems a small price to pay for restoring legitimacy to this aspect of Congress.

Personal Benefits Beyond Campaign Funds

The Federal Election Campaign Act sets $2,000 as the maximum fee an elected or appointed officer or employee of the federal government may accept for any appearance, speech, or article. In addition to the $2,000 maximum honorarium, the officer or employee may accept payment for (or provision of) actual travel and subsistence expenses for himself and his spouse or an aide.[12] The Senate and House codes of official conduct limit the total annual amount of honoraria a member may keep, requiring that any excess be donated to charitable organizations. For the 100th Congress the Senate yearly limit was 40 percent of salary ($35,000–$35,800) and the House 30 percent ($25,900–$26,800).

Common Cause studies of congressional honoraria showed that House incumbents in 1987 collected $6,530,000 and kept $5,100,000. About 25 percent were at or near the $25,900 limit. Senators received $2,980,000 and retained $2,200,000. Forty-one percent were at or near the $35,000 annual cap. Analysis of the top earners indicates that a majority are congressional leaders, members of the tax-writing committees, or committee chairmen or ranking minority members.[13] Subsequent studies focused on the sources of honoraria reported by members of the armed services, banking, and commerce committees.[14] Widespread awareness of the honorarium subject helped to make it an issue in several 1988 congressional contests,[15] and a concern in debates over the congressional pay raise in 1989.

In addition to honoraria, the associated travel and subsistence expenses are roundly criticized. Articles and books detail week-long, all-expense-paid stays at luxury resorts in balmy climes. Accompanying spouses or aides also receive free airfare, lodging, and meals. Many of these trips seem like vacations underwritten by corporations, trade associations, and lobbying groups.[16]

Groups and members of Congress who defend the honorarium system argue that it increases insight and allows for the exchange of information. Critics raise a number of issues. Allowing a member to receive \$25,000–\$35,000 in personal income[17] and free travel from groups with an interest in legislation casts an ethical cloud over congressional policy-making. Having a member appear at a group's conference in Honolulu in January may be a more effective means of gaining access than a \$10,000 PAC contribution to a large "war- chest."[18] Despite its noble appearance, giving excessive honoraria to charitable organizations in one's state or district may reap political benefits. Finally, being away from Capitol Hill too frequently may not be the most conscientious way in which to represent one's constituents. None of these charges has been formally proven, but their possibilities alone are enough to undermine trust in the system.

Simply banning honoraria, however, is only partial reform. The other part of the problem is the provision of vacations which may be designed to curry favor but which are disguised as necessary travel and subsistence expenses for members and their spouses. Non-wealthy members, lowly paid in recent years, may have been scurrying to earn honoraria to make ends meet, accepting travel money as incidental to earning the fee. With adequate pay they should not need the fees and, therefore, not make the trips. Yet a dilemma remains as to how to promote legitimate trips and eliminate junkets.

Tax-Exempt Organizations Affiliated with Candidates

During the 1980s a number of tax-exempt organizations affiliated with federal candidates have been established. Most are organized under section 501(c)(3) of the Internal Revenue Code as "public charities," meaning that they must have educational or philanthropic goals which serve a public purpose.[19] They are tax-exempt organizations, and they may collect tax-deductible contributions without limits as to source or amount. They are not required to disclose publicly information about their donors. In exchange for these benefits they must accept several restrictions. They may not participate in elections or support candidates; they may not exist primarily for the private benefit of an individual or a small group.[20]

The Center for Responsive Politics has produced a thorough, balanced study of 501(c)(3) organizations associated with federal politicians.[21] They investigated compliance with the requirements that these organizations be publicly supported educational or philanthropic operations benefiting the public and not involved in elections, concluding that there is potential for abuse, especially by organizations affiliated with presidential aspirants before official declaration of candidacy.[22] Other studies suggest that a large contribution to a candidate's tax-exempt organization is a vehicle for access or influence used by serious donors after they contribute to the principal campaign committee and the personal PAC, and pay an honorarium.[23]

The Internal Revenue Service is primarily responsible for monitoring the activities of 501(c)(3) tax-exempt organizations. The IRS regulations may be adequate, but their enforcement requires a costly and time-consuming examination of the actual activities of a particular tax-exempt. Pessimistic about a large increase in IRS enforcement, the Center for Responsive Politics recommends greater public disclosure as an alternative method for gaining compliance.[24]

These recommendations should be taken seriously. The elimination of honoraria could create an incentive for more members to establish 501(c)(3) tax- exempts. The reasons offered for pursuing honoraria (to help charities or to deliver a political message) would also lead inexorably to the setting up of tax-exempt groups. If so, unlimited and undisclosed donations to a "public charity" may replace disclosed fees limited to $2,000 per appearance. Reluctant donors may complain anonymously of extortion, while eager seekers of access may make contributions designed to be more noticeable than a $2,000 individual or $10,000 PAC donation to an abundant campaign coffer.

Abuses by Contributors

Contributor abuses of the rules of the campaign finance system range from stretching the spirit of the limits to violating the letter of the Act. Individuals may stretch the limits by giving to a personal PAC amounts they could not give to an authorized campaign committee; they may violate the FECA by giving amounts in excess of their statutory limits. Party committees and PACs are currently probing the boundaries of the regulatory system in two areas—the value of other-than-cash contributions and the method for "bundling" donations.

Individual Citizens

Remember that the Federal Election Campaign Act limits

an individual to an annual total of $25,000 in contributions to federal candidates and political committees involved in federal elections. No more than $20,000 per year may be given to a national party committee, $5,000 per year to any other political committee, or $1,000 per election to the committee of any federal contestant. Individuals may abuse the *spirit* of these limits by (1) giving more than $2,000 to a personal PAC or (2) contributing any amount to the personal PACs after donating $2,000 to the candidate's authorized campaign committee.

As for actual attempts to violate the law, the Act makes efforts to exceed the limits by channeling multiple small amounts into federal elections so time-consuming that the Act's major source of violations is "contributions in the name of another." To address what was a perennial problem in the pre- FECA era, the Act says that "no person shall make a contribution in the name of another person or knowingly permit his name to be used to effect such a contribution, and no person shall knowingly accept a contribution made by one person in the name of another person."[25]

The FEC and the Justice Department conduct civil and criminal investigations to enforce compliance with the Act. One recent FEC case dealt with allegations that contributions had been made in the name of minor children.[26] The Justice Department has studied individuals who were fundraisers for Senator Gary Hart's 1984 presidential race, and has successfully prosecuted a California video producer for having his employees make contributions which he reimbursed.[27] Four Californians have been indicted for a convoluted scheme in which they allegedly made in-kind contributions of $120,000 media buys in the names of others.[28] The Justice Department's investigation of savings and loan fraud has led to indictments against three former officials of a failed Texas savings and loan for reimbursing employees for $135,000 in donations which the employees made to two PACs.[29]

Detecting violations is difficult; they are often discovered in the course of a criminal investigation of another matter or uncovered when a complaint is filed. It is hard to know with any precision how common the practice is. Observers agree that there was virtually no illegal activity ten years ago when the Act was new. The impression is that violations began in the last five years, for a variety of reasons involving both the campaign finance regulatory system and other political and economic factors. Violations might decrease in the future if convictions and fines for campaign finance infractions act as a deterrent, but there is no guarantee.

Violators should be aggressively punished, for the morale of those who obey the law and the deterrence of potential abusers. Stretching or violating the limits of the FECA distorts the equality of access to policy-making and equality of political participation that the law aims for along with the prevention of corruption or the appearance of corruption. Individuals who want to do more than the law allows have the avenue of independent expenditures.

Parties and PACs

In their efforts to give maximum support to favored candidates, both major parties and a number of PACs have been aggressive pioneers at stretching the boundaries of the FECA limits. Parties have the incentive to be innovative because of their vast financial and technological resources, which they cannot use for independent expenditures. Thus, they supplement their direct contributions with coordinated expenditures, maximize the impact of their gifts by providing in-kind services rather than cash, and encourage "bundling" by individuals and PACs to increase the flow of funds to favored partisans. Because PACs face tighter contribution limits than parties to Senate candidates, cannot make coordinated expenditures, yet may be unsure about the value of independent spending, they mimic the parties' use of in-kind contributions and bundling as ways to increase their impact.

The FECA sets different limits for national party contributions to House and Senate candidates. The national committee may give $5,000 per election to each House contestant, as may the party's House campaign committee.[30] The national committee and the senatorial campaign committee may give a combined total of $17,500 to a Senate aspirant.[31] A state party committee and its subordinate local affiliates, however, may give a combined total of $5,000 per election to either a House or a Senate candidate.[32] A House campaign committee or a state party committee may not give its own separate $5,000 contribution allowance to its national committee.[33]

The Act also allows the national committee and the state party committees to make coordinated general election expenditures for their standardbearers.[34] These campaign expenditures are made in consultation with the candidate, but are paid for and reported by the party committee. The Supreme Court has supported the FEC's interpretation of the Act as permitting a state committee to name the national committee as its agent for purposes of this spending,[35] thus allowing the national committee to centralize a decision on how to spend its own plus a state's allowance for a particular campaign. The combined allowances are quite generous; they are adjusted every year to keep pace with inflation. In 1988 the party could spend a total of $46,100 in a House race. In the half-dozen statewide at-large House contests and the Senate races in sparsely populated states the party could spend $92,200. As the size of a state's population increases, so does the party's expenditure limit, reaching the maximum of $1,877,400 for California.

In 1986 Democratic political committees nationwide spent $65,913,700 in moneys raised under the FECA, of which 16 percent ($10,655,200) was reported as contributions to and general-election expenditures for Democratic contestants. Seven percent ($17,739,000) of the GOP's $258,879,000 was attributed to support of its federal candidates.[36] Observers of party behavior generally agree that some unknown amount of the Democrats' 84 percent and Republicans' 93 percent in other spending did assist congressional aspirants.[37] If only the Senate and House campaign committees are considered, the Democratic Hill committees spent $26,095,800 while reporting that 34 percent ($8,805,800) of that disbursement was for their contenders, and the GOP committees expended 13 percent ($16,342,400) of their $124,564,900 on their aspirants.

What happened to the rest of the money? Some substantial amount of the gap can be explained as the overhead associated with running party committees. Like non-connected PACs, party committees must pay their operating expenses from the funds which they raise from contributors. Another portion of the gap can be explained by the parties' expenses for generic advertising, which may indirectly benefit candidates but which is not reportable as campaign assistance. An additional expense is advertising which directly attacks the behavior of the opposition's incumbent but which does not advocate his defeat; this spending does not have to be allocated as support for the party's challenger.[38] But some of these funds may assist a candidate and yet not be legally reportable as campaign help. A party committee could spend $10,000 for a poll in a House district, for example, but not give the results to its standardbearer until sixty-one days after the survey was taken. The committee would report a $500 in-kind contribution to (or coordinated expenditure for) its House candidate and a $9,500 operating expenditure for itself.[39] If the committee kept the poll results and only recommended actions based on its knowledge of the survey findings to the campaign, the committee would report $10,000 as an operating expenditure and $0 as candidate assistance.[40] In both of these examples a campaign could receive substantial benefit that was not counted as party contributions to or expenditures on behalf of a candidate.

The previous examples begin to illustrate how providing in-kind campaign services rather than cash can risk abusing the contribution limits of parties and PACs. Such services have included training schools for candidates and campaign managers, field staff or campaign workers, polling or targeting data, issues research, advertisement production, fundraising assistance, and much more. In-kind contributions of goods or services or anything of value need to be properly valued to avoid stretching the Act's contribution limits.[41] The FEC has provided rules through its Regulations, advisory opinion decisions, and enforcement actions.

In-kind contributions have been made since the earliest days of the FECA era, but they are apparently increasing in popularity with the PAC community.[42] In 1986, 2 percent ($2,128,157) of PACs' $139,839,718 contributions to federal candidates were in-kind donations; unsponsored PACs made 60 percent of them ($1,282,898).[43] PACs make the same kinds of in-kind contributions the party committees make, and they make them for the same reasons—to increase their visibility in a campaign, to maximize the amount of support they give within the contribution constraints, and to control how their money is spent. As long as they are properly reported, in-kind donations need not become a violation of the spirit or letter of the law.

Bundling Contributions from Individuals and PACs

"Bundling" (or "conduiting" or "earmarking") occurs when an individual or a PAC makes a contribution through an intermediary or conduit. "A conduit or intermediary's contribution limits are not affected by passing on earmarked contributions, except where the conduit exercises any direction or control over the choice of the recipient candidate. If a conduit exercises any direction or control over the choice of the recipient candidate, the contribution shall be considered a contribution by both the original contributor and the conduit..."[44]

Since the beginning of the FECA period some PACs have had bundling systems of one kind or another. At one extreme are systems involving no PAC control, i.e., those where the PAC makes no recommendations and contributors make unassisted earmarking decisions. Somewhere in the middle are structures where the PAC sends its members a list of candidates' names with instructions to make any contribution check payable to a specific candidate's campaign. At the opposite extreme are methods wherein contributors earmark the money they give to the PAC for Democratic or Republican contenders; these amounts then count against the PAC's own per candidate limit because the PAC chooses the actual recipients. In terms of a PAC's support of a candidate, earmarking has two benefits. Individual contributions are clearly identified as PAC connected. And, if a PAC exercises no direction or control, it may forward moneys without affecting its own contribution limit. The only drawback is that the cost of the bundling operation counts as an in-kind contribution to the candidates who receive the donations.[45]

Bundling, which requires cumbersome bookkeeping and reporting, has been used by national Republican committees only in situations where a committee had already given its maximum support to a hard-pressed standardbearer. In the fall of 1984 and 1986 the National Republican Senatorial Committee urged its own potential individual and PAC donors who had not already given the statutory maximum to these endangered Senate contenders to make an earmarked contribution to them via the committee, instead of giving money directly to the committee. In 1984 the NRSC bundled $3 million in individual and PAC contributions to its competitive aspirants; in 1986 it conduited $6 million.[46] In 1988 the National Republican Congressional Committee began collecting contributions in the same way.[47]

Until 1986–87 the FEC's disclosure and regulation of bundling was routine and low-key. The regulatory environment then became turbulent, because of Advisory Opinion Request questions posed by several PACs and the controversial large-scale bundling by the NRSC. In the cases of the PACs' questions, the Commission deadlocked, three-three, on the Advisory Opinion answers for the PACs recommended by its General Counsel and, therefore, issued none.[48] Thus there is a regulatory uncertainty about three crucial questions: (1) who may pay for the costs of an earmarking operation (the PAC with FECA funds or the sponsor with non-FECA funds); (2) are the costs an in-kind contribution or an independent expenditure; and (3) what constitutes the "direction or control" necessary to cause a contribution to count against a PAC's own limit? In the NRSC case, the FEC resolved a complaint by Common Cause by unanimously finding that the committee had exceeded its allowed 1986 support of twelve candidates by $534,000, because it had not allocated bundling costs as in-kind contributions or coordinated expenditures. The NRSC argued, without success, that the costs of unsuccessful solicitations were not FECA candidate support. The Commission deadlocked, on party lines, over the question of whether the NRSC's methods constituted direction and control.[49]

Bundling is an instance where different political values are in conflict. In theory earmarking induces people to participate in their group's campaign effort while still retaining individual responsibility. It makes the group more accountable to its members. In practice bundling may abuse the Act's limits on contributions. Although the funds come from individuals, the agency that collects them may garner undue influence because of them. Such abuse is detrimental to the legitimacy of the campaign finance system. Finally, bundling complicates public disclosure and comprehension, requiring ever increasing amounts of Commission time, for guidance, compliance and enforcement, as other large political actors adopt the practice.

Loopholes

Whereas abuses arise in campaign financing when candidates, individuals, or political organizations attempt to circumvent explicit restrictions designed to prevent corruption or the appearance of corruption, loopholes emerge from unregulated activities that result in benefits for specific candidates. Originally, these activities were unregulated because they were considered to be valuable free speech and association only indirectly related to influencing elections. The funds used are not usually required to be disclosed, not limited in amount, and may come from corporate sources as well as individuals. These funds are commonly referred to as "soft money."[50]

There are three ways that individuals can legally spend unlimited funds in ways that might ultimately benefit candidates. Only independent expenditures made expressly to advocate the support or defeat of a specific candidate must be reported in any way. As Candice Nelson has noted, few individuals have opted for this loophole. More commonplace are the soft-money contributions individuals are making to national and state parties for the purchase or construction of office buildings, for state and local grassroots activities, and for national level "party building." Finally, individuals can give undisclosed and unlimited funds to tax-exempt (501)(c)(3) and (501)(c)(4) organizations. Some of these are tied to congressional candidates and others engage in political activities that are supposed to remain nonpartisan. Contributions to (501)(c)(3) public charities have the added benefit of earning tax deductions for the donors.

Corporate and interest group funds have also found their way back into federal elections, through contributions to the political parties and through other loopholes as well. Corporations, labor unions, and associations may use unlimited amounts of treasury money to urge the election (or the defeat) of a specific congressional candidate, but this advocacy may be directed only at executives or members and their families, and not at the general public.[51] This partisan advocacy may take any of the following forms: printed materials, appearances by the favored candidate, phone banks, and registration and get- out- the- vote drives. It is unlikely that Congress or the courts will move to restrict this private associational communication, even though it benefits a particular candidate.

Any electoral communications which corporations, unions, or organizations direct at the general public must be nonpartisan, with one exception recently created by the Supreme Court. In *FEC v. Massachusetts Citizens for Life, Inc.*, the Court held that small nonprofit groups which had simply taken the corporate form could make unlimited independent expenditures advocating the election (or the defeat) of a specific federal candidate to the general public. The key to the Court's decision to allow this corporation to spend its treasury funds was the fact that it took no contributions from for-profit corporations or labor unions. If the independent expenditures made by such a group total more than $250 per year, they must be reported under the FECA and the sources of the money disclosed.[52] It is very likely that other nonprofit corporations which do accept corporate and labor donations will test the Supreme Court's meaning when it granted this exemption to Massachusetts Citizens for Life because "it was not established by a business corporation or a labor union, and its policy is not to accept contributions from such entities." Allowing a nonprofit corporation which receives corporate or labor money to make independent expenditures would create another loophole.

Even the requirement that electoral activities aimed at the general public be nonpartisan can become a loophole. It is obviously easy to conduct a theoretically nonpartisan election effort which is in reality of direct partisan benefit to a particular federal candidate. This is especially true of registration and get-out-the-vote activities which can be undertaken in politically homogeneous areas. A determination of what is, in fact, a partisan effort is a complex enforcement problem, but it is one that the IRS must attempt. If the IRS discovers violations by corporations, unions, or associations in the course of its investigations, it should refer them to the FEC.

Tax-exempt organizations have also become loopholes by which candidates, corporations, groups, and wealthy individuals seek to increase their electoral influence. The creation of tax-exempt public charities to further the political ambitions of congressional candidates was discussed previously. Donations to such charities need not be revealed. Other foundations [(501)(c)(3)s] or lobbies [(501)(c)(4)s] receive unlimited funds from individuals, unions, or corporations to produce nonpartisan voter guides, conduct research, or carry out voter registration and get-out-the-vote drives. Of course, these "nonpartisan" activities can end up tailored to benefit specific candidates, unless the IRS steps in. Furthermore, there is another type of problem which seems to be growing. Some tax-exempt organizations are being misused to save money for their informally affiliated PAC, thus leaving the PAC with more money to spend on candidate contributions or independent expenditures.[53] Again, the extent of the problem is unknown; its existence has been discussed by the IRS and the House Ways and Means Committee. New IRS regulations, which took effect in February 1988, require 501(c)(3)s and 501(c)(4)s and PACs which are directly or indirectly affiliated to disclose that fact publicly,[54] providing the IRS with a new enforcement opportunity.

The manner in which the national parties are increasing their role in elections has led to charges that they are exploiting loopholes in the campaign finance regulatory system.[55] It is the parties' use of soft money that has most attracted attention to this issue. National and state parties may and do accept unlimited amounts from individuals, corporations, labor unions, and other groups for the purchase or construction and equipping of an office building. They are not required to disclose these donations.[56] The national committees, with increasing vigor and sophistication in each election cycle, also solicit what they call "non-federal" donations, arguing that these gifts need not be disclosed or limited in source or amount because they will not be used for "influencing" any federal election. Some of these moneys they place in their own non-federal accounts, and some they help channel to state committee non-federal accounts. Many of these donations, from individuals, corporations, unions, and groups, are very large. In 1986 the DCCC received $100,000 each from a number of labor unions.[57] In 1988 the DNC soft money efforts raised about $20 million, with $100,000 donations coming from corporations, unions, and 130 individuals; the RNC received about $25 million, with 250 gifts, of $100,000 or more, from individuals and corporations.[58]

The national committees use their non-federal accounts to pay for general party activity, e.g., generic ads in the media, a Democratic response to President Reagan's State of the Union messages, and lawsuits over congressional districting. The state parties use their soft money, raised either at the behest of the national committees[59] or on their own, for the following party-building activities: overhead expenses, support of state and local candidates, and grassroots activity in federal elections which the 1979 FECA Amendments exempted from disclosure and contribution/expenditure limitation.[60] If a state party performs an activity, such as a turnout drive, which benefits both state and federal candidates, it must determine the proportion that benefits the federal standardbearers and pay for that portion in FECA-raised "hard money." Obviously, the decision about how much should be allocated as the federal share is a critical regulatory concern. The FEC has been very slow in writing regulations on the allocation rules. It has been under court order since mid-1987 to write regulations which give specific guidance.

The FEC's inactivity, combined with the national parties' aggressiveness, and compounded by Dukakis fundraiser Robert Farmer's brazenness, has brought "soft money" to general public attention. Headlines and editorials equate 1988 with 1972. There certainly was centralized fundraising by the national committees from national donors who wanted to help a federal ticket. How much this money helped federal candidates is unknown. That some of it did in direct ways is inescapable. That much of it did in indirect ways is likely, because it paid for things which otherwise would have consumed hard money. Thus, it caused more hard money to be available for candidate support.

Even though raised in devious ways and used with questionable results, this non-federal money, at both the national and state level, has had positive consequences. Citizens have been stimulated and informed, and parties as electoral institutions have been strengthened. But these benefits have been purchased at the cost of governmental legitimacy. This money has come from sources—corporations, unions, and "fat cats"—which are unacceptable to the American public.

This public reaction is not simply knee-jerk cynicism. It is valid to raise the question of whether these large donors are purchasing unequal access to federal office-holders. Fundraising techniques for $100,000 gifts are not like those for direct mail. They involve a party broker in a personalized appeal to a big contributor. That broker will introduce the donor to members of Congress as a staunch party supporter. The willingness of the party broker to vouch for the large contributor means that the latter could, in some cases, receive as much unequal access (or appearance of such) as if he had donated his $100,000 directly to the incumbent's personal PAC's non-federal account.

Unlike the parties' "fat cats," the topics of political misuse of tax- exempt organizations and of corporate and union partisan wolves in nonpartisan sheeps' clothing have not become front-page items. Among political participants the corporate/group electoral activity raises no eyebrows, while the behavior of tax-exempts does. There is no sense that these uses of loopholes are common, but they do seem to be growing in popularity. Even though the democratic benefits of an illegally partisan registration or turnout drive are theoretically great in terms of more citizen participation, they are purchased at the possible price of decreased public trust and enhanced access to office-holders by the violators.

Conclusions

The major values threatened by abuses and loopholes in campaign finance laws are effectiveness and legitimacy. When enforcement of the letter or spirit of the FECA is ineffective, doubts arise about the legitimacy of our campaign finance system and, ultimately, about the government it serves to elect.

Many of the practices discussed, especially those that are loopholes, are defended as promoting political liberty and increasing avenues for participation in campaign funding. Since several of them simply allow wealthy individuals or corporate and labor donors to regain influence the FECA attempted to reduce, however, such loopholes and abuses also undermine political equality and distort the accountability of elected representatives to voters.

Fortunately, several potential problem areas such as debt retirement and in-kind contributions are adequately addressed by careful enforcement of current laws and the self-restraint of candidates and contributors. Several other areas are in need of reform in order to preserve the values of legitimacy, effectiveness, accountability, and political equality.

1) Many of the abuses engaged in by Members of Congress—even if not widespread—need to be halted in order to prevent corruption or the appearance of corruption and to restore public trust in our government. These include eliminating personal PACs, repealing the grandfather clause, ending the use of honoraria, and placing controls on the acceptance of travel funds by members and their spouses. Personal PACs too easily allow contributors and candidates to circumvent the contribution limits of the FECA. The personal uses of campaign funds as retirement bonuses provide no public benefits yet undermine citizen trust of government. Honoraria and travel expenses are of only slightly less questionable status. One solution to promoting valuable legislative trips rather than potentially corrupting junkets would be to use public funds for all travel by members of Congress. A less costly approach would require strict rules on travel and subsistence comparable to those regulating executive branch employees. Such rules would require adequate disclosure and meaningful enforcement by the House and Senate ethics committees.

2) Another abuse that provides few benefits in exchange for its costs is bundling. This practice circumvents the spirit of contribution limits, thereby weakening their effectiveness and legitimacy. It may also encourage elected officials to feel more accountable to PACs that provide bundled funds than to their constituents. Because eliminating bundling will not severely curtail the participation or political liberty of individuals or organizations, it should be abolished.

3) Other campaign finance problems can best be addressed by vigorous enforcement of the laws by the FEC, IRS, and Department of Justice. These include individual attempts to skirt

contribution limits by gifts in the name of others, in-kind contributions by PACs and parties, and candidates' use of tax-exempt organizations for electoral objectives.

4) The potential for tax-exempt organizations to use unrestricted contributions from individuals and corporations to benefit candidates is best addressed by stronger IRS enforcement to assure that activities are nonpartisan. In addition, such organizations should be required to disclose the sources and sizes of their contributions so that proper scrutiny can be given to them.

5) Disclosure is also the most obvious first step in addressing the other uses of soft money, especially those of the political parties. The party building and voter education activities supported by such contributors are valuable. Nonetheless, concerns about "fat cats" and corporate donors receiving privileged access to policy-makers because of their partisan support suggests that, ideally, limits may need to be extended to soft money contributions to national and state parties.

6) Partly to offset the restriction of soft money contributions to the parties and to reduce their incentive to use such funds to benefit federal candidates, the coordinated general election spending limits for parties should be raised. This reform would allow us to reap the continued benefits of stronger parties: increased political participation and education as well as enhanced competition in elections. Routine audits by the FEC could assure that the parties do not abuse their privileged status.

7) The Federal Election Commission structure should be changed to one with seven Commissioners. With staggered terms, the Democrats would have a majority for two years, and then the GOP would be temporarily ascendant. The reason for the proposal is that, on many of the issues reviewed here, partisan deadlock occurred on enforcement or advisory opinions when the stakes were very high. It may be time to consider a more conventional number of regulators. Abstentions should be made more difficult. Appeal to the courts would still be available to candidates and committees who disagree with a Commission action.

8) Perhaps the most beneficial and practical reforms can come through self-regulation by the actors in our campaign finance system. Too often candidates, parties, and PACs are choosing clever tactics for short-term benefits without recognizing the long-term damage their behavior may be inflicting on the campaign finance system. Participants need to exercise more financial and ethical self-control. Such self-restraint may be our

only hope for restoring legitimacy in the face of certain abuses and loopholes described in this chapter.

NOTES

1. PACs are allowed to give $1,000 or $5,000 per election to a candidate, depending on their status (2 U.S. Code, sec. 441a(a)(4)), and parties have the most generous contribution and support allowances.

2. For a detailed treatment of such personal PACs, see Clyde Wilcox's chapter in this volume.

3. 11 Code of Federal Regulations, sec. 110.10, 100.7(a)(1)(i) and (b)(11). If a PAC or party committee decides to make a loan, its contribution limit amount applies.

4. Joseph E. Cantor, *Campaign Financing in Federal Elections*, Report No. 86-143 GOV of the Congressional Research Service (Washington: Library of Congress, 1986), 41–42.

5. Jeremy Gaunt, "Winners Have No Trouble Retiring Debts," *Congressional Quarterly Weekly Report*, Vol. 45, No. 36, 2134–36.

6. See, for example, "PACs Doing Senatorial Flip-Flops," *The Washington Post* (March 21, 1987) and Dale Russakoff, "The Fickle Affections of PACs," *The Washington Post* (January 5, 1989).

7. 2 U.S. Code, sec. 441(a)(1) and (2), and 432(e)(3)(B).

8. 2 U.S. Code, sec. 439a.

9. Brooks Jackson, *Honest Graft*, (New York: Alfred A. Knopf, 1988), 312.

10. Ed Zuckerman, "188 in House Have $100,000-Plus Banked for '88," *PACs & Lobbies*, Vol. 8, No. 2, 1–6.

11. Center for Responsive Politics, *Money and Politics: Spending in Congressional Elections* (Washington: 1988), 18–20.

12. 2 U.S. Code, sec. 441i. Executive branch ethics codes further restrict federal employees. Section 441i of the Act defines an honorarium as payment for an "appearance, speech, or article." The Federal Election Commission Regulations, in giving a fuller description of those terms, say that an article "means a writing other than a book" (11 C.F.R., sec. 110.12(b)(4)).

13. David S. Cloud, "Leaders, Tax Experts Top Hill Honoraria Rolls," *Congressional Quarterly Weekly Report*, Vol. 46, No. 24, 1572–73; also "Survey of Honoraria Earned by Congressmen in 1987 Released," *Campaign Practices Reports*, Vol. 15,

No. 12, 4.

14. "The Defense Industry and Capitol Hill," *The Washington Post* (July 7, 1988), and Tom Kenworthy, "Courting the Key Committees," *The Washington Post* (August 3, 1988). The correlation between committee jurisdiction and honorarium source may be confounded by a factor reported by Jackson (*Honest Graft*, 211). Anthony Coelho is quoted as saying he asked groups to extend invitations to colleagues who were in financial trouble.

15. Brooks Jackson, "Easy Money," *The Wall Street Journal* (November 1, 1988), reports on the anti-honoraria campaign commercials of three House challengers.

16. Eric Pianin and Charles R. Babcock, "Congress' Business Vacations," *The Washington Post* (June 20, 1988) also report a Common Cause study on the increase in travel expenses between 1980 and 1985; Dan Morgan, "Company Reaps Subsidies with Congress as Partner," *The Washington Post* (June 13, 1988); Thomas B. Edsall, "Congress' Free Rides," *The Washington Post* (June 14, 1987); Jackson, *Honest Graft*, 211–13; and Philip M. Stern, *The Best Congress Money Can Buy* (New York: Pantheon Books/Random House, 1988), 51–55 and 91–94.

17. Members must give any honoraria over their body's limit to charity, thus on the face of it deriving no personal financial benefit from any excess amounts. Charles Babcock reports, however, that the tax-sheltered Keough retirement plans set up by ten Senators and at least thirty House members may give them incentive to earn excess fees even if they must donate them. A member with no other outside income would have an incentive to earn up to $120,000 in honoraria, in order to raise his income base and make the maximum donation to his Keough. "Hill Lawmakers Find Tax Haven in Honoraria," *The Washington Post* (August 7, 1988).

18. Stern, *Best Congress*, 55, 156, 160.

19. Internal Revenue Code, sec. 501(c)(3). They must also pass a public support test contained in either section 509(a)(1) or (2). Public support distinguishes them from the much more regulated 501(c)(3) privately funded "foundation."

20. 26 Code of Federal Regulations, sec. 1.501(c)(3).

21. Center for Responsive Politics, *Public Policy and Foundations: The Role of Politicians in Public Charities* (Washington: 1987). Also see Judith Havemann, "Lawmakers Lobbying for Endowments," *The Washington Post* (May 28, 1988).

22. If personal PACs were the first-generation enhancement

in the post-FECA candidate product line, then 501(c)(3) public charities are the second- generation product.

23. Morgan, "Company Reaps Subsidies," *The Washington Post* (June 13, 1988), and Stern, *Best Congress*, 77–88.

24. The Center's findings and specific recommendations are contained on pages 42–45, 54, 61–63, and 67–74. As of February 1, 1988 federal law now requires these tax-exempt organizations to make their annual tax return available for inspection at their offices and to disclose on it any direct or indirect relationship with a lobbying group or a PAC. Ed Zuckerman, "New Law in Effect for Tax-Exempts," *PACs & Lobbies*, Vol. 9, No. 2, 1, 4–5.

25. 2 U.S. Code, sec. 441f.

26. Matter Under Review 2579 of the FEC (1988), which was closed with "no reason to believe" a violation had occurred. To contribute legally children must use their own money and be old enough to have "donative intent."

27. Charles R. Babcock, "Hart Supporter Guilty of Illegal Donations," *The Washington Post* (August 4, 1988), and "Former Hart Supporter Fined for Campaign Law Violations," *The Washington Post* (December 8, 1988).

28. Charles R. Babcock, "4 Californians Indicted on Election Law Charges," *The Washington Post* (December 15, 1988).

29. Ruth Marcus, "Three Former Officials of Texas S&L Indicted," *The Washington Post* (January 13, 1989).

30. 11 Code of Federal Regulations, sec. 110.3(b).

31. 11 C.F.R, sec. 110.2(c).

32. 11 C.F.R, sec. 110.3(b). The $5,000 amount applies to multi-candidate committees (11 C.F.R, sec. 100.5(e)(3)). The national, House, and most state party committees are multicandidate committees. State committees which are not are limited to a $1,000 per election contribution.

33. Nothing in the Act or in court decisions allows the House or state party committees to delegate their contribution allowances. Transfers of money, however, between different levels of party organizations are permitted without limit (2 U.S.C., sec. 441a(a)(4)). Therefore, a national committee with ample funds could transfer funds to an impecunious state committee; the latter could then use the money for contributions to House candidates.

34. 2 U.S. Code, sec. 441a(d) and 441a(c).

35. The Republican committees began the practice in 1978. The Democrats challenged them, but the FEC and the Supreme

Court agreed with the GOP's interpretation. *FEC v. Democratic Senatorial Campaign Committee*, 454 U.S. 27 (1981).

36. Federal Election Commission, *FEC Reports on Financial Activity, 1985–86, Final Report, Party and Non-Party Political Committees* (Washington: 1988). The parties' spending figures are their net disbursement amounts (i.e., their total disbursements minus transfers to affiliated party committees).

37. See, for example, Larry J. Sabato, *The Party's Just Begun* (Glenview, IL: Scott, Foresman and Company, 1988), chapt. 3 and Frank J. Sorauf, *Money in American Elections* (Glenview, IL: Scott, Foresman and Company, 1988), chapt. 5.

38. Jackson, *Honest Graft*, 177–80, 184–85; Ed Zuckerman, "Lawsuit's Real Issue Is FEC's Political Power," *PACs & Lobbies*, Vol. 8, No. 18, 1–5; Ed Zuckerman, "Appeals Court Says FEC Deadlocks Can Be Reviewed," *PACs & Lobbies*, Vol. 8, No. 21, 1, 4; and "DCCC Wins Point Against FEC Dismissal," *Campaign Practices Reports*, Vol. 14, No. 22, 4.

39. 11 Code of Federal Regulations, sec. 106.4(f) and (g) for the rules on depreciating the value of surveys.

40. Paul S. Herrnson, *Party Campaigning in the 1980s* (Cambridge, MA: Harvard University Press, 1988), 79. A party official argues that when the party keeps the findings there is no candidate "acceptance of poll results." FEC Regulations (11 C.F.R., sec. 106.4(b)) define "acceptance" as the mechanism which triggers the obligation to report a contribution to a campaign.

41. FEC Regulations (11 C.F.R., sec. 100.8(a)(1)(iv)) require that the value of donated goods or services reflect ordinary market prices.

42. Larry J. Sabato, *PAC Power* (New York: W. W. Norton & Company, 1984), 93–95; Margaret Ann Latus, "Assessing Ideological PACs," in Michael J. Malbin, ed., *Money and Politics in the United States* (Chatham, NJ: Chatham House Publishers, 1984), 151–67; Walter K. Moore, "The Case of an Independent Political Action Committee," and Paul M. Weyrich, "The New Right," in Michael J. Malbin, ed., *Parties, Interest Groups, and Campaign Finance Laws* (Washington: American Enterprise Institute for Public Policy Research, 1980), 56–67 and 73–75; and Sorauf, *Money in American Elections*, 110, 118–20.

43. *FEC Reports on Financial Activity, 1985–86, Final Report, Party and Non-Party Political Committees.*

44. 11 Code of Federal Regulations, sec. 110.6(d). See

sec. 110.6(c) for the complex reporting requirements for earmarked contributions.

45. For indications of the relative rarity of earmarking in past years see Sabato, *PAC Power*, 63–64; Edward Handler and John R. Mulkern, *Business in Politics* (Lexington, MA: Lexington Books/D. C. Heath, 1982), 78–82; and Ann B. Matasar, *Corporate PACs and Federal Campaign Financing Laws* (New York: Quorum Books, 1986), 53. Specific PACs' bundling procedures are described in Bernadette A. Budde, "Business Political Action Committees," and Stephen W. Thomas, "Commentaries," in Malbin, ed., *Parties, Interest Groups, and Campaign Finance Laws*, 22, 81–86; Latus, "Assessing Ideological PACs," in Malbin, ed., *Money and Politics*, 151–61; and Stern, *The Best Congress Money Can Buy*, 170–72.

46. Herrnson, *Party Campaigning*, 71–72; Sabato, *The Party's Just Begun*, 104; and Sorauf, *Money in American Elections*, 319–23.

47. "NRCC 'Bundles' PAC Contributions from Reagan Fundraiser to Help Beleaguered GOP House Incumbents," *Campaign Practices Reports*, Vol. 15, No. 19, 5.

48. Ed Zuckerman has analyzed the draft Advisory Opinions and discussion of them at Commission meetings in the following articles in PACs & Lobbies: "FEC Bundles Itself in Partisan Knot," Vol. 8, No. 10, 7–8; "FEC Gets Key 'Bundling' Questions," Vol. 8, No. 21, 1–2; "FEC Stalls Answer on 'Bundling' Plan," Vol. 8, No. 22, 1, 4; "'Loose Bundles'," Vol. 9, No. 12, 3; and "FEC Partisan Deadlock Leaves AMA/AMPAC to Ponder Fundraising Plan," Vol. 9, No. 13, 1, 5–6. Also the *Campaign Practices Reports* articles "FEC Delays Decision on LUPAC 'Bundling' Plan," Vol. 14, No. 22, 1–2 and "FEC Declines to Approve AMPAC's Variations on 'Bundling' Theme," Vol. 15, No. 13, 2–3.

49. Matter Under Review 2282 of the FEC (1988).

50. Herbert Alexander has described and analyzed all the activities which are discussed in the following paragraphs. He has also made estimates, where possible, of the amounts spent on elections through 1984. See Herbert E. Alexander, *'Soft Money' and Campaign Financing* (Washington: Public Affairs Council, 1986). Also see his book with Brian A. Haggerty, *Financing the 1984 Election* (Lexington, MA: Lexington Books, 1987).

51. 2 U.S. Code, sec. 431(9)(B)(iii) and 11 Code of Federal Regulations, sec. 114.3, 104.6, and 100.8(b)(4). The cost of

this communication does not have to be disclosed unless it exceeds $2,000 per election for all federal candidates. Labor unions predominate among those who file these communication costs reports. Corporations, unions, and associations may also spend unlimited and undisclosed amounts of treasury funds to set up and operate a "separate segregated fund" (or PAC) to receive political contributions from its executives or members. 2 U.S. Code, sec. 441b(b)(2)(C).

52. *FEC v. Massachusetts Citizens for Life, Inc.* 479 U.S. 238 (1986). See Ed Zuckerman's articles in *PACs & Lobbies* on the repercussions of this decision: "Non-Profit Group Tests High Court Ruling," Vol. 8, No. 5, 8; "'Express Advocacy' Opinion Opens Political Rift," Vol. 8, No. 7, 1–4; "'Express Advocacy' Ties FEC in Partisan Knot," Vol. 8, No. 8, 7–8; "Judge Tells NOW: 'Surrender Data to FEC'," Vol. 9, No. 10, 1, 10–11, 13; "FEC Seeks Advice for Rulemaking," Vol. 9, No. 20, 1, 4; and "FEC Gets Conflicting Advice for Rulemaking," Vol. 9, No. 23, 5–6. See also "Business Corporations Seek to Expand Permissible Role in Election Activity," *Campaign Practices Reports*, Vol. 15, No. 23, 2–3.

In September 1988 a U.S. Appeals Court panel, relying on Massachusetts Citizens for Life, ruled that the Michigan Chamber of Commerce could make indirect expenditures in Michigan elections. The Chamber is a nonprofit corporation which receives the majority of its funds from corporations. "Federal Appeals Court Declares Michigan Ban on Independent Expenditures by 'Non-Traditional' Corporations Unconstitutional," *Campaign Practices Reports*, Vol. 15, No. 19, 6.

53. The use of the tax-exempt loophole seems particularly attractive to unsponsored, non-connected PACs. These PACs may solicit contributions from anyone, but they must pay their overhead from what limited and disclosed contributions they do receive. If one of these PACs sets up a tax-exempt organization, the latter can be used to pay for research/policy papers, for creating and refining a mailing list, and for some allocated share of overhead. The temptation is to inflate the overhead allocation and to have the tax-exempt do things which are partisanly election related.

54. See Ed Zuckerman's reports on tax-exempt organizations in *PACs & Lobbies*: "Hearing Focuses on Tax-Exempt Lobbies," Vol. 8, No. 6, 1–4; "House Panel OKs Political Curbs for Tax-Exempts," Vol. 8, No. 15, 1–2; "New Law in Effect for Tax-

Exempts," Vol. 9, No. 2, 1, 4–5; "IRS: 501(c)(3)s Can Have PACs," Vol. 9, No. 4, 1–2.

55. Brooks Jackson (*Honest Graft*, 8, 12–15, 142–66) provides the most detailed look at soft money in congressional campaigns, with his case study of the 1986 operation of the DCCC under Representative Tony Coelho (D-CA). Others who have described and analyzed the evolution of national party soft money during the 1980s are: Alexander, *'Soft Money' and Campaign Financing*; Elizabeth Drew, *Politics and Money* (New York: Macmillan Publishing Company, 1983), 111–18; Sabato, *The Party's Just Begun*, chapt. 3; Sorauf, *Money in American Elections*, chapts. 5 and 10; and Stern, *The Best Congress Money Can Buy*, 161–65. The Center for Responsive Politics provides a succinct summary of activity through 1984 in its publication *Money and Politics: Soft Money—A Loophole For the '80s* (Washington: 1985).

56. 11 Code of Federal Regulations, sec. 100.7(b)(12). See Alexander (*'Soft Money' and Campaign Financing*, 29–32) and Jackson (*Honest Graft*, 143–54) for data on national committee building funds.

57. Jackson, *Honest Graft*, 8, 15, 155–65.

58. Brooks Jackson, "Bush, Dukakis Presidential Campaigns Each Spent More Than $100 Million," *The Wall Street Journal* (December 12, 1988). The committees voluntarily disclosed the lists of names of large donors; the DNC released a list in August and another after the election, while the RNC's releases were post-election. See Charles R. Babcock's articles in *The Washington Post*: "Democrats Disclose Big Donors," (August 17, 1988); "Names of 40 Who Gave Democrats $100,000 Each Disclosed," (November 3, 1988); "Big Donations Again a Campaign Staple," (November 17, 1988); "GOP Discloses Names of Big Donors," (January 24, 1989); and "Paying Dearly To Be Top Fans of a Winning Team," (February 1, 1989).

59. National party fundraisers look for a match between donor and state law, i.e., if a labor union wants to give $100,000, the fundraiser will suggest that the money be given to a party committee in a state which permits unlimited union gifts.

60. The exemptions are for things like slate cards and bumper stickers distributed by volunteers and for registration and get-out-the-vote drives conducted by volunteers. 11 Code of Federal Regulations, sec. 100.7(b)(9), (15), and (17).

6

The Unaccountability of Political Money

David Adamany

The sources and spenders of campaign money should be accountable, or so we are told. But why should political money be accountable? Accountable to whom? And what procedure would satisfy the requirement for accountability? Although much has been written about campaign finance, there has been little specification of what the accountability of campaign finance means.[1]

Accountability emphasizes the need to check both the misuses and the untoward consequences of campaign money. It assumes that because money is needed to present alternatives in campaigns substantial expenditures are necessary.[2] But it also assumes that those who use money in politics should be made responsible for the way they use it. Furthermore, since candidates seeking election or re-election must obtain funds to wage their campaigns, contributions must be regulated to diminish the possibility that once in office, representatives will be influenced by those who provide financial resources rather than those who cast votes.[3]

To whom should campaign money be accountable? First, and foremost, political money should be accountable to the voters,[4] because elections are intended to allow them to select officials by casting equally weighted, but also fully informed, votes. Second, donors who make contributions or organization members who pay dues should have some control over the political uses of those funds.

Third, the use of campaign funds by committees that are sponsored by another institution could be accountable to the parent organization.[5] The clearest cases are connected PACs, the political committees sponsored by corporations, labor unions, trade associations, and other institutions. Similarly, the senatorial and congressional campaign committees of the two parties in Congress are "connected" to the party caucuses.

The question of how campaign money should be made accountable captures two separate concerns. First, what relationship between voters, donors, or parent organizations and those who deploy campaign funds meets the standard of accountability? Does accountability require that voters, donors, or parent organizations have the opportunity to influence or control the use to which their contributions are put by candidates, political parties, or political committees? Does accountability require that voters, donors, or parent organizations have means to impose retrospective sanctions on those who deploy campaign funds? What kinds of sanctions should those be?

Second, how should accountability be implemented? Sometimes accountability rules are written into law. Sometimes they are written into the formal rules of organizations. Labor union constitutions, for instance, typically require that representative bodies, such as elected executive committees or union conventions, must endorse candidates who will receive labor contributions. And finally, accountability may occur because of patterns of behavior followed by donors, members, and leaders of political organizations. Organizational leaders may, for instance, poll donors or members about the allocation of campaign funds, even though they are not required to do so. Here there is de facto accountability, even though it is not required by law or associational charter.

Striving for Accountability

Current American law and practice emphasize several techniques for achieving accountability and several that ameliorate the need for accountability. In the first category are laws requiring the disclosure of campaign funds, rules and institutional practices that give members or donors some control over the use of campaign funds, and the individual's option to "exit"—that is, to withhold contributions or forswear organizational membership—if she does not approve of the way political funds are used. The second category includes laws that promote equality among persons in funding politics, such as contribution limits or public financing.

Reformers have long seen disclosure as a means of promoting accountability to voters and to donors. Following revelations before an investigating committee of the New York State Senate that massive corporate contributions had been made to Theodore Roosevelt's 1904 presidential campaign, the National Publicity Bill Organization was formed to promote the disclosure of campaign contributions and expenditures.[6] With the development of the publicity movement, proponents also argued that the electorate should "know before the election who gave how much to which candidates and could judge for itself the political indebtedness of the various candidates."[7]

The theory of disclosure is that sanctions will be imposed on those who engage in offensive campaign finance practices. The assumptions about effective disclosure are that information is disclosed, that it is in usable form, that it is disseminated, that appropriate audiences (voters, donors, members, stockholders, etc.) obtain and comprehend the information, and that those audiences act on the information. Faced with disclosure and its consequences, those who collect and deploy political funds would engage in anticipatory self-restraint.

Grave doubts have been raised about the effectiveness of disclosure.[8] First, so much information is reported under federal and state laws that citizens, candidates, and the media cannot analyze it rapidly enough to make finances a campaign issue. Even public agencies responsible for reviewing campaign finance reports may be swamped by the volume of filings.[9]

Second, disclosed information may not be publicized. The media unevenly cover campaign financing. Opposition candidates cannot be relied on to raise campaign finance issues: they may not have the resources, or they may prefer to devote campaign resources to other issues, or they may fear retaliation on the funding issue by opponents in an age when virtually all candidates receive special interest funds.

Third, the media may bring bias to campaign finance coverage. In 1972, papers that endorsed Richard Nixon were much less likely to carry early Watergate stories or place them on the front page than were McGovern-endorsing papers.[10] More recently, Frank Sorauf has argued that media coverage of campaign finance reflects a "neo-Progressive outlook" stemming from journalists' biased assumption that campaign money, especially from organized interest groups, is inevitably corrupt.[11]

Fourth, the public may not pay much attention to campaign finance disclosures. In one of the few studies of the public's knowledge of campaign finance practices, 1972 survey respondents viewed campaign finance information through partisan lenses: Republicans found little wrong with GOP financing practices but were critical of Democratic campaign funding; Democrats took the opposite view.[12]

Fifth, of course, campaign finance information may not be available at all. Historically, disclosure laws have been rent with loopholes.[13] The Federal Election Campaign Act's (FECA) disclosure provisions were tightly written, and the independent Federal Election Commission (FEC) was established to administer and enforce the law's provisions. Indeed, disclosure was extensive under the Act for about the first decade of its life. Recent campaign finance practices—especially the extensive use of "soft money"—have undermined disclosure.

Sixth, even if a candidate's financial practices are known to voters and are regarded as offensive, voters may still not vote against him. Offensive campaign funding practices may not appear to a thoughtful voter to be sufficient reason to abandon a candidate with whom she agrees on great issues of national security, economic policy, or civil rights.

These reservations do not mean that campaign finance can never be an issue. The National Conservative Political Action Committee (NCPAC) became so visible for its negative advertising campaigns against liberal Democrats that some candidates and political committees purchased advertising to make NCPAC's spending the issue and succeeded. Indeed, in one instance NCPAC's favored candidate was also damaged by its negative campaigning as well as the opposition counterattack. There are also a handful of reported instances when challengers made such an issue about purported connections between PAC contributions and an officeholder's record that the incumbent was defeated or very severely challenged.[14]

Finally, even if the preconditions for disclosure occur, it is probably least effective in regulating those who offer contributions and most effective in limiting those who receive them. It is the political party and especially the candidate who may suffer voter retaliation at the polls, for instance. Only rarely is the donor in jeopardy of losing institutional office or suffering legal sanctions when adverse campaign finance disclosures occur.[15]

Disclosure may have positive effects. It may assist in enforcing campaign finance laws.[16] It may stimulate efforts to improve campaign finance rules.[17] And it may allow comparison of policy decisions or legislative votes by officials with their sources of campaign funds, thus suggesting patterns of interest group activity or influence. But it is not a promising means for holding candidates accountable by provoking voter retaliation.

Membership or Donor Control

Frank Sorauf has pointed out that the mass of state legislation regulating the internal life of political parties often makes party leaders accountable to party members for party operations, including the leaders' decisions about fundraising practices and political expenditures.[18]

Non-party organizations are rarely subject to such legal constraints. But some write methods of accountability into their formal rules. Labor union spokesmen point out that under union constitutions, labor leaders are selected by the same members who provide financial contributions to labor political committees; and, in some unions at least, candidate endorsements are made by representative bodies elected by union members.[19]

Other rules may give members or donors considerable control over political funds, but these rules are not widespread. Some corporate PACs, for instance, permit donors to earmark their contributions for specific candidates or parties—what Larry Sabato has called "pure democracy in the PACs"[20] By his count, 37 percent of PACs allow earmarking but only 4 percent of contributors choose this option.[21] Indeed, corporate PACs tend not to encourage earmarking, because it can lead to split-giving to candidates in the same race or to contributions to candidates at odds with the PAC's goals.[22]

Most PACs welcome member suggestions about candidate endorsements, and some aggressively solicit such information.[23] Moreover, PACs must pay attention to recommendations of PAC representatives from local plants or various divisions in diversified companies. In trade association PACs organized on a federated basis, the state or regional affiliates will have considerable influence on national PAC spending decisions; and these local units may have considerable internal democracy in selecting officers and perhaps even in making political decisions. Nonetheless, PAC members generally play a small role in actually governing PACs or in making decisions about political funds.

One method of donor control requires neither laws nor organizational rules: the decision to stop making contributions. Sorauf has characterized this behavior as "exit."[24] Donors may withdraw their financial support from a candidate or political organization because they disagree with policies or personalities or political practices. The decline in donor support for the Republican party in the aftermath of Watergate may be an extreme example. In 1989, a dramatic decline in fundraising by the Democratic National Committee was attributed to disenchantment by donors and fundraisers with party chairman Ron Brown.[25]

But the evidence is generally that exit, especially in PACs, occurs for other reasons. Donors may become exhausted by repeated appeals by an organization or by a torrent of appeals from kindred groups. A number of studies have pointed out that PAC donors tend to be less politically active and less well informed than givers to parties or candidates.[26] They may therefore be less sensitive to political events than others and, thus, less likely to exit for political reasons. On the other hand, as Sorauf has pointed out with respect to donors to corporate PACs, their gifts may be intermittent in any case, so the concept of "exit" as a means of influencing organizational behavior is not very relevant.[27] Moreover, in corporate PACs and perhaps labor union PACs, the main incentive among regular givers may be broadly conceived loyalty to the parent organization or a sense of community of interest with others in it. This loyalty is not likely to be discarded by exit because of some particular disagreement about candidate support or political advocacy.

If exit occurs among small donors, or only a few donors, or only intermittently, it may not have much influence on candidate or organizational behavior. Both candidates and organizations are continually in the process of expanding their base of participation, replacing lost supporters with new ones, and renewing the interest of former supporters. Exit may be taken more as a challenge to stimulate renewed interest than a mandate to change direction.

Limits on Contributions

The purpose of Congress in adopting contribution limits was at least partly to advance political equality by reducing the extent of "multiple voting" by donors.[28] Congress sought to protect the equality of each voter by diminishing the unequal influence of big donors in campaigns. And to the extent that contribution limits have had the effect of promoting equality among voters during election campaigns, there is less need to hold contributors accountable. There may still be a need for accountability in making expenditures, however. Members or donors may legitimately expect to influence the character or content of campaign messages which they help fund.

Individual contributions of $1,000 per election to candidates allowed by the FEC do not make a significant impact in candidate campaigns in an era when incumbent members of the House of Representatives spend on average $334,000 and their challengers spend $125,000 and when sitting Senators spend an average of $3.3 million and their opponents spend $1.7 million.[29] Political Action Committees are permitted to give up to $5,000 in each primary and general election. Again, this is not a large amount in today's world of costly campaigns, although $10,000 contributed in the primary and general election combined would be a large percent of the funds received by an average challenger in a House campaign. But only in rare cases do PACs give the maximum to challengers.

For both individuals and political committees, therefore, the FECA's contribution limits are low enough to prevent extensive multiple voting and to mitigate concerns about accountability.

Public Funding of Campaigns

The Federal Election Campaign Act allows presidential candidates to choose public financing of their campaigns. In primaries, candidates receive public funds to match small private contributions they receive; in the general election, they receive a fixed sum, adjusted each election for inflation. Candidates who accept public funds must also accept limits on their total expenditures. Public funding, if extended to congressional elections, could promote greater equality in the resources available to candidates, as it has in presidential elections. If so, it could ameliorate concerns about accountability.

Accountability Problems in Campaign Finance

Several significant problems with promoting accountability have not been resolved by current laws and practices:

PAC Accountability to Donors and Voters

Donors or members have, at best, slight control over PACs. Most contributions to PACs are in small sums: a 1981–82 survey showed an average contribution of $100, ranging from $14 by union members to labor PACs to $160 by executives and managers to corporate PACs.[30] Consequently, individual members do not have "financial clout" within the PACs. And, as mentioned previously, small givers to PACs are not likely to have the information or motivation to "exit" en masse to show discontent with PAC political activities.

The accountability of PAC leaders to their members may be represented by labor unions, at one poll, and non-connected ideological PACs, at the other. Union members elect union officers, who either serve on PAC executive committees or select those who do. In many unions, conventions or other representative bodies endorse the candidates who will be eligible for labor support. Membership and professional PACs may also have a degree of accountability to members, because association officers are elected by the members. As with labor unions, however, interest in political activities among members may be low, reducing attention to PAC activities.

By contrast, non-connected PACs are generally instruments of political entrepreneurs or small groups of cause- oriented activists. Their members are simply persons who once or repeatedly mail a contribution in response to solicitation. They play no role in the selection of officers or decisions about candidates or issue campaigns. Their gifts are generally so small and their participation so intermittent that neither protest nor exit will affect organizational leaders.

The role of members in the operation of corporate PACs falls somewhere between these poles. Formally, at least, members of corporate PACs have little to say about how the PAC is administered or to whom it contributes. PAC committees and managers in corporations are generally selected by and report to the chief executive officer or some other senior executive.

Studies differ on the extent to which members are included on PAC governing boards. One study reports only 10 percent of PACs make room for "volunteers;"[31] another argued that almost all PAC boards include representatives of the contributing middle management group;[32] and a third says that about 31 percent of PACs include "non-specialist amateurs" to represent contributor perspectives and participate actively in making contribution decisions.[33]

Most corporate PACs make substantial efforts to inform contributors about PAC activities. Reports generally include statements of funds raised, contributions made, and the "win/loss" record of candidates who received financial support.[34] Of course, to the extent that contributors or members must rely on the PAC itself for information, they are likely to receive reports that are calculated to retain their support.[35]

Another aspect of corporate and union PAC operations bears on the degree of internal accountability: the increasing use of payroll deduction as a means for collecting PAC pledges. About 80 percent of corporate PACs and 50 percent of labor PACs reportedly use the payroll deduction.[36] And 80 percent of corporate contributions and 30 percent of labor contributions are collected in this way.[37] When a donor disagrees with a PAC, his contributions continue unless he acts to end them. Once one agrees to a payroll deduction, however, accountability by exit may be lost to inertia. One corporation that eliminated its payroll deduction system suffered a 30 percent loss of contributions over two years.[38] Payroll deduction places PACs that use it at a distinct advantage, and weakens a channel of donor control. Candidates, parties, and non-connected PACs are dependent upon repeated acts of support from their donors while corporations and unions can obtain continuing support without review by a donor who has made an initial commitment through payroll deduction.

Sponsoring Administrative Expenditures

Special accountability problems also arise for connected PACs that pay operating costs from the sponsor's treasury. The FECA permits corporations, unions, and other "parents" to use institutional funds (so-called treasury funds) to establish, administer and solicit contributions for a PAC. Other political organizations, such as parties and non-connected PACs, pay these costs from political contributions they receive.

Treasury subsidies for PACs are in reality a "pass through" of institutional funds to candidates, for without treasury subsidies the administrative costs of PACs would be paid from contributed receipts and those moneys would no longer be available to make gifts to candidates. In 1980 PAC contributions to candidates were $55.2 million, but $30 million (54.3 percent) of this was indirectly subsidized by parents' expenditures for PAC operations.[39] In 1984, PAC gifts to candidates were $106.8 million while treasury funds for administration were $75 million (70.2 percent).[40]

The payment of PAC administrative costs from treasury funds raises accountability problems at every level. First, treasury funds diminish political equality in two ways. Unlimited amounts from a single source are being committed to politics. Moreover, the sources of treasury funds used to influence elections are economic institutions that are not citizens entitled to vote in elections. Second, PAC parents apparently are not legally required to disclose PAC administrative expenses even to members or stockholders, thus diminishing accountability to them. Third, expenditures of treasury funds are also not disclosed to voters, depriving them of information needed to evaluate candidates supported by the connected PAC.

Independent Expenditures

Although independent expenditures have consistently drawn wide attention and criticism, they are relatively modest in amount, as is pointed out by Candice Nelson elsewhere in this volume. Nonetheless, independent expenditures pose a far greater problem of accountability than do other uses of political money.

The non-connected PACs that engage in independent expenditures cannot easily be curbed by voters at the polls. Independent spenders are not on the ballot. Conversely, if voters strike at candidates supported by independent spenders, those candidates are unfairly being held accountable for spending they have not controlled or approved.

Soft Money

"Soft money" raises substantial issues of accountability.[41] First, very large contributions, many totaling $100,000 or more, create political inequality among citizens well beyond the modest differences anticipated by the contribution limits of the FECA. Second, soft money contributions from unions and corporations permit economic institutions that are not citizens possessing the vote significantly to influence elections. Third, contributions and expenditures are not fully disclosed, thus preventing the media, opposition candidates, and voters from considering funding practices as an election issue.

Out-Of-District Contributions

Contributions sent from one state or district to another raise an accountability issue that has been termed the "two constituency problem"[42]—that is, differences between a candidate's electoral constituency and his campaign resource constituency. This discrepancy could be a problem even for within-district donors and supporters if their ideological and socioeconomic characteristics were vastly different from the voters at large. But the problem is accentuated when substantial campaign resources come from outside the district, since these contributors may influence elections in which they cannot vote and officeholders who do not represent them in any legal sense.

Some suggest that out-of-district contributions reflect "the national interest" that senators and representatives must consider in addition to the interests of their constituents.[43] This argument assumes that out-of-district donors are representative of the national public at large, which is highly unlikely. Moreover, it mistakenly assumes that an official has an obligation to represent those outside her district when, in fact, a representative's "national" responsibility is to understand how policies may strengthen the nation as a whole in order to benefit the people of his district as part of that whole.

Out-of-district money has become increasingly prominent in campaigns, especially for incumbents. Grenzke has shown that in the early 1980s, House incumbents received 61 percent of their individual contributions of $500 or more—the contributions most likely to be remembered by the candidate—from outside their districts, about 28 percent from elsewhere in the state and 33 percent from outside the state. Only about 2 percent of PAC gifts came from within the district and about 14 percent from within the state.[44] This pattern has almost certainly heightened over time. There are also reports that out-of-state individual donors increasingly play a role in U.S. Senate campaigns. Wealthy donors in "political money centers" such as California, Florida, New York, Texas, and, to a lesser degree, Atlanta, Boston, and Kansas City are wooed by senators up for re-election.[45]

To the limited extent that present disclosure rules inform the electorate, voters may evaluate candidates in part on their potential commitment to out-of-district donors rather than within-district citizens.

Aggregating Political Contributions

Limits on individual and committee contributions have enhanced political equality by bringing financial disparities within acceptable limits, but these disparities are re-introduced into American political life by the aggregation of contributions. The aggregation of funds has two faces. Positively, the mobilization of political resources by candidates, parties, and associations is valued because the association of donors or political workers in a common cause is citizen activism at its best. Conversely, the aggregation of campaign money allows a few persons who raise and disburse those funds to acquire substantial influence over the electoral process and perhaps over public policy as well. In short, those who mobilize political money—but not the many citizens who give it—cast multiple votes on a massive scale.

Resource aggregation by candidates poses few problems of accountability under present law. Limits on the size of contributions, disclosure of fund sources, and potential scrutiny and criticism by the press and the political opposition create checks on candidates. Voters can impose sanctions at the polls on candidates whose use of money is excessive or offensive; and even though disclosure is only intermittently effective, candidates must continually engage in anticipatory restraint.

A special problem of fund aggregation is the contribution of funds raised by one candidate to another. Clyde Wilcox, in his subsequent chapter, details such member-to-member giving and the accountability problem it generates: Those who give to a candidate may neither intend nor approve of the use of their gifts to support other candidates whose views may differ widely from the giver's.

Individual fundraisers have historically played a role in American politics. Contribution limits curb the amount a fundraiser can obtain from each person he solicits, so it would take vastly more effort now than in the past to raise huge sums of money. Nonetheless, fundraisers do influence the electoral process by aggregating funds, and there seems little doubt that they also acquire access to elected officials for whom they raise money. Yet, the degree of accountability of fundraisers is very slight. Indeed, it is difficult even to formulate a policy to hold them accountable.

One variant of fundraising has, however, prompted calls for regulation. "Bundling" occurs when an individual or organization not only solicits contributions but collects the individual checks and transmits them to the candidate in the donor's name. The gift is attributed to the donor on campaign reports, but it is the fundraiser who most significantly takes the political "credit" for the bundled gifts. There is no limit on the money that an individual or organization can aggregate by bundling. The organization that engages in bundling is not directly accountable to members for the allocation of organizational funds. And neither an individual or an organization that engages in bundling discloses their fundraising activities to voters. A recent New York City ordinance requires the disclosure of bundling, but despite some very preliminary favorable reactions to this regulation, its effectiveness remains largely untested.[46]

Political parties are the most widely accepted and perhaps the most benign of those who aggregate political resources. The relatively generous limits on combined contributions and expenditures by party committees certainly allow them to make a substantial impact on elections. Moreover, the Republican party raises much more than the Democrats, thus introducing another form of disparity into the political process.

The substantial inequality arising from the parties' aggregation of funds is largely offset by other factors, however. Party officials are elected by party members and political spending is thus subject to some membership control. The party label appears on the ballot, and voters may take a party's funding practices into account in casting their votes. Finally, elected officials may be reasonably well insulated from influence by party officials even when party financial support has been generous.[47]

Quite different is the aggregation of PAC contributions. The contribution limits imposed on individual PACs by the FECA are low enough to ameliorate serious problems of political equality. But when PACs act in unison, sometimes as a result of coordination but often without concerted action, they may concentrate financial resources that very significantly influence elections and policy.

The concentration of PAC funds occurs both formally and informally. The U.S. Chamber of Commerce and the Business & Industry Political Action Committee actively seek to guide business PACs in contributing to candidates. Labor's Committee on Political Education provides similar guidance to union PACs. There are also informal networks of PAC managers who share contribution strategies. And the national political parties work closely with PACs to steer campaign money to preferred candidates. What seems clear is that the aggregation of PAC funds is largely deliberate and calculated.

There is, of course, wide diversity among PACs. But they have tended in recent years overwhelmingly to support incumbents and, in the aggregate, to support Democrats over Republicans. As Maisel notes in a subsequent chapter, the concentration of PAC support for incumbents tends to undermine effective competition in elections and, thereby, reduces the accountability of representatives to voters.

Toward Accountability

Although money is essential to conduct campaigns, all political money should meet either a standard of rough equality or rigorous accountability. Where there is equality, there is less concern about accountability. Where accountability is required, it should be first and foremost to voters, since it is the equal value of their votes that accountability devices are intended to protect. In addition, accountability to donors should be enhanced to reduce the unchecked influence of group leaders. The following reforms would promote accountability to voters and/or donors.[48]

Disclosure and Disclaimers

Although disclosure's effectiveness is modest, it adds some measure of accountability, and this accountability is greatest when the disclosure or disclaimer is addressed to attentive audiences.

1. PACs, therefore, should be required to inform donors about their uses of campaign funds. These disclosures should be directly provided to donors of $100 or more. (The cost of disclosure to smaller donors would be prohibitive.) Disclosures should include the PAC's total receipts, the amount and percentage of those receipts spent for administrative and solicitation expenses, the amount contributed to candidates, and the amount of independent expenditures. Candidates supported and the amounts given to each candidate should be listed. In defining categories of expenses, solicitation expenses should be broadly defined to avoid reporting of issue-oriented solicitation letters as independent expenditures, a technique used by some independent expenditure PACs to exaggerate reports of their political activities. Armed with this kind of information, donors would be better able to hold PAC leaders accountable or, where donors do not participate in organizational affairs, to exit.

2. PACs should be required also to file these reports with the FEC as full disclosure to voters. In addition, PACs should file copies of their solicitation letters with the FEC. This would heighten accountability to voters by permitting public scrutiny of PAC characterizations of politicians and issues.

3. Disclosure also provides one of several means for addressing the "two constituency" problem created by out-of-district contributions. Candidates should be required to report the number of gifts and the amount of money they receive from within their district and from elsewhere. Although some funds from

out-of-district PACs and party committees may actually be raised within a candidate's district, the available evidence suggests these amounts are small. It would, therefore, not be a distortion to require that contributions from committees whose principal offices are outside the district be reported as out-of-district funds. Disclosure of this information would allow the press and the opposition to raise questions with voters about any substantial extent to which a candidate's financial constituency is different from her geographic constituency.

4. Disclaimers would heighten the effectiveness of these disclosures to voters. Candidates receiving more than a certain percentage of their funds from outside their district could be required to include a disclaimer on campaign literature and print advertising acknowledging that more than one-third or one-half of their funds came from outside their constituency. The disclaimer could be simple and direct. A spoken disclaimer—rather than the indecipherable printed disclaimers that now appear on TV ads—on any electronic advertising of 30 seconds or more would also inform voters effectively.

5. Similarly, disclaimers would be the most effective means for alerting voters about the funding sources for independent expenditures. These expenditures cannot constitutionally be subject to statutory spending limits. Printed and spoken disclaimers pointing out the percentage of out-of-district funds of independent expenditure committees would provide direct accountability to voters.

6. The accountability problems created by "soft money" can also be partially addressed by additional disclosures. FECA disclosure regulations should be extended to state and local candidates and party committees that make expenditures jointly with federal office candidates or national political party committees for grassroots activity or voter mobilization. A more troublesome question is whether FECA disclosure provisions can also be extended to the national political parties' non-federal accounts used for organizing activities and for institutional party advertising. It is not clear whether the Supreme Court would regard such expenditures as direct advocacy of the election or defeat of a candidate that would fall within the scope of regulation permitted by the *Buckley* case.

7. Finally, disclosure could introduce some accountability to voters where bundling creates multiple voting. It is difficult to fashion a regulation that does not sweep too broadly, and conse-

quently attention should be paid to the New York City ordinance. But a promising approach would require a political committee or candidate to file a report identifying anyone who personally transmits gifts from others that in the aggregate exceed a certain dollar level.

Limits on Contributions

Present limits on campaign contributions are set at levels that generally promote political equality. Several additional limits could heighten equality or extend accountability where inequality occurs.

1. FECA contribution limits should be extended to state and local committees and candidates that engage in jointly funded grassroots activity and voter mobilization with federal candidates and committees. There is no doubt that grassroots activity is advocacy on behalf of a candidate, but voter mobilization efforts that do not identify specific candidates might not fall within the scope of regulation approved by the Supreme Court. Nonetheless, voter mobilization and other campaign activities are so intertwined, especially when these efforts are jointly funded by national, state, and local party committees engaged in candidate advocacy, that it seems quite likely that the FECA's contribution limits could be extended to the state and local as well as national committees. This would curb the extraordinary multiple voting due to soft money contributions.

2. A prohibition on candidate-to-candidate contributions by candidate campaign committees would instill further accountability to donors. This would not bar the creation of candidate-sponsored PACs. But it would require that candidates seek money either for their own election campaigns or for PACs that would contribute to other candidates without mingling funds for the two separate purposes. Donors would be informed when solicited of the purpose of their gifts, and they could withhold contributions from a candidate PAC if they were concerned about the candidates to whom such funds would be transferred.

3. PAC contribution limits should also be reconsidered. The present contribution limits of $5,000 per election are not so high as to allow any individual PAC to greatly influence any election campaign. Moreover, most PAC contributions are substantially less than the legal limit. Nonetheless, an aggregate limit on PAC contributions to candidates has been repeatedly proposed. It would have the advantage of reducing the pack behavior of

PACs. On the other hand, it might also drive some PACs, especially those whose contributions were rejected after a candidate's aggregate limit was reached, to use their funds for independent expenditures.

On balance, some additional limitation on PAC contributions seems warranted, especially if public funds reduce candidates' reliance on PAC money in order to wage competitive campaigns. A reduction in the PAC contribution limit from $5,000 to $3,000 has been proposed in Congress, and it could be a sound first step. If combined with a limit on aggregate PAC contributions to each candidate, it might allow virtually all PACs to make contributions within the aggregate limit while assuring that neither the size of particular PAC gifts nor aggregate PAC contributions would constitute significant multiple voting.

4. The use of institutional treasury funds for PAC administration and solicitation costs should be repealed. These are not funds contributed by citizens but, rather, are from the resources of economic institutions that have no franchise. Prohibiting the use of treasury funds for PAC administrative and solicitation expenses would simply put PACs on an equal footing with candidates, political parties, and non-connected PACs.

Public Financing

The essential element for making political money fully accountable to voters is to provide substantial public financing in primary and general election campaigns for Congress as well as for President. Public funding can assure sufficient campaign funds to stimulate competitive elections even as campaign finance regulations diminish the role of large private contributions. But public funds should be considered as a "floor" of competitive funding that can be supplemented by closely regulated small gifts, rather than as a "ceiling" on expenditures. This would allow citizens to participate in campaigns by making small donations; and it would allow additional campaign funds to flow into districts with highly competitive races, a diffusion of media outlets that drive up costs, or other special characteristics that increase the costs of waging campaigns.

Public funding does not raise issues of voter equality or disproportionate influence by individuals or groups during the campaign. The only accountability devices needed are those that verify eligibility, audit the uses of funds and verify that private giving remains within carefully specified, low contribution limits. Fully specifying a system for public financing that promotes equality and accountability is beyond the scope of this chapter, however.

Additional Accountability to Donors

Finally, although accountability to donors is not as important as accountability to voters, two additional steps would broaden the accountability of political money by increasing donor control over their gifts and reducing the power of PAC leaders to aggregate and allocate funds.

1. All PACs should be required to offer donors an earmarking option. It is not clear how many PAC donors would use such an option, especially in connected PACs where institutional loyalty rather than candidate preference is an important donor motivation. But earmarking would assure donors control over their gifts if they wanted it.

2. Payroll deductions beyond a period of one year should be eliminated, requiring connected PACs to renew their appeals to donors annually. This would put connected PACs on the same footing as political parties, candidates, and non-connected PACs, all of whom must repeatedly seek the renewed support of donors. Requiring connected PACs annually to renew their appeals to donors would also heighten accountability, since greater efforts would be required to inform donors of PAC activities and perhaps also to assure that PAC contributions and expenditures were acceptable to donors. Inertia would be on the side of PAC donors rather than PAC leaders, reflecting the relationship between political leaders and their followers in all other realms of American political life.

Conclusion

Campaign funds in the United States continue in many respects to defeat political equality, requiring attention to the preservation of accountability. Yet, accountability to voters in campaign giving and spending is often attenuated, at best. Democracy in elections is therefore weakened.

The regulations proposed above will not eliminate all multiple voting or instill complete accountability. Continual revision of campaign finance laws is necessary to address new funding practices, because in the long term "no law can weaken the resolve of the powerful forces behind that money to influence federal elections."[49] But these proposals will help promote democracy in campaign finance as part of continually evolving legal regulations to achieve that purpose.

NOTES

1. The principal exception is Frank J. Sorauf, "Accountability in Political Action Committees," *Political Science Quarterly*, Vol. 99 (1984–85), 591–614.

2. In addition, both expenditures and contributions enjoy some degree of constitutional protection, and banning them outright would be unconstitutional. See *Buckley v. Valeo*, 424 U.S. 1, 14–23 (1976).

3. David Adamany, "PACs and the Democratic Financing of Politics," *Arizona Law Review*, Vol. 22 (1980), 594–596.

4. Sorauf, "Accountability in Political Action Committees," 608–11.

5. Sorauf, "Accountability in Political Action Committees," 605–607.

6. Robert E. Mutch, *Campaigns, Congress, and Courts* (Praeger Publishers, 1988), 8.

7. Max McCarthy, *Elections for Sale* (Houghton Mifflin, 1972), 189. For a similar viewpoint, see also Herbert E. Alexander, *Money in Politics*, (Public Affairs Press, 1972), 227.

8. David Adamany and George Agree, *Political Money* (Johns Hopkins, 1975), 95–115.

9. Peter Kerr, "Campaign Donations Overwhelming Monitoring Agencies in the States," *New York Times*, December 27, 1988, A1, col. 1.

10. Ben H. Bagdikian, "The Fruits of Agnewism," *Columbia Journalism Review*, Vol. 11 (1973), 15–16.

11. Frank J. Sorauf, "Campaign Money and the Press," *Political Science Quarterly*, Vol. 102 (1987), 25–42.

12. Adamany and Agree, *Political Money*, 108–110.

13. Mutch, *Campaigns, Congress, and the Courts*, 8–16, 24–29.

14. Larry Sabato, *PAC Power* (W.W.Norton, 1984), 102, 107.

15. But there are rare occasions when donors face criminal penalties and the loss of institutional positions. See, Caryle Murphy and Ruth Marcus, "Two Admit Illegal Hill Donations," *Washington Post*, January 28, 1989, A1, col. 6; Warren Weaver, Jr., "2 Admit Illicit Political Donations in Military Procurement

Inquiry," *New York Times*, January 29, 1989, A1, col. 1; Charles R. Babcock, "4 Californians Indicted On Election Law Charges," *Washington Post*, Dec. 15, 1988, A15, col. 1.

16. This purpose was recognized by the Supreme Court as a justification for upholding disclosure provisions of the Federal Election Campaign Act against the challenge that they invade the constitutional right of associational privacy. *Buckley v. Valeo*, supra, 64–68.

17. Disclosure "would enhance the ability of government to identify and regulate specific trouble spots in political finance." Alexander Heard, *The Costs of Democracy* (University of North Carolina Press, 1960), 462.

18. Sorauf, "Accountability in Political Action Committees," 608.

19. David Jessup, "Can Political Influence Be Democratized? A Labor Perspective," in Malbin, ed., *Parties, Interest Groups and Campaign Finance* (American Enterprise Institute and Chatham House, 1984), 43.

20. Sabato, *PAC Power*, 63. One-third of corporate PACs permitted earmarking in the survey conducted by Catherine Morrison, *Managing Corporate Political Action Committees* (Conference Board, 1986), 20.

21. Sabato, *PAC Power*, 64.

22. Morrison, *Managing Corporate Political Action Committees*, 20; Edward Handler and John R. Mulkern, *Business in Politics* (Lexington Books, 1982), 79–80.

23. Morrison, *Managing Corporate Political Action Committees*, 20; Handler and Mulkern, *Business in Politics*, 82–84.

24. Sorauf, "Accountability in Political Action Committees," 602–606.

25. Richard Berke, "Democrats Trail in Fund Raising, And Many Blame New Chairman," *New York Times*, July 17, 1989, A1, col. 1.

26. Ruth Jones and Warren Miller, "Financing Campaigns: Macro Level Innovation and Micro Level Response," *Western Political Quarterly*, Vol. 38 (1985), 203–205; Ruth Jones, "Campaign Contributions and Campaign Solicitation: 1984," paper presented to the annual meeting of the Southern Political Science Association, Nashville, TN, November 6–9, 1985; Frank J. Sorauf, *What Price PACs?* (Twentieth Century Fund, 1984), 82–83.

27. Sorauf, "Accountability in Political Action Commit-

tees," 104–105.

28. David Adamany and George Agree, "Election Campaign Financing: The 1974 Reforms," *Political Science Quarterly*, Vol. 90 (1975), p 211; Mutch, *Campaigns, Congress, and the Courts*, 65–66. On the concept of "multiple voting" see Heard, *The Costs of Democracy*, 48–49.

29. The 1986 figures are reported in Frank J. Sorauf, *Money in American Elections* (Scott, Foresman, 1988), 163.

30. Sabato, *PAC Power*, 59.

31. Morrison, *Managing Corporate Political Action Committees*, 13.

32. Sabato, *PAC Power*, 35.

33. Handler and Mulkern, *Business in Politics*, 70, 71–72.

34. Handler and Mulkern, *Business in Politics*, 89–90; Sabato, *PAC Power*, 167–69.

35. Sabato, *PAC Power*, 168.

36. Ibid., 62.

37. Ibid.

38. Handler and Mulkern, *Business in Politics*, 47.

39. Alexander, *Financing the 1980 Election*, (Lexington Books, 1983), 127.

40. Alexander, *Financing the 1984 Election*, 83.

41. Soft money is described in detail in Anne Bedlington's chapter of this volume.

42. Adamany, "PACs and the Democratic Financing of Politics," 594–596.

43. Herbert E. Alexander, *The Case for PACs* (Public Affairs Council, n.d.), 14.

44. Janet Grenzke, "Campaign Contributions to U.S. House Members From Outside Their Districts," *Legislative Studies Quarterly*, Vol. 13 (1988), 83–103. In 1984, only 25.8 percent of corporate PAC contributions in House races were made to candidates in the same states as the PACs' headquarters. Theodore Eismeier and Philip Pollock, III, *Business, Money, and the Rise of Corporate PACs in American Elections* (Quorum Books, 1988), 67.

45. Maxwell Glen, "Early-Bird Fund Raising," *National Journal*, Vol. 19 (1987), 1591–92.

46. Frank Lynn, "Finance Law for Candidates Achieving Some of Its Goals," *New York Times*, July 20, 1989, A22, col. 5.

47. David Adamany, "Political Finance and the American Political Parties," *Hastings Constitutional Law Quarterly*, Vol.

10 (1983), 548–53.

48. I have previously proposed many of these ideas elsewhere. See Adamany and Agree, chapt. 11; Adamany, "PACs and the Democratic Financing of Politics," 597–602; David Adamany, "Political Action Committees and Democratic Politics," *Detroit College of Law Review* (1983), 1013–28.

49. Mutch, *Campaigns, Congress, and the Courts*, 191.

Part II: Problematic Consequences

Having explored difficulties that arise from the "inputs" of the campaign finance system, we turn to several issues that have been considered to be potential consequences of this system: lack of competition in elections, undue influence over congressional behavior, the proliferation of "candidate PACs," and the challenge all PACs pose to the primacy of political parties.

L. Sandy Maisel suggests serious problems for accountability, representation, and participation result when the campaign finance system exacerbates the advantage of incumbency and discourages viable competition. According to Maisel, incumbent war-chests, early money given to incumbents, and the patterns of PAC support, so stack the deck against challengers as to undermine competition and with it, the accountability of elected representatives. He recommends the following reforms in order to help attract more qualified challengers into the electoral arena: Turn surplus campaign funds over to the Federal Election Campaign Fund; prevent PACs from contributing to campaigns until April 1 of the election year; and allow candidates to accept no more than 25% of their funds from PACs.

Janet Grenzke undertook her analysis of the influence of campaign funds on congressional behavior because many values would be threatened if corruption is as widespread as critics such as Common Cause believe. The influence of moneyed interests on Congress could weaken governmental effectiveness and legitimacy; distort representation and accountability if Members of Congress favor donors over voters; and reinforce the political inequality that can result from unequal economic resources. Her careful review of studies on the influence of PACs suggests that corruption is less extensive and harder to prove than commonly believed. Nonetheless, because campaign funds may influence congressional behavior in special circumstances, and because other values such as competition and political equality need to be supported, Grenzke endorses a system for public financing that includes matching funds for primary elections and diminishing the disparities in campaign spending between incumbents and challengers in general elections.

Clyde Wilcox explores a different influence on congressional behavior, the growing trend toward "personal PACs" and other contributions or fundraising by one Member of Congress on behalf of another. With reinforcement provided by the FECA, such activities are increasingly important ways to seek power in Congress, especially party leadership positions. Wilcox argues that while member-to-member giving, including contributions by candidate PACs, often focuses on highly competitive races, it worsens the fragmentation of Congress, weakening party unity. Members of Congress may view such activities as reflections of their political liberty, but Wilcox claims that this liberty comes at the expense of the effectiveness of Congress as an institution. He also questions whether donors to one candidate can hold her accountable for how she uses their funds to contribute to colleagues.

The proliferation of PACs and their competition with political parties is the consequence of the campaign finance system that Larry Sabato explores. Sabato characterizes the relationship between PACs and parties as symbiotic and parasitic rather then purely competitive. Based upon a review of the criticisms against PACs, Sabato supports PACs as an avenue for participation and political liberty, but is concerned that they undermine the effectiveness, legitimacy, and accountability of Congress. As discussed by Grenzke and Maisel, PACs also tend to exacerbate political inequality and diminish competition. Whether because of the PAC challenge or despite it, the Democrats and Republicans are reinvigorating their electoral capacities, a positive development to Sabato. His argument for why parties deserve preferred status over PACs precedes proposals to strengthen the role of the parties in elections in order to enhance the promotion of governmental effectiveness, legitimacy, and accountability.

7

The Incumbency Advantage

L. Sandy Maisel

> *When 99.2% of all incumbents get re-elected, many of them without opposition, there is more than the PAC issue at stake. Democracy is at stake.*
>
> House Minority Leader Robert Michel
> Remarks to the Republican Conference
> December 6, 1988

Competition Versus the Incumbency Advantage

The link between competitive elections and representative democracy is indisputable.[1] The ability of voters to express their views on governmental policy, and to have those views reflected in subsequent decisions by those whom they elect, is a function of whether or not the voters are presented with a meaningful choice on election day. A minimal criterion for an effectively functioning election system is that officeholders are held accountable for their actions in frequent elections; if officeholders do not represent their constituents responsibly, they can be turned out of office. However, in the case of the United States House of Representatives, incumbent officeholders are almost never turned out of office. Thus, we are concerned about the ways in which the congressional election system serves our representative democracy.

Is a high incumbency re-election rate a problem with which we should be concerned? Scholars, political journalists, and politicians are fond of pointing out that in every election save one since 1972 at least 90% of the incumbents seeking re-election to the House of Representatives have been returned for another term. When retirements are few, as they have been in the past three elections, turnover is very low. Thus, the composition of the House changes very little; any changes in public sentiments are not reflected in changes in who is to represent those sentiments in Congress. How one evaluates that depends on how one defines the role played by the Congress. Nelson Polsby claims, "Longevity promotes competence. You have to actually advocate incompetent legislators to get the turnover you want.... Everything in the government is being professionalized, and if there were enforced or high turnover, members wouldn't have much influence vis-a-vis the executive branch or the institutional congressional bureaucracy."[2] Most members of Congress who are re-elected would concur with that view.

Others claim that the House is ossifying, that the built-in Democratic majority insured by low turnover guarantees that changing public perceptions will not be reflected in legislation. Dave Hoppe of the Heritage Foundation reflects this view: "[Conservative policy ideas] really get short shrift.... Freezing in the status quo means you really only get one side of the debate—one side of the coin being examined. And that's not good for democracy."[3]

Table 7.1 presents the most recent data on incumbents' re-election success. A number of factors stand out. First, the number of incumbents retiring has in fact decreased in recent years. Turnover would have been lower even if re-election rates had stayed the same. Second, primaries are a less significant obstacle for incumbents seeking re-election because of the advantages which incumbents have over challengers—which are increased in the absence of a possibly negative partisan cue—and the fact that fewer districts in the South are now one-party districts in which the only competition is within the Democratic Party. But most important to see from this table is the fact that over 98% of the incumbents seeking re-election in each of the last two election years have been re-elected. While the percentage of incumbents winning re-election has been high for some time—it has only fallen below 90% five times (and below 80%, once) since 1946—the 98% in the last two elections are the highest percentages reached. In fact, as many incumbents died in the 100th Congress as were defeated in their efforts to win re-election to the 101st. When combined with the few retirements, this re-election rate meant a return rate of 92.4% to the 101st Congress, the highest in at least the last forty years. The 1988 election was unique because it combined an extremely low number of retirements with a record high incumbency re-election rate. That combination has caused concern among some who felt that the situation did not merit concern earlier.

Table 7.1

Incumbency Success in House Elections 1972–1988

Year	Incumbents Seeking Re-election	Defeated in Primaries	Defeated in General Election	Percentage Re-elected
1972	390	12	13	94
1974	391	8	40	88
1976	384	3	13	96
1978	382	5	19	94
1980	398	6	31	91
1982	393	10	29	90
1984	411	3	16	95
1986	393	3	6	98
1988	407	1	6	98

Source: Compiled by the author.

The high re-election rate of incumbents is coupled with the increasingly high margins of their victories, which in turn is buttressed by the large number of incumbents who run unopposed.[4] Table 7.2 shows that there is cause for concern. The last three elections particularly lead one to question whether the congressional election process as it is currently constituted performs the function it is designed to perform in a representative democracy. These were the election years in which most incumbents ran without major party opposition. That is, more incumbents were given a "free ride" in 1984, 1986, and 1988 than had been the case before.[5] Furthermore, in the last two elections, those winning incumbents who faced major party opponents won re- election by wider margins than had previously been the case. Thus, to beat these incumbents, challengers would have to "swing" a larger percentage of voters' support away. Of course, it is too early to know whether this is a new trend or merely an aberration. Still, one need not be an alarmist to wonder whether the experiences in 1986 and 1988 indicate a serious diminution of the ability of congressional elections to reflect the will of the people on policy matters.

Table 7.2

Mean Vote of Contested Incumbents in House Elections, 1972-1988 (in percentages)

Year	Vote	N	Vote	N
1972	65.6	310	71.2	378
1974	64.0	322	69.5	383
1976	65.8	329	70.2	381
1978	65.8	309	71.8	377
1980	66.1	336	70.8	392
1982	65.0	315	71.0	383
1984	65.6	318	72.8	408
1986	68.2	319	74.1	393
1988	68.6	335	73.9	407

Source: Data for contested elections for 1972-1984 are from Jacobson, *The Politics of Congressional Elections*, 32. The remaining data were compiled by the author.

The Decision to Challenge an Incumbent

The most recent explorations of "incumbency advantage" have confirmed that incumbents are preferred because of their name recognition and reputation, but they have also revealed that challengers are perceived by the electorate to be weak—often unknown—candidates. Thus, among the most important advantages enjoyed by victorious incumbents seems to be the relative weakness of their opponents' campaigns.[6]

Why do more "qualified" candidates not contest congressional elections against incumbents?[7] Gary Jacobson and Samuel Kernell argue that politicians act strategically in that they are most likely to run for an office when the chance of their succeeding is greatest (as weighed against what they will be giving up by undertaking a race).[8] While seemingly simple on its face, the strategic politician model is in fact rich in subtlety. "Qualified" candidates are deemed to be sophisticated politicians. Sophisticated politicians know they cannot wage successful campaigns against incumbents without adequate financing. They think it unlikely that they will receive adequate financing unless those who give generously to campaigns feel that the incumbent might be beaten, because contributors tend not to spend their money on lost causes. Large contributors think incumbents might be beaten in either of two situations: (1) when the incumbent has shown him or herself to be vulnerable (either through a close call in the last election, implication in a scandal, or other evidence that he or she has lost touch with the district); or (2) when the national trend seems to be away from the incumbent's party. The second of these circumstances then links "qualified" candidates running with national trends, e.g. the status of the economy or the public's assessment of presidential performance, which in turn others have claimed reflect on the likelihood that incumbents of the President's party will be successful candidates for re-election. That is, more "qualified" candidates run—and therefore better campaigns are run—when incumbents of the President's party might be vulnerable in any case. The two factors reinforce each other.[9]

Our understanding of which individuals decide to challenge incumbents is incomplete. Most of the work focuses on declared candidates and much of that depends on their recall of factors leading to their decision to run.[10] Thus, the decision not to run is not examined, though it is equally important.[11] Other work stresses the importance of national partisan tides, reflected by perceptions of the state of the economy and assessments of the performance of the President.[12] Yet, individual decisions to run for Congress depend on local contextual factors as well. Unfortunately, most of the work which has stressed local context has dealt with case studies which have not permitted generalization across districts.[13] Others have looked at factors which permit generalization (e.g. the incumbent's vote in the previous House election or measures of ideological discrepancy between the incumbent and the district) but do not capture the richness of local context.[14] Finally, in addition to national partisan tides and local context, others have examined the role of campaign financing in challengers' decisions of whether or not to run for office, arguing that incumbents raise and spend money pre-emptively to discourage challengers.[15]

Given the many reasons quality challengers may decide not to run, thereby reducing competition in congressional elections, the only available remedy to promote turnover, short of restricting terms of office, is to alter campaign finance laws. Little can be done by way of legislation to change either national partisan tides or local context. Therefore, if one is concerned about lack of competition faced by incumbents for Congress and about decisions by qualified challengers not to run for Congress, it is necessary to take a longer look at how campaigns are financed.

The Incumbency Advantage in Fundraising

Four facts about our current campaign finance system affect the shortage of qualified candidates: (1) the total cost of campaigns has continued to rise; (2) incumbents have little difficulty raising money; (3) challengers do; and (4) political action committees have abounded and give most of their money to incumbents.

The data in Tables 7.3 and 7.4 make these conclusions clear. The costs of campaigns have risen astronomically. Figures compiled by the Center for Responsive Politics show that in competitive House races in 1986—those in which the winner polled 55% of the vote or less—the average winner spent approximately $564,000, up from under $200,000 in every election before 1980; the average loser in these close races spent approximately $450,000, more than three times what was spent on the average race less than a decade earlier.[16] Frank Sorauf has shown that the expenditure ratio of incumbents to challengers has risen sharply, from 1.7:1 in 1980 to 2.7:1 in 1986.[17]

Table 7.3

Average Expenditures By General Election Candidates 1978–1986
(in thousands of dollars)

	1978	1980	1982	1984	1986
Democrats					
Incmbs.	103	157	245	279	312
Challs.	76	78	127	102	143
Open	207	188	267	360	419
Republicans					
Incmbs.	127	177	287	282	366
Challs.	75	113	130	145	110
Open	191	227	318	401	456

Source: Various releases of the Federal Election Commission.

Table 7.4

Political Action Committees: Growth and Giving Patterns 1978–1986
(in percentages)

	1978	1980	1982	1984	1986
Number	1653	2551	3371	4009	4157
Incmbs.	60.4	65.8	66.8	75.6	75.7
Challs.	18.8	20.8	17.9	14.9	10.5
Open	20.8	13.4	15.3	9.5	13.7

Source: Various releases of the Federal Election Commission.

It is equally clear that political action committees have contributed significantly to this growth–and to the disparity in funds available to incumbents and challengers.[18] The cumulative influence of these organizations on congressional campaign financing is beyond question. In the 1986 election cycle, PACs gave nearly $140 million to candidates for the House of Representatives. Of that number nearly $105 million went to incumbents and barely $15 million to challengers. Certainly this is not a very encouraging picture for those seeking to unseat incumbents.[19]

One more piece must be added to this picture of incumbents' advantage in financing their campaigns for re-election. Because incumbents who do not face serious challengers can raise more money than they need in any election cycle,[20] they frequently have a great deal of money left over after one campaign ends. Under the current law they are allowed to carry that money over into their next campaign. After the 1986 election, those elected to the 100th Congress cumulatively had over $48 million left over to apply to their 1988 campaigns.[21] The percentage of money left over after winning campaigns has risen from 5.5% in 1978, to 6.2% in 1980, to 6.7% in 1982, to 9.5% in 1984, to 13.5% in 1986—while the total dollar amounts on which these percentages are based have also been rising.[22] Thus, not only do incumbents have an advantage in raising money, but they also have a significant headstart.

Factors Discouraging Qualified Challengers

One cannot prove that lack of an incumbents' campaign fundraising advantage will lead to qualified challengers; rather the best one can do is to demonstrate that incumbents who had a significant fundraising advantage did not face difficult competition. The two major advantages to explore are "war-chests" and early money channeled to incumbents from PACs.[23]

War-chests from Previous Campaigns

Incumbents have no difficulty raising money for re-election; many of them have no need to spend a great deal. Therefore, a growing number of winning incumbents have an increasingly large amount of money left over after their campaigns. Challengers considering a race against an incumbent might well be dissuaded when they know that that incumbent already has on hand more money than the challenger can think about raising. And the incumbent's money is making more money—as it sits in a bank gaining interest.

Table 7.5

Incumbents with Large Surpluses after 1986 Election

	N=17	N=17	N=39
Surplus (in dollars)	400,000+	300,000+	200,000+
Electoral Status			
Average 1986 Winning Percentage	83	79.1	76.8
Unopposed in 1986	5	4	9
<60% in 1986	0	0	1
Qualified Challenger in 1988	0	0	2
Average 1988 Winning Percentage	77.5	76.2	78.8
Unopposed in 1988	3	3	11
<60% in 1988	0	1	3
Unopposed in 1986 and 1988	2	2	6

Source: Compiled by the author from FEC releases.

At the end of the 1986 campaign, 160 winning incumbents had over $100,000 left in their campaign accounts. Anecdotal material relates how challengers have been put off by the task of matching these amounts, but the data in Table 7.5 those 1986 victors who had over $200,000 in surplus is dramatic.

First, these data show that those with large surpluses in 1986 were in fact those who won big in that election. Only two incumbents who had close races in 1986 had large surpluses left after those races. One of those was Fernand J. St. Germain (D-RI), the Chairman of the House Banking Committee, who, despite a scandal hanging over his head, had little trouble raising much more money than his opponent. As a group, the average winning percentage of these incumbents was considerably higher than that of all winning incumbents. In addition, 18 of these 73 1986 winners had no major party opposition in that election at all; that is, they had huge surpluses left from campaigns against no one.

Second, those who had large war-chests left after the 1986 campaign—with only two exceptions—did not face qualified challengers in 1988.[24] Again, some particular examples are worth noting. Congressman St. Germain did not draw a qualified challenger by this definition, despite his relatively close call in 1986 and the scandal which tainted his reputation. However, when the scandal worsened, his challenger was able to raise more money, to run a strong campaign, and eventually to upset St. Germain. One of the exceptions was Democratic State Senator Gary Hart (did name similarity help?) in California. Hart's State Senate District was nearly co-terminous with Congressman Robert J. Lagamarsino's Congressional District; state senators in California have a good deal of name recognition and thus Hart did not have to overcome odds as high as many other challengers. He raised more early money than did any other challenger—nearly $700,000 before his primary—and came within 2,200 votes of upsetting the incumbent.

Third, those who had large war-chests left after 1986, on the whole, won impressively in 1988. Again, 17 had no major party opposition whatsoever. Ten of these were among the 17 who had not had opposition in 1986.[25] Only four from this group polled less than 60% in 1988; only one (St. Germain) lost. Two of the others who faced relatively close elections were opposed by qualified challengers.

One can only draw inferences, not reach conclusions from these data. But the inference that large campaign surpluses deter qualified opponents and contribute to subsequent victories without serious competition seems warranted. This inference is reinforced when one notes that incumbents with only modest war-chests were much more likely to face challengers than those discussed above; about 10% of those who had surpluses under $200,000 had qualified opponents and their average winning percentage was approximately 5% lower than those analyzed above.

Patterns of PAC Support

Most political action committees are pragmatic. Among their goals are aiding candidates with a record of support for their views and seeking to maximize their access to elected officials. Both criteria point to a bias toward incumbents, a bias which further reinforces the incumbency advantage. The Democratic Congressional Campaign Committee relies upon the general PAC preference for sitting representatives to underpin its strategy of protecting potentially vulnerable incumbents. By encouraging political action committees to target early money to troubled incumbents, the DCCC capitalizes on PAC preferences for known commodities and hopes to generate a self-fulfilling prophecy that even vulnerable incumbents can become sure bets if the betting is done early.[26] Presumably such early money serves two key purposes: allowing threatened incumbents an early start in mending their political fences and discouraging underfunded potential challengers from entering the race.

Does early money from political action committees deter qualified challengers? We must first consider when potential challengers make their decisions about entering a congressional race, because PAC money at the time of the decision might enter into that calculus. Some argue that these decisions are made quite early,[27] whereas others state that the relevant date is much later, when the prospective candidate can no longer withdraw from the race gracefully.[28] In fact, a majority of congressional candidates do not even register with the Federal Election Commission until March of the election year.[29] Nonetheless, those who enter the race officially—as signified by registering a principal campaign committee with the FEC—have had to take significant and often irreversible steps earlier. Certainly many who decide not to enter a race have undertaken their personal analyses of factors which will determine the election's outcome well before spring of the election year.

One relevant piece of data available to potential candidates for Congress in the election year is the incumbent's end of previous year's filing with the FEC. According to filed reports covering the period from January 1 through December 31, 1987, 52 House incumbents had raised more than $100,000 from political action committees.[30] The average for this group was nearly $150,000. Their average total receipts in 1987 were just over $250,000; thus, just under 60% of their early money came from PACs. Did the early PAC money received by these incumbents deter qualified congressional challengers?

Eleven of these 52 incumbents ran unopposed. None of the 41 challengers who did run reached the $100,000 plateau in PAC funds by the end of 1987. All save one of these 52 incumbents went on to win re-election in 1988. Their average winning percentage was over 74%. Only eight of these incumbents faced qualified challengers. Five of these eight were freshmen, seeking re-election for the first time. They all won. One of the others, Joseph DioGuardi (R- NY), had faced a tough race in 1986, to hold a seat he had taken from the Democrats as an open seat in 1984. He was the one incumbent in this group who lost.

Challengers need not only worry about early PAC giving, they might also be deterred because of patterns in PAC giving later in campaigns. In 1986 the patterns of PAC giving meant that incumbents received over 40% of their total receipts from PACs while challengers received only around 5%. This represents an increase in the percentage of incumbent money from PACs—up from under 30% in all elections prior to 1984. The pattern of increased incumbent reliance on PAC contributions to fund their campaigns was continued in 1988. Thus, "strategic" challengers might well be deterred not only by early PAC support for incumbents, but also by indications that PACs will continue to fund significant proportions of incumbent campaigns while challengers cannot look forward to this largesse.

If one leaves PAC receipts and looks at total receipts in 1987, a pattern similar to that described above appears. A total of 75 members of the 100th Congress reported receipts of at least $200,000 by December 31, 1987. Of these, 38 had received at least $100,000 from PACs. Qualified challengers ran against 14 of these 75. Six of the qualified challengers took on incumbents who had polled less than 60% in 1986; two of these (Democrats Nita Lowey over DioGuardi in New York and Ben Jones over Pat Swindall in Georgia) won. Six of the qualified challengers took on freshmen. They all lost. Twelve of the 75 Members who had at least $200,000 raised by the end of 1987 ran unopposed in 1988. The other 49 faced weak opponents and won easily.

Thus, a somewhat mixed picture emerges. If local factors

seemed to indicate a vulnerable incumbent, early fundraising did not deter qualified opponents, though few of these opponents emerged victorious. However, in the absence of easily identifiable local factors, the vast majority of those who raised significant amounts of early money were successful in keeping at bay any qualified opponents who might have considered a challenge. In those cases at least, early money—which was frequently early PAC money—was associated with a lack of competitive races.

The Effects of Proposed Reform on Increased Competition

Recently incumbents have so cemented their hold on congressional seats that real competition is a rare exception. Among the factors that have helped more than 90% of the incumbents seeking re-election win with increasingly higher margins of victory is the incumbency advantage in fundraising. The other factors which favor incumbents might not be subject to policy reform to promote increased competition, but reforms of the campaign finance system can work to enhance or undermine electoral competition, especially as they impact on two major resources which aid incumbents—war-chests retained from previous campaigns and storehouses of early money from political action committees.

In the 100th Congress at least 20 Representatives and 15 Senators proposed legislation to reform campaign finance laws governing congressional elections. How would these proposals affect the competitiveness of elections? The proposals can be grouped according to the reform strategies they follow, but the consequences for competition are as dependent upon how these strategies are implemented as they are on the strategies themselves.

Public Financing of House General Elections

A number of proposals call for public financing of House (and Senate) general elections, adopting the philosophy of campaign financing which structures presidential elections. The differences between these proposals and the way in which presidential elections are financed are: (1) most proposals only call for public funding of general elections, not the pre-nomination phase of the process as is the case in presidential elections; and (2) most proposals call for a matching system of public and private financing, not the outright grant which the major party presidential candidates receive.

Public funding proposals often include an overall limit on campaign expenditures and/or a limit on receipts from particular sources, e.g. PACs or personal wealth. These proposals are often combined with suggestions for raising the money necessary to pay for these campaigns and/or with proposals for encouraging small contributions to campaigns, e.g. re-instituting tax credits. Variations on these proposals call for public subsidy of broadcast costs and/or postal costs for candidates for federal office.

A number of philosophical points underlie these proposals. First, those interested in reform in this direction generally are concerned about the overall costs of campaigns. They see public financing as a constitutional way to limit spending. Second, they are concerned about the influence of private money on subsequent actions by those who are elected. Public funding is viewed as cleaner and neater. They feel that the experience with presidential elections has been a positive one which should be repeated for other federal offices. Third, public funding is seen as a means for promoting competition, by equalizing the financial resources of challengers and incumbents. Given the other advantages of incumbency, however, the level of support challengers receive must allow them to wage a viable campaign; or public funding would only further ensconce incumbents.[31]

Reducing Campaign Costs

Various proposals do not go so far as calling for public financing, but still seek ways to reduce the costs of elections, which might also reduce some of the pressure on challengers to maximize their financial resources. Reformers following this track feel that campaign costs have escalated largely because of increased costs for media and that these escalating expenses can be effectively held in check through legislation.[32] A variation of these reforms calls for free response time when a candidate is a target of independent expenditures (H.R. 166 [Howard, D-NJ]). The theory behind these proposals is that campaigning is essentially a public activity and that broadcasters, whose use of the airwaves is a public grant and a public trust, should not get wealthy providing this public service. As with public funding, however, attention should be paid to assuring that adequate media are available to challengers to offset the name recognition advantage of incumbents.

Limiting Political Action Committees

Political action committees were frequent targets of reformers in the 100th Congress. Most of those concerned with political action committees worried about the increasing amount of money they were giving to individual campaigns, frequently in connection with the decreasing amount which was coming from individuals. The philosophical concerns relate to the values of legitimacy and accountability, a worry about the relationship between these contributions to candidates and legislation of concern to the special interests sponsoring the PACs on which successful candidates must vote. In addition, limiting political action committee contributions might also further competition in elections, because most of the PAC money goes to incumbents.

PAC reform has proceeded in a number of different directions. Some feel it is necessary to lower the amounts which PACs can give to a campaign (from the current $5000 to say $3000). Others say what is needed is to increase the amount which individuals can give, from the current $1000 to an amount closer to that which political action committees can give. Some, of course, combine these two ideas.

Others feel that the problem stems not from the individual contribution limits but from PAC influence in the aggregate. Reformers have proposed two approaches to correct this perceived evil. Some claim that PACs should have an aggregate limit on the amount they can contribute to all campaigns, similar to the limit in effect for individuals. A limit such as that proposed would reduce the overall influence of any one political action committee. Another approach restricts the amount candidates can receive from PACs in the aggregate. The theory here is that it is not the giver whose influence we must fear but the recipient who might be influenced. Reformers following this tack also stress the importance of individual contributions to campaigns.

Only the last of these approaches to reducing the influence of political action committees might increase the level of competition for congressional seats. If the cap on aggregate PAC contributions were set fairly low or limited to a modest proportion of funds raised (e.g. under 25%), incumbents would lose one of the major advantages in gaining financial resources that they now enjoy. Of course, it is unclear what political action committees would do with the money they did not give to incumbents. They might give it to challengers, but contributions to challengers would not meet the goals which PACs have generally established for their giving. It is just as likely that a reform such as this one, rather than increasing competition, would lead to unintended negative consequences, such as an increase in independent expenditures.

PAC reform has been on the legislative agenda virtually since the time political action committees began to make substantial contributions to congressional campaigns. Reform efforts have rarely been bi-partisan (the Obey-Railsback bill which emerged in various forms in the late 1970s is a notable exception). How one feels about political action committees has tended to be a function of how much support one can expect to receive from PACs and what alternate sources of contributions were likely to replace PAC contributions.[33] The uncertain consequences of PAC reform are likely to remain constant in the years ahead.

Reforms to Increase Meaningful Competition

Because those who must improve campaign finance reform are incumbents with a vested interest in a system that protects them, we should not be surprised that few reforms are proposed with the expressed aim of increasing competition in elections. Yet, representative democracy is not well served if officeholders are not held accountable by the electorate for their actions. In the United States Congress, incumbents have become all but insulated from electoral defeat, and in many cases even from serious challenge. Incumbent safety is, to a large extent, the result of unqualified candidates running underfunded campaigns against incumbents. While we do not know all of the reasons why qualified contenders choose not to run for Congress, we do know that the campaign finance system is structured in such a way as to discourage challengers. The following proposals are specifically intended to reduce the incumbency advantage in funding in order to encourage more challenges by qualified candidates.

Eliminate Surplus War-chests

All campaign funds remaining after an election cycle should be required to be turned over to the Federal Election Campaign Fund. Allowing Members of Congress to carry excess campaign funds over from one election cycle to the next has a significant impact on deterring qualified challengers from running against those incumbents who enter an election cycle with sizable war-chests in place. Legislation which called for surrendering any campaign surplus to the Federal Treasury, to be applied to the Federal Election Campaign Fund, would reduce one advantage that many entrenched incumbents currently enjoy.

Such legislation would also end the incentive for incumbents to raise excess funds. In addition, this change might reduce PAC contributions to Members of Congress who face no or little opposition because political action committees would not like to see their funds turned over to the U. S. Treasury. However, a reduction of this type would depend on the extent to which PAC managers wanted to receive credit for supporting a powerful and safe incumbent, even if all concerned knew that that contribution meant nothing in terms of the election. All of the consequences of the proposed reform which have been mentioned would impact positively on the democratic values served by elections; none appears to have negative consequences for the ways in which elections should be contested in a democracy.

Limit Early Money

Political action committees should be prohibited from contributing to congressional campaigns until April 1 of the election year.[34] The campaign finance system should be altered so that early money is less of a deterrent to challengers than it now appears to be. This proposal would restrict the role that political action committees play in the early stages of the electoral process. Incumbents could still raise money early, but they would have to do so from individuals, presumably largely from individuals who live within their district. This proposal also furthers another value significant in our system, representation. Electoral representation in the United States is geographically based. Those in Congress also represent interests, interests which span congressional districts or even states. When they are working in their committees, this kind of functional representation is often very important. The problem is to devise an electoral system which balances these two forms of representation.

Those who fear PAC influence today claim that while we elect our representatives from geographic constituencies, the power that determines who will win those elections is interest group power. Early PAC money may even reduce the likelihood that there is a contest at all. Thus, interest groups have insulated incumbent Members of Congress from the pressures of electoral competition in order to assure that the economic interests of those groups are advanced.[35]

This proposal reduces the power of PACs without ignoring the legitimate interest which those contributing to political action committees have in influencing who in Congress decides on legislation of importance to them. The early PAC money restriction promotes both forms of representation—geographic and issue—by allowing the district to define the contest before political action committees intercede. Political action committees would be prohibited from contributing to campaigns prior to April 1 in the election year. By that time challengers would have had a chance to start their campaigns without facing a mountain of political action committee money in their opponents' coffers. In some districts real competition might appear where none seemed likely before. At the specified date, political action committees could contribute. Many would still support incumbents, but others might well decide that challengers in some districts merit attention—because they seem to be mounting serious attacks on incumbents or because they are expressing views more in line with the interest group's views and might become serious candidates with an infusion of funds.

Prevent PAC Dominance

Congressional campaigns should be restricted to receiving no more than 25% of their receipts after April 1 from political action committees. As a corollary to the second reform, this proposal aims at the deterrent effect caused by prospective challengers knowing that an incumbent is likely to be supported heavily by political action committees. Political action committees are recognized as having a legitimate stake in the process, but they are prohibited from dominating the process. If a candidate can raise money from individuals, then he or she can receive money from political action committees. But if that candidate cannot demonstrate the ability to raise money from individuals, then his or her campaign cannot be excessively funded by "outside" "special" interests. Not only does this reform balance geographic and interest representation, it also prevents elected officials from feeling more beholden—hence accountable—to PACs than to their constituents, thus impacting positively on two basic values of our electoral system in addition to fostering more competitive elections.

Neither these reforms nor the three approaches discussed earlier would solve all problems. Campaign managers are expert at finding loopholes in legislation and exploiting those loopholes.

I am certain these reforms would fall prey to some of those efforts. But they would be just that—exploitation of loopholes—and they could be exposed as such. For example, if campaigns had huge infusions of funds on one day, the press would have a field day. And the voters would be able to make appropriate evaluations. Furthermore it must be recognized that any reforms which seek to promote certain values may have unintended consequences for other values.

The purpose of the reforms discussed here is to correct those aspects of the system which work to prevent effective competition. Qualified challengers will not run if they think they have no chance of winning. They will not run if they fear that the campaign finance system is stacked in favor of those in power. Considerable evidence points to the conclusion that qualified challengers view the system in that way and, furthermore, that they are correct in doing so.

Reformers can change some aspects of the system—and three suggestions (with some alternatives) have been proposed here. But to change is not necessarily to reform, if "reform" implies bringing to a better state. The logic behind these proposals seems clear. But their impact is only hypothesized. To be able to predict the impact of these reforms before they are implemented with any accuracy requires research into the decision-making of those who consider running for Congress but who decide not to do so. This research involves looking not only at the impact of national partisan tides, local contextual factors, and the campaign financing system, but also at the personal factors which motivate potential qualified candidates for Congress and the connections which various candidates make among these factors. That research should be high on the agenda for political scientists interested in the effective functioning of our representative democracy.

Notes

1. See, as examples, E. E. Schattschneider, *Party Government* (New York: Holt, Rinehart, and Winston, 1942); Herman Finer, *The Theory and Practice of Modern Government* (New York: Holt, 1949); and V. O. Key, Jr., *Politics, Parties, and Pressure Groups*, 5th ed. (New York: Thomas Y. Crowell, 1964).

2. Julie Rovner, "Turnover in Congress Hits an All-Time High," *Congressional Quarterly Weekly Report*, November 19, 1988, 3362.

3. Rovner, "Turnover in Congress," 3363.

4. Gary C. Jacobson, *The Politics of Congressional Elections* (Boston: Little, Brown, 1987), 32, presents similar data for elections from 1952 through 1984, showing the mean (and median) percentages in elections contested by the major parties. He notes (31) that though the winning percentages rose about 5% between the 1950s and 1970s, incumbents' chances of losing did not change appreciably. The data presented in Table 7.2 lead one to qualify his conclusion in two ways. Jacobson does not present data on seats in which only minor party or independent candidates oppose incumbents or seats in which incumbents run totally unopposed. When those data are added, the winning percentages rise appreciably. Furthermore, in 1986 and 1988, when a higher percentage of incumbents won re-election, they also won by wider margins.

5. Peverill Squire, "Competition and Uncontested Seats in U.S. House Elections," *Legislative Studies Quarterly*, forthcoming.

6. See, as examples, Alan I. Abramowitz, "A Comparison of Voting for U.S. Senator and Representative in 1978," 74 *American Political Science Review* 633 (1980) and his "Party and Individual Accountability in the 1978 Congressional Election" in Louis Sandy Maisel and Joseph Cooper (eds.), *Congressional Elections* (Beverly Hills, CA: Sage Publications, 1981); Barbara Hinckley, "House Re-elections and Senate Defeats: The Role of the Challenger," 10 *British Journal of Political Science* 884 (1980); Thomas E. Mann and Raymond E. Wolfinger, "Candidates and Parties in Congressional Elections," 74 *American Political Science Review* 617 (1980); Glenn R. Parker, "Incumbent Popularity and Electoral Success," in Maisel and Cooper, *Congressional Elections*; Gary C. Jacobson, "Congressional Elections: The Case of the Vanishing Challengers," in Maisel and Cooper, *Congressional Elections*; and John R. Johannes and John C. McAdams, "The Congressional Incumbency Effect: Is It Casework, Policy Compatibility, or Something Else?" 25 *American Journal of Political Science* 512 (1981).

7. The word "qualified" is in quotation marks because scholars disagree over how to operationalize the concept of a qualified candidate. Definitions range from ever having held elective office (e.g. Gary C. Jacobson and Samuel Kernell, *Strategy and Choice in Congressional Elections*, 2nd ed. [Boston: Little, Brown, 1983]) to more sophisticated, but perhaps no more

accurate scales of challenger quality (e. g. Jon R. Bond, Cary Covington and Richard Fleisher, "Explaining Challenger Quality in Congressional Elections," 47 *Journal of Politics* 510 [1985]; or Jonathon S. Krasno and Donald Philip Green, "Pre-empting Quality Challengers in House Elections," 50 *Journal of Politics* 920 [1988]).

8. Jacobson and Kernell, *Strategy and Choice.*

9. The strategic politician model has not gone unchallenged. Richard Born, "Strategic Politicians and Unresponsive Voters," 80 *American Political Science Review* 599 (1986), has challenged Jacobson and Kernell's model on the question of when strategic politicians make their decisions and on whether or not "qualified" candidates win more votes than do other candidates. However, Gary Jacobson has refuted that argument in "Strategic Politics and the Dynamics of House Elections, 1946-1986," a paper delivered at the 1988 Annual Meeting of the American Political Science Association. Others have questioned the way in which Jacobson and Kernell (and Jacobson elsewhere) have defined "qualified" challengers (see David T. Canon, "Political Conditions and Experienced Challengers in Congressional Elections, 1972-1984," a paper delivered at the 1985 Annual Meeting for the American Political Science Association; Bond, Covington, and Fleisher, "Explaining Challenger Quality in Congressional Elections"; Donald Philip Green and Jonathon S. Krasno, "Salvation for the Spendthrift Incumbent: Re-estimating the Effects of Campaign Spending in House Elections," 32 *American Journal of Political Science* 884 [1988]; and Krasno and Green, "Pre-empting Quality Challengers in House Elections"). Jacobson uses a simple dichotomous variable, whether or not the challenger has ever held elective office of any kind. The others claim that more sophistication can be added by examining other challenger qualities. The conclusion that better candidates run better campaigns and therefore have better chances for success seems to be accepted by all, despite controversies over definitions.

10. Louis Sandy Maisel, *From Obscurity to Oblivion: Running in the Congressional Primary*, rev. ed. (Knoxville: University of Tennessee Press, 1986).

11. But see, Thomas A. Kazee, "The Deterrent Effect of Incumbency on Recruiting Challengers in U. S. House Elections", 8 *Legislative Studies Quarterly* 469 (1983) and Linda L. Fowler and Robert C. McClure, *Political Ambition: Who Decides to Run for Congress* (New Haven: Yale University Press, 1989).

12. See Alan I. Abramowitz, "National Issues, Strategic Politicians, and Voting Behavior in the 1980 and 1982 Elections," 28 *American Journal of Political Science* 710 (1984); William T. Bianco, "Strategic Decisions on Candidacy in U. S. Congressional Districts," 9 *Legislative Studies Quarterly* 351 (1984); and Canon, "Political Conditions and Experienced Challengers."

13. See Leo M. Snowiss, "Congressional Recruitment and Representation." *American Political Science Review* 60 (1966): 627; Linda L. Fowler, "The Electoral Lottery: Decisions to Run for Congress," 34 *Public Choice* 381 (1979); Thomas A. Kazee, "The Decision to Run for the U. S. Congress: Challenger Attitudes in the 1970s," 5 *Legislative Studies Quarterly* 79 (1980); Kazee, "The Deterrent Effect of Incumbency on Recruiting Challengers"; Maisel, *From Obscurity to Oblivion*; and Fowler and McClure, *Political Ambition.*

14. Krasno and Green, "Pre-empting Quality Challengers in House Elections"; Bond, Covington, and Fleisher, "Explaining Challenger Quality in Congressional Elections."

15. Edie N. Goldenberg, Michael W. Traugott, and Frank R. Baumgartner, "Pre-emptive and Reactive Spending in U. S. House Races," 8 *Political Behavior* 3 (1986); Krasno and Green, "Pre-empting Quality Challengers in House Elections"; Green and Krasno, "Salvation for the Spendthrift Incumbent"; and Gary C. Jacobson, *Money in Congressional Elections* (New Haven: Yale University Press, 1980); and "Enough is Too Much: Money and Competition in House Elections, 1972-1984," in Kay L. Schlozman, ed., *Elections in America* (New York: Allen and Unwin, 1987).

16. Center for Responsive Politics, *Spending in Congressional Elections: A Never-Ending Spiral* (Washington: Center for Responsive Politics, 1988).

17. Frank J. Sorauf, *Money in American Politics* (Boston: Scott, Foresman, and Company, 1988), 163.

18. Open seats are not included in this discussion because we are concerned only with competition faced by incumbents.

19. See Chuck Alston, "Campaign-Finance Gridlock Likely to Persist," *Congressional Quarterly Weekly Report*, December 17, 1988, 3525-9, and Brooks Jackson, *Honest Graft: Big Money and the American Political Process* (New York: Alfred A. Knopf, 1988).

20. Gary C. Jacobson, *Money in Congressional Elections*, points out the interesting phenomenon that incumbents who are

in trouble have little difficulty in raising money, but he also concludes that late incumbent fundraising and spending is one sign that that incumbent might well face difficulty in the coming election.

21. Jackson, *Honest Graft*, 291.

22. Sorauf, *Money in American Elections*, 157; see also Maxwell Glen, "Early-Bird Fundraising," *National Journal*, June 20, 1987, 1589.

23. One cannot prove causality, because the dependent variable is the decision by a prospective qualified candidate not to run. That variable cannot be explained by any independent variables—for example, the existence or lack of a campaign warchest—unless one knows many other factors about the prospective qualified candidate, not the least of which is his or her identity.

24. For the purposes of this analysis, challengers deemed to be qualified were those who met at least one of the following criteria: (1) holding elective office either at the time they were running or having held office in the biennium immediately before they were running, if the districts overlapped considerably; (2) having run credible campaigns in the immediately preceding congressional race; or (3) having been rated as a serious challenger in the Congressional Quarterly Weekly Report analysis of the district before the primary was held. This definition is different from those used by others, but seems most appropriate for this analysis. The first two criteria are, of course, objective and are clearly relevant for congressional candidates. By restricting our definition to current or recent officeholders and those whose districts overlapped with the congressional district, we eliminated some anomalies which Jacobson faced, e.g. including Harold Stassen, who ran in Minnesota in 1988 among his qualified candidates. We did include those who had shown the requisite skills and had the appropriate experience in the appropriate context. The third criterion, while somewhat subjective, draws on the acknowledged expertise of an organization whose track record is admirable; I use the pre-primary analysis, not the pre-election analysis, because I am interested in identifying challengers whose qualities were recognized before they started campaigning and raising money. As an example, this criterion would have allowed us to include David Price, the political scientist and former state party chair who unseated an incumbent in North Carolina in 1986.

25. This seems to contradict the conclusion of Squire, "Com-

petition and Uncontested Seats in U. S. House Elections," that most of those who are unopposed in one election face competition in the next election. That conclusion may well bear re-examination in the case of those who have large surpluses left after the campaign in which they are unopposed.

26. See Jackson, *Honest Graft*; and Sorauf, *Money in American Elections.*

27. Maisel, *From Obscurity to Oblivion.*

28. Jacobson, "Strategic Politics and the Dynamics of House Elections," or Jacobson and Kernell, *Strategy and Choice.*

29. Clyde Wilcox, "The Timing of Strategic Decisions: Candidacy Decisions in 1982 and 1984," 12 *Legislative Studies Quarterly* 565 (1987).

30. As a point of reference, 32 of these 52 went on to raise at least $200,000 from PACs by June 30, 1988. They were 32 of the 40 top PAC recipients at that time.

31. Jacobson, *Money in Congressional Elections.*

32. See Edie N. Goldenberg and Michael W. Traugott, *Campaigning for Congress* (Washington: Congressional Quarterly Press, 1984).

33. See Frank J. Sorauf, *What Price PACs? Report of the Twentieth Century Fund Task Force on Political Action Committees* (New York: Twentieth Century Fund, 1984); Sorauf, Money in American Elections; and Larry J. Sabato, *PAC Power* (New York: Norton, 1984).

34. Alternatively one could specify that no political action committee funds could be received until after major primary nominations have been determined. This would have much the same effect but would be more difficult to administer. In addition, such a federal restriction might well lead to changes in state laws to help incumbents, an undesirable consequence.

35. Jackson, *Honest Graft.*

8

Money and Congressional Behavior

Janet Grenzke

Our current campaign finance system is giving us "the best Congress money can buy." So say journalists, Common Cause, Citizens Against PACs and numerous other critics of campaign financing in general and PACs in specific. Important values are at stake if corruption is as commonplace as popular critics would have us believe: (1) Governmental effectiveness and legitimacy, because PAC money may undermine the congressional capacity to act or distort and corrupt the actions that are undertaken; (2) Representation and accountability, because incumbents are increasingly reliant on PAC funds rather than the resources of their constituents to stay in office. Thus, they may become more accountable to and more concerned about representing moneyed interests rather than voters. Finally, political equality, because PAC money reflects and reinforces the unequal distribution of wealth in America that translates into unequal political power. If PACs have undue influence in Congress, then elections become meaningless as a way for the less privileged to use their votes to direct their representatives or to hold them accountable.

Issues in Assessing PAC Influence

Anecdotes and popular studies about PAC influence purport to prove that PACs are having all the pernicious impact noted above—that Congress is "for sale to the highest bidder." Common Cause produces some of the most visible examples of this approach. They examined contributions to members of the Finance Committee and concluded that the members are "bought." *Newsweek* entitled a selection on the 1988 election, "For Members Only–No Outsiders need apply to Congress, where incumbents get fat on PACs." Jackson argues that PAC contributions to Fernand St. Germain and other members largely explain how individuals in the savings and loan industry received preferential treatment that eventually cost the taxpayer billions of dollars for bailouts.[1]

In contrast to these claims, most scholarly evidence suggests that popular claims grossly exaggerate the impact of contributions. Unfortunately, the two camps usually talk past each other, with academics dismissing the validity of popular claims in a few paragraphs and the popular press ignoring the research of scholars or quickly rejecting its methods and conclusions as irrelevant. Activists argue that money influences congressional behavior but that statistical models cannot uncover the relationship. What follows not only clarifies what we do and don't know about the influence of PAC money, but also attempts to show the merits and flaws of both the popular and scholarly approaches.

Academics are troubled by three aspects of the popular case against PACs. First, the coincidence of congressional roll-call votes and PAC contributions is used as evidence that money buys member votes. This interpretation ignores the likelihood that members of Congress respond to pressures from their district, party, and the President, that they consider their own ideology, and that the interest groups' other activities influence members. In short, members may vote as they do, regardless of whether PACs contribute. Furthermore, the coincidence of PAC contributions and congressional voting could exist because PACs contribute money to help re-elect supporters, not because PAC contributions influence member votes.

Second, academics are critical of the superficial examination of PAC attempts to influence policy (e.g. giving money to party and committee leaders who face minimal electoral opposition) and the leap to the assumption that these strategies are successful, in spite of considerable evidence to the contrary.[2]

Third, academics are skeptical of the quotations in the popular literature from members of Congress who contend that their colleagues are influenced by contributions. Of course, the person interviewed is rarely guilty, and the "others" are unnamed. Assessments by members of what others are doing are usually based upon anecdotes, and the evidence varies from Drew's accusations that nearly all members are bought to surveys conducted by The Center for Responsive Politics that report that 20% of congressional members feel money influences member votes.[3]

Most of the academic analyses as well as the popular analyses that conclude that PAC contributions influence member votes, either in general or under particular conditions, do not use a methodology that adjusts for the extent to which PACs react to, rather than influence, members' votes in Congress.[4] Some of these scholars use a time sequence to try to accommodate the simultaneity of the relationship between PAC money and members' votes, but these efforts are not entirely satisfactory. For example, Langbein and Lotwis find a relationship between contributions from the NRA and Handgun Control PAC between 1983 and April 1986 and members' votes on the Firearms Owners Protection Act after April 1986. However, the relationship could be spurious, rather than causal, if members' votes in 1986 are highly correlated to their earlier position on gun control, and if PACs reacted to, rather than caused, members' earlier positions on gun control.[5]

Even though analyses that ignore the simultaneity of contributions and members' votes may exaggerate the impact of PAC contributions, several of these studies find very limited support for the thesis that money influences votes.[6] Wright finds that contributions from four of the five association PACs he studies appear to increase the probability of voting with the PAC, but "in none of the cases were the effects of contributions great enough to change the voting outcome" Because he examines some of the most influential PACs, and because he uses a methodology that may exaggerate the impact of PAC contributions, his findings represent the upper limits of PAC influence, limits which "pale in comparison to the unbounded influence that many scholars, journalists, and politicians have imputed to PACs"[7]

An early study by Chappell clearly boosts the argument for a simultaneous methodology when he demonstrates that the relationship between contributions from specific PACs and member votes on seven varied pieces of legislation appear to influence members on six of the votes when a single equation methodology is used, but on only one of the votes when a simultaneous model is used.[8]

In addition to Chappell, several other researchers employ simultaneous models to investigate the impact of PAC money on members' votes, and they reach conflicting conclusions.[9] These works reach conflicting conclusions because their models differ with respect to whether they examine voting on particular bills or a series of votes combined into ratings by interest groups; contributions of individual PACs or groups of PACs; actual votes and contributions or changes in them. Their models also differ in how they control for the propensity of members to vote in the absence of contributions. This includes separating the impact of contributions on members' votes from the influence of voters in the district, party, and their own ideology. It also involves separating the impact of the interest group's lobbying and voter mobilization efforts from the impact of campaign contributions. Although studies using single equation techniques also differ along these dimensions, the discussion that follows focuses on interpreting the conflicting conclusions drawn from simultaneous models.

Successful studies of whether PAC money influences votes must control for the influence of the legislator's constituency, ideology, party, the President, fellow legislators, and interest group activity beyond contributions, on members' roll-call votes. There are problems with the way in which many of these factors are measured, however, and inadequate measures lead to questionable results. For example, census data that describes the economic and demographic composition of the district may capture the essence of the constituency only if these factors are closely related to the bill or policy domain under investigation.[10] The ideological disposition of the district, measured by the district's presidential vote, also taps district concerns. However, many districts are heterogeneous, and these measures do not indicate which parts of the district are most politically influential. The legislator's ideology is generally measured by a rating by a broad based interest group (i.e. ADA, ACA, COPE) or by the members' conservative coalition support scores, but the legislator's votes on the bills in the summary scores may be influenced by interest group activity, including PAC contributions, reintroducing a problem of simultaneity.[11] Members' party affiliation is usually added to the equations, as an indicator of members' ideology, influence from party leaders and fellow legislators, and even influence from the President. Even this measure is not perfect, however, for conservative Democrats are often more similar to Republicans than to their own partisans.

One way to control for these other influences on member votes is to use a dynamic model, which examines changes in member votes and contributions.[12] If one assumes that the other influences on the legislator are relatively stable, then these variables drop out of the equations, and many measurement problems are avoided. Alternatively, one can carefully choose measures of the other influences on the legislator, and recognize the way in which errors in these measures may result in an overestimation or underestimation of the influence of PAC contributions.

Some studies examine the impact of contributions on specific bills.[13] While this approach may be useful for uncovering influence on particular legislation, the generality of such studies is always debatable. Others examine the impact of contributions from either a major PAC or group of PACs on voting in an entire issue domain, to determine the pervasiveness of PAC influence.[14] For example, Grenzke finds that contributions to incumbents from 120 PACs representing 10 interest groups rarely influence a pattern of voting (measured as a rating) in the issue domains of education, labor, business, abortion, and insurance between 1977 and 1982. The relationships between actual contributions and rating, as well as between changes in contributions and changes in ratings, are examined to determine that contributions neither maintain nor change members' overall voting in an issue domain. Instead, members are influenced by their district, party, and their own ideology. Even when the statistics suggested that PAC money influenced votes, PAC officials insisted that their lobbying efforts and their voter mobilization activity was crucial, and that PAC contributions were simply surrogate measures of this more extensive activity.

Recognizing that the contribution may be a surrogate measure of an interest group's efforts to lobby and mobilize votes in the district is an important step toward reconciling the different conclusions reached by Grenzke, Wilhite and Theilmann, and Wilhite on the impact of labor contributions on member votes on labor legislation.[15] All three studies use simultaneous statistical models with controls for district influence and party (or a combination of party and member ideology) to explain member COPE scores. Grenzke's interviews with PAC officials indicate that the positive statistical relationship between House member votes and contributions from COPE and 78 of its affiliates for 1977–78 tapped the impact of COPE's lobbying and voter mobilization efforts. The relationships for the 1979–1980 and 1981–1982 Congresses were not significant. On the other hand, Wilhite and Theilmann uncovered a significant statistical relationship between contributions from the entire labor community and COPE scores for 1980 and 1982 in the House and the Senate. If one adopts the perspective that contributions are surrogate measures of labor's other activities, then it is not surprising that contributions, lobbying, and voter mobilization on the part of the entire labor community have an impact on labor legislation, while the activities of COPE and its PAC affiliates alone do not. This reconciliation of the differing conclusions is further supported by Wilhite's suggestion that labor money did not influence the COPE scores of Senators or Representatives in 1984, because the labor community may have been divided.

In a study of the impact of contributions from the entire labor and corporate community on House member COPE scores in 1979–1980, Saltzman also concludes that contributions influence member votes. However, once again, the possibility that the contributions could be surrogates for lobbying and vote mobilization efforts from both the labor and corporate community is not considered.[16]

Malbin argues that campaign contributions are insignificant when compared to the resources employed in lobbying campaigns.[17] For example, the business community spent about $5 million on a single bill involving revisions to the labor law in 1979, whereas $9 million was contributed by all corporate PACs during the same year. Sabato estimates that lobbies spent $350 million to influence congressional legislation in 1982, while all PACs contributed $83 million to congressional candidates in both 1981 and 1982.[18] In 1986, the National Committee to Preserve Social Security estimates it spent over $3 million, primarily to generate 8 million pieces of mail to Congress, whereas it contributed just over $700,000.[19] In spite of the importance of lobbying efforts, they are difficult to measure, and consequently have rarely been included in the statistical models which seek to assess the impact of campaign contributions.

Two studies that do control for lobbying efforts reach different conclusions about the impact of campaign contributions. Wright's study of voting on the re-authorization of the Comprehensive Environmental Response, Compensation and Liability Act ("superfund") in the Ways and Means committee indicates that while lobbying efforts were related to member voting, "the total direct and indirect effects of campaign contributions are extremely small."[20] Langbein and Lotwis find that anti-gun lobbying, measured by letters to members of Congress, was related to the number of times House members voted to support gun control legislation in 1986.[21] They also claim that contributions from the National Rifle Association (NRA) and Handgun Control influenced voting over and above each group's lobbying efforts. However, Langbein and Lotwis base their conclusion on a model that does not account for the simultaneous relationship between contributions and member votes, as discussed above, and is likely to exaggerate the impact of contributions.

Given the difficulty of measuring lobbying efforts, Wright suggests that the impact of contributions may be isolated from lobbying by looking at an issue where little lobbying occurs, where large PACs are involved, and where the legislators are responsive to group demands.[22] Welch's study of voting on price supports for the dairy industry in 1974 satisfies these criteria, in that dairy PACs are some of the largest campaign contributors, they have a strong constituency base, and a survey of newspapers during the votes indicates that lobbying efforts were minimal.[23] Welch concluded that campaign contributions had very little influence on votes for price supports.

It is also important, and difficult, to separate the impact of campaign contributions from the influence of groups' nonmonetary electoral activities. These include endorsements, internal communications, and voter mobilization activities which can be for or against a candidate. For example, the NRA has a potent grass roots organization of members who feel strongly enough about gun control to base their vote on that issue alone.[24] PAC officials representing the Communication Workers of American (CWA) and the AFL-CIO Committee on Political Education (COPE) argued that their ability to deliver votes to candidates was much more important than their contributions. An official from the National Abortion Rights Action League (NARAL) gave an example of a Congressman who changed his voting from pro-life to pro-choice in order to get NARAL's endorsement, and he did not accept campaign contributions from any PACs.[25]

The above discussion of the systematic research on the impact of campaign contributions on member votes argues that claims of widespread vote buying on Capitol Hill are grossly exaggerated.[26] Whereas contributions may facilitate access, even these claims may be exaggerated. Groups that are large enough to make contributions are often powerful enough to gain access without a contribution. Conversely, groups that are politically unimportant are least likely to contribute enough to significantly improve their access or to present a convincing case once they obtain access.[27] If contributions were essential for access, and if one only needed access in order to influence, the relationship between contributions and member votes would emerge more strongly than it does. Thus, both popular and scholarly studies on whether PAC contributions influence votes in Congress have serious difficulties to overcome. The best analyses seem to indicate that the influence of PAC money is insignificant compared to the other means interest groups use to influence votes and the other factors that enter members' voting decisions.

When Might PAC Money Matter?

Those who believe that PAC money is pernicious will probably not be convinced otherwise by the above discussion, and some of their doubts may be well founded. Focusing primarily on roll-call votes may keep scholars preoccupied with studying this behavior because of its ease of measurement while overlooking other important but less easily observable arenas of influence, such as the committee and subcommittee level. PAC money may be a more important factor in structuring decisions before they reach the level of roll-call votes or in preventing matters from ever being seriously considered.[28] Finally, even concluding that PAC money only reinforces the other lobbying efforts of groups or that it buys access rather than influence may not be benign. Our interest group system is already marked by great inequalities that may undermine important values such as governmental legitimacy and effectiveness, representation and accountability, and political equality. PAC money need not be encouraged to worsen that situation.

In fact, scholars have begun to turn their attention to some specific areas where PAC money might be expected to be significant. Most of these studies show only weak influence, if any, and once again their focus is primarily on floor votes rather than other types of behavior. Nonetheless, such studies represent important attempts to focus on areas where popular sentiment and sound logic suggest PACs might more readily gain influence.

First, interest groups and their contributions may be more influential for votes that attract little publicity, and for issues where the public is indifferent, divided, or ignorant.[29] Jones and Keiser find stronger relationships between contributions and low visibility labor votes than between contributions and high visibility labor votes.[30] Frendreis and Waterman suggest that trucking legislation created little publicity, and therefore contributions were important to member votes.[31] Schroedel contends that contributions were more important for the Bank Underwriting Bill than for two other bills that concerned the financial sector, because the Bank Underwriting Bill received little publicity.[32]

As a corollary, less publicity is likely when the organized groups agree and when the opposition is either absent or unorganized. Evans suggests this scenario is likely when the bill's costs are dispersed and the benefits are concentrated.[33] Thus, she finds that contributions and lobbying (their separate impact is not determined) are more important on a consensual vote such as the loan to Chrysler than on a more conflictual vote such as the windfall profits tax. On both issues, however, the impact of contributions is overshadowed by the importance of party and member ideology. Welch[34] examines dairy price supports in 1975, where the costs are also dispersed and the benefits are concentrated, and finds that contributions from the wealthy dairy PACs are statistically significant, but less important to members' voting than dairy production in the members' districts, their ideology, and party affiliation.[35]

Second, in addition to low visibility bills, there are low visibility settings, such as committee meetings, where campaign contributions may influence member votes.[36] The only study addressing this possibility is Wright's examination of decisions of the Ways and Means Committee on an excise tax to pay for the cleaning of toxic waste sites.[37] He concludes that when one controls for groups' lobbying efforts, contributions do not influence decisions, either directly or indirectly by easing access for lobbies.

Third, just as contributions may be more influential in certain settings and on certain types of bills, PAC money may influence some members more than others. Feldstein and Melnick examine House members who receive contributions from the American Medical Association and state medical political action committees (MEDPACs) and find that members who faced close elections in 1978 were slightly more likely to support MEDPAC positions when they voted on the Gephardt Amendment to hospital containment legislation.[38] Frendreis and Waterman report that the relationship between contributions from the American Trucking Association (ATA) and votes on trucking deregulation in 1980 was stronger for senators who faced an election in 1980 than for those whose elections were in 1982 and 1984.[39] Ginsberg and Green report that contributions from a variety of interest groups are more strongly related to the votes of uncommitted members than to those of members exhibiting the most and least support for the interest. Again, however, it is unclear whether some members are influenced by contributions, or by the groups' entire package of political activity.

The scope of the potential problem of PAC influence in cases of low visibility and low conflict issues, low visibility settings, or certain types of members of Congress is difficult to assess. The good news is that most members of Congress do not seem to be influenced by PAC money alone on issues of major significance and publicity. The bad news is that much legislation is of low visibility and low conflict where money may matter. Many decisions are made at the subcommittee and committee level—or in private—where PAC money may alter the choices that emerge or prevent some issues from emerging at all. Finally, even if only select members are susceptible to influence in specific circumstances, these few votes could be pivotal at the subcommittee and committee level, if not on the floor. Without systematic analyses of these avenues for influence, however, neither complacent confidence nor constant cynicism about congressional behavior can be justified—merely continued cautious concern.

What Reform is Warranted?

The extent and nature of the problems should direct the remedies we seek. Since PACs do not generally influence votes in Congress, although they may influence behavior under certain circumstances, attempts to restrict PACs alone may be unnecessary. If governmental legitimacy and effectiveness are weakened, that is likely due to the pressures of interest groups in general, although the effect may be exacerbated and more easily observed because of PACs. Even radical campaign finance reforms cannot alter the basic reality of the unequal power of interest groups in their lobbying and electoral power. Some interests have tremendous resources with which to promote their cause, and contributions are only a part of these resources. Those interests with resources do, in fact, influence public policy, not because they contribute to campaigns, but because they can activate constituents to pressure representatives on a bill and mobilize voters to support or defeat a candidate at the polls.

On the other hand, the protection of other fundamental values may require reforms that might also restrict the influence of PACs. Such reforms could restore the linkages of representation and accountability between members and their constituents by alleviating those circumstances under which PAC money may be influential. They could further enhance these values by increasing the likelihood of competitive elections. Finally, they might improve political equality in two ways. First, they allow for the more equal access of candidates to the resources necessary for a viable campaign. Second, they reduce the unequal influence that moneyed interests may have in select instances because of their contributions.

The reforms I have in mind rely on a voluntary system for public financing of primary and general congressional elections. In the general election, the reforms are designed to bring about more competitive elections and more equality by supplementing the campaigns of those candidates—generally challengers—who lack the resources to communicate with voters.[40] While the reforms will not result in equally well funded campaigns, the proposal will guarantee that candidates with support in the district have sufficient funds to run viable campaigns. The reforms for the primary elections will help less wealthy candidates, although not enough to significantly challenge an incumbent's likely nomination. More importantly, the primary election reforms are necessary to alleviate some of the side effects caused by the general election reforms. The main result is a set of primary and general election reforms that work together to produce a choice in the general election between at least two candidates with viable campaigns.

The reform proposal for the general election involves public funding, but is very different from funding in the presidential elections. Each month after the primary, the contributions from PACs and individuals, independent expenditures, and family money spent by each candidate will be compared, and a gap between the two candidates of more than $10,000 will be eliminated by federal funds.[41] A candidate who is behind the first month, receives federal funds, and in the second month accumulates more money in contributions than his or her opponent, will return whatever federal money is necessary to close the gap again. Federal funds will equalize the resources of the two campaigns up to $500,000 for House races (indexed for inflation) and will match a decreasing proportion of the opponent's resources above $500,000, an amount high enough so that challengers can begin to overcome the advantages of incumbency, and an amount low enough so that a few particularly expensive races will not bankrupt the program.[42] For House candidates spending between $500,000 and $1,000,000, $.50 of every dollar collected by the opponent is matched to lessen the gap, and $.25 of every dollar above that. A comparable point will be chosen for Senate races, varying according to the voting age population. Participation will be voluntary, but it is unlikely that candidates with fewer resources than their opponents will refuse federal funds. In order to qualify for public funding in the general or primary election, candidates must demonstrate support in their district by raising more than $10,000 in individual contributions of up to $100. A tax check-off similar to that for the presidential campaign will be supplemented by general treasury funds as necessary. Unspent money at the end of the two year cycle, up to the amount of the public money received by the candidate, is returned to the general fund. In the general election, the proposal supplements the campaigns of those without resources, enhancing equality and electoral competition.

Some may object that the proposal does not do enough, that candidates will still have unequal resources. For example, 16 House candidates (10 incumbents, 2 challengers, 4 open seat candidates) spent over $1 million in their general election campaigns.[43] A proposal that provides opponents of these big fund raisers with equal amounts of money would be prohibitively expensive. The proposal does, however, provide candidates with sufficient funds to run a viable campaign that communicates with a significant part of the district. This seems to be a minimal requirement for democratic elections. Furthermore, the return on each additional dollar spent in these very expensive campaigns declines, so that the opponent is not as disadvantaged as the difference in total spending suggests.

As with any reform, there probably will be unintended consequences. The general election reforms could encourage well funded candidates to spend large amounts of money in the primary, and little in the general election. Candidates with few resources would not get matching funds in the general election because their opponents would not raise money, and they would not be able to overcome the lead the well funded candidates established in the primaries. The following proposal for the primaries is designed to alleviate this side effect.

The reform proposal for primary elections again involves public financing, but this time small contributions to a candidate, up to $100 from individuals and PACs (located within and outside the district) are matched with public money to the same candidate, providing the candidate agrees to limit primary campaign expenditures to $75,000 (inclusive of public money) for House campaigns, and a comparable limit for Senate campaigns, depending on the size of the voting age population. As stated earlier, candidates must demonstrate support by raising $10,000 in amounts up to $100 from individuals within the district. If one candidate exceeds the spending limit, the other candidates in the same party will receive double the matching funds, $200 for the first $100 of individual and PAC contributions, until they reach a spending limit of $150,000, inclusive of public funding.[44]

The primary proposal diversifies the sources of campaign funds, thereby expanding this aspect of participation, and it will provide some assistance to candidates with support in the district, but with few resources. The primary proposal does not claim to bring about equality among the primary contenders. Because many more candidates compete in the primary election, it is unfeasible to use government funds to fund everyone at the level of the wealthiest candidate. Whereas the use of public money to support candidates who win a small proportion of the vote in general elections is justified because meaningful elections require competition between parties, widespread competition within parties may be neither affordable nor necessary for a viable democracy. From the perspective of the larger political system, it is more important for citizens to choose which party wins than to choose which Democrat or Republican candidate contests the general election. This remains true regardless of the policy positions held by either the primary or general election candidates.

Two aspects of the primary and general election reforms require further explanation. First, contrary to many proposals that seek to discourage PACs and encourage individual contributions, this proposal does not restrict PAC contributions in the general election, and even matches the first $100 of PAC contributions in the primaries. This is based upon the premise that the influence of PAC money on votes in Congress is not nearly as important as inequalities in the total resources that individuals and groups use to lobby and mobilize votes. The solution is based upon the Madisonian argument that we cannot control the efforts of interest groups to generate district pressure on members to support or defeat legislation, or their use of communication networks to mobilize support or opposition for candidates during elections. The reforms should encourage as much diversity and competition between interest groups as possible. Furthermore, interest groups, including PACs, aggregate individual interests. While wealthy individuals may influence politics without an aggregating institution, the poor and the middle class cannot. Ideally the aggregating structures would be political parties, and reforms that allow larger contributions to parties would work toward that end. However, American parties, in spite of recent rejuvenation, are limited by the American context.[45] By matching small PAC contributions, small PACs will form and contribute, and large PACs will spread their money more widely. This brings about more diversity in the PAC community, and members' campaigns will be less dependent upon any single interest.

Furthermore, a system that matches individual contributions but not PAC contributions encourages PACs to give bundles of individual contributions instead of PAC contributions, a practice that will be virtually impossible to eliminate, and one in which sophisticated PACs will be able to engage much more easily than the smaller PACs. Bundling is problematic because it is difficult for the public to characterize a candidate on the basis of the names and occupations of more than a thousand individual contributors. It is relatively easy for the public to determine the interests that support a candidate when the money is identified with a PAC. The candidate is aware of the source of the money under either system.

A second unusual feature of this proposal is that out- of- district contributions are not discouraged, and in fact are matched in the primary election. Objections to this provision will come from persons who want to restrict the legislator's funding constituency to the candidate's geographic constituency. When coupled with a spending limit of $75,000, a primary proposal that matches only contributions from within the district would accentuate the power of the wealthy within that district. Those who have more trouble raising money, either challengers or candidates who represent the less advantaged in the district, can only be competitive if their opportunities for raising money are expanded to include out-of-district sources and PACs.[46] Note, however, that this argument applies only when there is a spending limit. If there is no spending limit, and out-of-district funds are matched, incumbents who are better known than challengers, and well funded candidates with more professional organizations may raise enough out-of-district money to preclude serious competition.

A second argument in favor of matching out-of-district contributions (when there is a spending limit) concerns the representation and participation opportunities of citizens whose interests are not served by any of the candidates in the primary. Because we have single member districts, the candidate nominated in the primary, and the winner in the election in an heterogeneous district can only represent the issue positions of a portion of the district. In the absence of multi-member districts with proportional representation, PACs and cross- district contributions provide the minority the opportunity to support the election of a candidate they like by contributing to candidates in other districts and to PACs who will funnel resources to candidates who promote their cause.

The combination of public financing at the primary and general election stages should produce the following scenarios. First, candidates will raise and spend as much as possible during the primaries, because some of the money they raise will be matched, whereas it will be negated at the general election by public money to their opponent. While it is hoped that most candidates will choose to stay within the $75,000 primary limit, there will be some who choose not to participate, in spite of the boost this would give to their opponent's campaign. When a well funded candidate spends much more than $75,000 in the primary, the opposition will begin the general election at a considerable disadvantage. This scenario is familiar today, particularly with incumbents in one-party districts. These reforms constitute an improvement because with public money, the spending of resource-poor candidates will approximate that of the wealthier opposition for the several months immediately preceding the election. Such a reformed system is certainly better than the current system, where well funded candidates may spend over $1 million shortly before the general election, when the opposition may not have the funds or time to respond.

Second, when a strong incumbent and weak challenger emerge from the primaries, it is in the incumbent's interest to turn over contributions remaining after the primary to the public financing general fund. The incumbents benefit from greater recognition and support accumulated from previous elections and tenure in office, and will have little motivation to spend money that will be matched by public funds to their opponents. In races with weak challengers, the cost to the government of general election races will be low, and the public financing general fund may even make money which can be distributed to other races.

Third, the appearance of an attractive challenger in the other party's primary will cause both candidates to begin to raise money. It is possible that only one candidate would raise money, but the other candidate would be somewhat disadvantaged by the month waiting period for public money. The difference between the current situation and the one likely to emerge with the reform is that as the spiral heightens, and one candidate begins to fall behind, the government will narrow the gap. Generally, this will help attractive challengers stay even up to a point ($500,000 in House elections), so that the incumbent will not win just because the challenger lacks funds to communicate with voters. If both candidates stay about even in a very expensive campaign, there will be no need for government involvement because no disparities should occur, and voters will choose between two viable candidates.

Conclusion

Review of the reliable evidence about whether PAC money is corrupting Congress suggests that the problem is less extensive and less easy to prove than common charges would have us believe. Those previously concerned about governmental legitimacy, effectiveness, representation, and accountability might reasonably conclude that PACs have not significantly altered either the advantages or limitations of our pluralist system of government. In fact, reformers who give primacy to the value of political liberty might argue for reducing the restriction on PACs. I believe that there may be limited cause for concern about the influence of PACs in certain circumstances, but that our greater goal should be to reduce the way PACs and our campaign finance system in general reinforce political inequality and reduces competition.

The public financing scheme I offer attempts to promote as many of the fundamental values of elections as possible without appreciably harming others. In improving the prospects for viable competition, it also enhances representation and accountability. By matching small contributions in the primaries, it promotes broadened participation. By reducing the incentives for candidates to rely heavily on PACs and by enhancing competition, it restores governmental legitimacy. It also enhances the political equality of individuals and candidates in elections, with related improvement of representation and accountability. Yet, it does not significantly reduce the political liberty of PACs, individuals or candidates. Such a system of public financing might truly give us "the best Congress money can buy"—an effective, legitimate, representative and accountable Congress that is obtained by a combination of public and private funds and serves all the people, not merely those with economic clout.

NOTES

1. Common Cause, *Financing the Finance Committee* (Washington, D.C.: Common Cause, 1986); George Hackett and Eleanor Clift, "For Members Only–No Outsiders Need Apply to Congress," *Newsweek*, November 14, 1988, 22–23; Brooks Jackson, *Honest Graft* (New York: Knopf, 1988). See also Common Cause, *Looking to Purchase or Rent*, (Washington, D.C.: Common Cause, 1984), and *A Common Cause Guide to Money, Power and Politics in the 97th Congress*, (Washington, D.C.: Common Cause, 1981); Elizabeth Drew, *Politics and Money: The New Road to Corruption* (New York: Macmillan, 1983); Philip M. Stern, *The Best Congress Money Can Buy* (New York: Pantheon Books, 1988).

2. Fred Wertheimer, "Commentary," in Michael Malbin, ed., *Parties, Interest Groups and Campaign Finance Laws* (Washington, D.C.: American Enterprise Institute, 1980).

3. Drew, *Politics and Money*; Peter Lindstrom, Congress Speaks (Washington, D.C.: The Center for Responsive Politics, 1988).

4. Examples of this work include R. Kenneth Godwin, "The Policy Impact of Party Inequality in Campaign Finance." paper presented at the annual meeting of the American Political Science Association, Washington, D.C., 1988; Woodrow Jones, Jr., and K. Robert Keiser, "Issue Visibility and Effects of PAC Money," *Social Science Quarterly* 68 (March 1987): 170–176; John Frendreis and Richard Waterman, "PAC Contributions and Legislative Behavior: Senate Voting on Trucking Deregulation," *Social Science Quarterly* 66 (June 1985): 401–412; Kirk Brown, "Campaign Contributions and Congressional Voting," paper presented at the annual meeting of the American Political Science Association, Chicago, Ill., 1983; Jean Reith Schroedel, "Campaign Contributions and Legislative Outcomes," *Western Political Quarterly* 39 (September 1986): 371–389; Jonathan Silberman and Garey C. Durden, "Determining Legislative Preferences on the Minimum Wage: An Economic Approach," *Journal of Political Economy* 84 (April 1976): 317–329; D. Gleiber, J. King, H.R.

Mahood, "PAC Contributions, Constituency Interest and Legislative Voting: Gun Control Legislation in the U.S. Senate," paper presented at the annual meeting of the Midwest Political Science Association, Chicago, Ill., 1987.

5. Laura Langbein and Mark Lotwis, "Electoral Margins, Policy Positions, and Campaign Contributions: The Firearms Owners Protection Act in the House," a revision of the paper presented at the annual meeting of the American Political Science Association, Washington, D.C., 1988. See also W.P. Welch, "Campaign Contributions and Legislative Voting: Milk Money and Dairy Price Supports," *Western Political Quarterly* 35 (December 1982): 478–495; G. Saltzman, "Congressional Voting on Labor Issues: The Role of PACs," *Industrial and Labor Relations Review* 40 (January 1987): 168. Ginsberg and Green use a time sequence and report that contributions change member voting in the subsequent session. However, these results are problematic because their measure of change in member's voting is a proportion that has the same value for members undergoing very different amounts of change. Benjamin Ginsberg and John Green, "The Best Congress Money Can Buy," in Benjamin Ginsberg and Alan Stone, eds., *Do Elections Matter* (Armonk, New York: M.E. Sharpe, 1986).

6. John Wright, "PACs, Contributions and Roll-Calls: An Organizational Perspective," *American Political Science Review* 75 (June 1985): 400–414; W.P. Welch, "Campaign Contributions and Legislative Voting: Milk Money and Dairy Price Supports;" Diana Evans, "PAC Contributions and Roll-Call Voting," in Allan Cigler and Burdett A. Loomis, ed., *Interest Groups and Politics* (Washington, D.C.: Congressional Quarterly Press, 1986).

7. Both quotations are from John Wright, "PACs, Contributions, and Roll-Calls," 411.

8. Henry Chappell, "Campaign Contributions and Congressional Voting: A Simultaneous Probit-Tobit Model," *Review of Economics and Statistics* 64 (February 1982): 77–83.

9. Arguing that contributions influence member votes are Saltzman, "Congressional Voting,"; James B. Kau and Paul Rubin, *Congressmen, Constituents and Contributors* (Boston: Martinus Nijhoff, 1982). Arguing that contributions generally do not influence votes is Janet Grenzke, "PACs in the Congressional Supermarket: The Currency is Complex," *American Journal of Political Science* 33 (February 1989): 1–24. Wilhite and Theilmann find that contributions influence votes in 1980 and 1982, but not

in 1984. Allen Wilhite "Union PAC Contributions and Legislative Voting," *Journal of Labor Research* 9 (Winter 1988): 79–89; Allen Wilhite and John Theilmann, "Labor PAC Contributions and Labor Legislation: A Simultaneous Logit Approach," *Public Choice*, 53 (Fall 1987): 267–276.

10. The haphazard way in which Kau and Rubin control for other influences on the members' voting raises doubts about the validity of their model and their conclusion that contributions influence votes. They attempt to isolate the impact of one set of contributions, for example labor contributions, from other possible causes of member votes on eight economic bill in 1979 with a simultaneous model that includes 13 district characteristics, seniority, members' electoral margins, and contributions from other PACs, grouped according to the FEC categories. Different variables are included in the equation for each vote, but the choice of variables does not seem to be related to any underlying theory about what influences members' voting decisions. For example, should high seniority and a narrow electoral margin encourage one to support or oppose the debt limit? Why should total contributions received from individuals be included in the model, if we cannot establish how the contributors would like the member to vote? The regression is cluttered with many variables whose theoretical relationship to the members' voting is questionable and the coefficients are unstable, raising doubts about their conclusions. For example, with ADA rating included in the equation, the coefficients reported in Table 7.2 of Kau and Rubin, *Congressmen, Constituents and Contributors* differ significantly from those from the equations without ADA rating, in Table 1 of Kau, Keenan, and Rubin, "A General Equilibrium Model of Congressional Voting," *The Quarterly Journal of Economics* (May 1982): 271–293. Also, probit analysis is more appropriate for a dichotomous dependent variable. John Aldrich and Charles Cnudde, "Probing the Bound of Conventional Wisdom: A Comparison of Regression, Probit, and Discriminant Analysis," *American Journal of Political Science* 19 (August 1975): 571–608.

11. Keith T. Poole, "Dimensions of Interest Groups Evaluation of the U.S. Senate 1969–1978," *American Journal of Political Science*, 25 (February 1981): 49–67.

12. Janet Grenzke, "PACs in the Congressional Supermarket."

13. Kau and Rubin, *Congressmen, Constituents and Con-*

tributors; Chappell, "Campaign Contributions and Congressional Voting."

14. Grenzke, "PACs in the Congressional Supermarket;" Wilhite and Theilmann, "Labor PAC Contributions and Labor Legislation;" Wilhite, "Union PAC Contributions and Legislative Voting;" Saltzman, "Congressional Voting on Labor Issues."

15. Grenzke, "Shopping in the Congressional Supermarket;" Wilhite and Theilmann, "Labor PAC Contributions;" Wilhite, "Union PAC Contributions."

16. Saltzman's statistical model is different from Grenzke, Wilhite and Theilmann, and Wilhite, in that it appears to include corporate contributions as an exogenous variable. As the inverse relationship between and labor and corporate contributions is so strong, including corporate contributions in the model may negate the effect of the first stage regressions used to control for the simultaneity of the relationship between contributions and member votes.

17. Michael J. Malbin, "Looking Back at the Future of Campaign Finance Reform," in Malbin, ed., *Money and Politics in the United States* (Chatham, NJ: Chatham House, 1984); Michael J. Malbin, "Of Mountains and Molehills: PACs, Campaigns, and Public Policy, in Malbin, ed., *Parties, Interest Groups and Campaign Finance Laws* (Washington, D.C.: American Enterprise Institute for Public Policy Research, 1980), 179.

18. Larry Sabato, *PAC Power* (New York: Norton, 1984), 125.

19. Federal Election Commission, *FEC Reports on Financial Activity, 1985–1986, Party and Non-Party Political Committees*, (Washington, D.C.: Federal Election Commission, 1988) vol. 4, 707; *The New York Times*, June 1, 1987, B7.

20. John Wright, "Contributions, Lobbying, and Voting in the U.S. House Ways and Means Committee," paper presented at the annual meeting of the American Political Science Association, Washington, D.C., 1988, 16.

21. Langbein and Lotwis, "Electoral Margins, Policy Positions, and Campaign Contributions."

22. Wright, "Contributions, Lobbying, and Voting in the U.S. House Ways and Means Committee."

23. Welch, "Campaign Contributions and Legislative Voting."

24. Frank Sorauf, *Money in American Elections* (Glenview, IL: Scott, Foresman, 1988), 310.

25. Interviews were conducted by the author with PAC officials, 1986.

26. See also Sabato, *PAC Power*, 135–140, and Sorauf, *Money in American Elections*, 307–317, for similar assessments of the literature.

27. Grenzke, "PACs in the Congressional Supermarket;" Sorauf, *Money in American Elections*, 314; Wright, "Contributions, Lobbying, and Voting in the U.S. House Ways and Means Committee" and "PAC Contributions, Lobbying and Representation," paper presented at the annual meeting of the Midwest Political Science Association, Chicago, IL.

28. Peter Bachrach and Morton S. Baratz, "Two Faces of Power," *American Political Science Review*, 56 (December 1962): 947- 52.

29. Sorauf, *Money in American Elections*, 314; Sabato, *PAC Power*, 135–140; Arthur Denzau and Michael Munger, "Legislators and Interest Groups: How the Unorganized Interests Get Represented," *American Political Science Review* 80 (March 1986): 89–106.

30. Jones and Keiser, "Issue Visibility and Effects of PAC Money."

31. Frendreis and Waterman, "PAC Contributions and Legislative Behavior."

32. Schroedel, "Campaign Contributions and Legislative Outcomes."

33. Evans, "PAC Contributions and Roll-Call Voting."

34. Welch, "Campaign Contributions and Legislative Voting."

35. Two methodological comments are relevant to assessing the studies that argue that contributions influence members on low visibility votes. First, none control for other interest group activity when they establish that campaign contributions influence member votes. Second, none of these studies use a simultaneous model. While the single equation technique may exaggerate the impact of contributions, comparative statements about the relative impact of a group's activities on high and low visibility issues seem valid, as the extent to which the group contributes to reward members should not vary with the vote's visibility.

36. Malbin, "Looking Back at the Future of Campaign Finance Reforms," 248.

37. Wright, "Contributions, Lobbying, and Voting."

38. Paul J. Feldstein and Glenn Melnick, "Congressional

Voting Behavior on Hospital Legislation: An Exploratory Study," *Journal of Health Politics, Policy and Law* 8 (Winter 1984): 686–701.

39. Frendreis and Waterman, "PAC Contributions and Legislative Behavior."

40. When the values of citizen equality and electoral conflict, I opt for more competitive elections. For example, the values conflict when conservative candidates in liberal districts get public money to promote interests supported by a small minority in their district. Because their resources become more equal to those of the liberal, majority candidate, each conservative resident in the district has more political power in the campaign than each liberal resident.

41. While it is possible that candidates may encourage bogus independent expenditures against themselves in order to receive more public funding, this practice is risky and unlikely to be common. Primaries in 15 states are held in September, and should be held earlier to allow time for those with less money in the primaries to receive public funds and to conduct general election campaigns. There will be a some lag between when the better funded candidate spends money and when the less well funded candidate receives public funds. However, candidates may borrow money with the knowledge that public funds are forthcoming, just as presidential candidates do now.

42. Gary Jacobson, "Enough is Too Much: Money and Competition in House Elections, 1972–1984," Thomas P. O'Neill, Jr. Symposium "Elections in American" Boston College, Nov. 4–5, 1985.

43. Federal Election Commission, *FEC Reports on Financial Activity 1985–86 Final Report U.S. Senate and House Campaigns*, 1988, 46.

44. Grants of money seem superior to subsidized media time, because they are simpler to administer, they accommodate districts with very different types of media markets, and they are less likely to meet opposition from broadcasters.

45. Leon Epstein, *Political Parties in the American Mold* (Madison, WI: University of Wisconsin Press, 1986).

46. Janet Grenzke, "Comparing Contributions to U.S. House Members from Outside their Districts," *Legislative Studies Quarterly* 13 (February 1988): 83–103.

9

Member to Member Giving

Clyde Wilcox

Members of Congress usually raise more money than they need for their re-election campaigns. In 1988, the median House incumbent finished the election cycle with nearly $100,000 in the bank; the largest sum was $1.2 million. The median 1988 Senate incumbent finished the election cycle with $166,000 in the bank; the largest sum was nearly one million.[1] The interest on these sums generates considerable revenue: several House incumbents received over $100,000 in interest during the 1988 election cycle, often more than a third of their total revenue. Some, like Rep. William Archer, no longer actively solicit funds, but campaign with the interest from their savings. Others use their surplus funds to contribute to charities, to entertain constituents, and for personal expenses.[2] And, as Maisel notes, members believe that a sizable bankroll acts as a deterrent to potential challengers.

Members also increasingly use their excess funds to contribute to the campaigns of candidates for statewide or national office. This is not the only way that incumbents aid other candidates: some members form PACs to raise and distribute money to candidates, and a number of members engage in a variety of other activities to aid their current and potential colleagues in their fundraising. How do these "member to member" contributions and fundraising activities affect the operations of Congress? Do they enhance or undermine congressional effectiveness and legitimacy? How do they affect the promotion of other values such as accountability, competition, equality, or liberty?

While campaign money has always been a valuable commodity on Capitol Hill, in recent years members have more openly used fundraising and contributions to seek and maintain power. The three candidates for Senate Majority Leader in 1988, Senators Mitchell, Inouye, and Johnston, all stated that such activity was probably a prerequisite for leadership selection. In the House, Rep. William Gray openly courted PAC contributions to his own PAC in an effort to influence the outcome of the race for chairman of the Democratic caucus.

The role of money in these contests was disquieting to many members. One junior member of the House noted "It diminishes the stature of the House when Bill [Gray] openly raises money as part of a leadership election."[3] Others call the practice disgraceful, some find it demeaning. A few members go even further, calling for legislation to limit member financial activity on behalf of other members.

An Historical Perspective

Although fundraising assistance by incumbents to other candidates has increased in recent years, it has a long history on Capital Hill. Rep. Gray notes that in 1914, the House of Representatives determined that the Pendelton Act did not restrict incumbents from contributing money to or raising money on behalf of other candidates. Sam Rayburn used his ties to Texas oil money to aid Democratic candidates.[4] Rep. Lyndon Johnson took over the Democratic Congressional Campaign Committee (DCCC) in 1940, and used that position to increase his power and prestige in the House.[5] By raising large sums from independent oil operators in Texas, Johnson was able to increase the funds available to the committee, and to surprise his current and potential colleagues with relatively large contributions in an election in which early predictions were for a large gain by the Republicans.

Although Johnson provided other services to candidates including endorsements and political information, it was the financial assistance which the candidates wanted most. To those candidates whom he chose to assist, Johnson gave significantly more money than previously had been available. Caro concluded:

> Through cloakrooms and Speaker's Lobby spread a realization that, in some way most of them did not understand, this young, junior, rather unpopular Congressman... had become a source—an important source—of campaign funds.... This realization... abruptly altered Johnson's status on Capitol Hill. When Congress had left Washington in October, he had been just one Congressman among many. Within a short time after Congress returned in January, the word was out that he was a man to see, a man to cultivate.[6]

More recently, Rep. Thomas (Tip) O'Neill held the position of head of the DCCC while serving as his party's appointed Whip, a position which enabled him to dispense largess and which helped him in his bid to succeed the late Rep. Hale Boggs as House Majority Leader.[7] Yet his elevation to Majority Leader seemed to be assured by the institutionalized ladder of succession for House Democrats. Through 1974, fundraising does not seem to have been a normal part of active campaigning for leadership or power in the Congress.[8]

The contest to succeed O'Neill as Majority Leader in 1976, however, involved active fundraising as a campaign strategy. Rep. Phillip Burton, John McFall, and Jim Wright all raised money from interest groups and individuals for Democratic House candidates, and all four contestants (including Rep. Richard Bolling) actively campaigned on behalf of candidates.[9]

During the 1984 election cycle, Senator Robert Dole's PAC contributed over $300,000 to other candidates as part of his bid to succeed Howard Baker as Senate Majority leader, and Senators Richard Lugar and Ted Stevens contributed substantial amounts as well. Peabody has argued that Dole's activity was "really critical in the case of one or two Senators."[10] (Dole won by three votes.)

The use of political money in internal House elections became more visible in the 1986 Democratic contest for House Majority Whip. Tony Coelho had served six years as chairman of the DCCC, and had directed funds and services to many candidates. In addition, however, his PAC increased its contributions from under $20,000 in 1984 to well over $500,000 in 1986. His principal opponent, Rep. Charles Rangel, contributed nearly $220,000 through his PAC, and another $45,000 through his campaign committee, while Rep. Martin Sabo and Rep. Norm Mineta contributed somewhat smaller amounts.

In late 1988, two contests for party leadership in the coming session of Congress attracted a good deal of attention, in part because of the conspicuous role that money played in the campaigning. In the race to succeed Robert Byrd as Senate Majority leader, all three candidates, Senators Bennett Johnston, Daniel Inouye, and George Mitchell, actively raised money for their current and potential colleagues. All three of the leadership candidates held fundraisers for Senate candidates and solicited money on their behalf. Johnston and Inouye went even further, forming Political Action Committees which jointly contributed more than $450,000 to candidates. Mitchell's bid was helped by his stint as head of the Democratic Senatorial Campaign Committee (DSCC), from which he directed party funds to Senate candidates, including several successful challengers in the 1986 election. Johnston estimated that the three candidates raised or contributed over a million dollars during the campaign.

In the House, two of the three contestants for chairman of the Democratic Caucus also used campaign contributions and fundraising as one part of their campaigns. Rep. Bill Gray, the eventual winner, attracted attention by openly soliciting contributions to his PAC by stressing his potential leadership role. His fundraising letters asked for funds to help him "build active support within the Democratic members of Congress to win this key leadership position." In addition, he established a monthly breakfast program for those who contributed large amounts to his PAC to "discuss in detail what needs to be done to enable me to become Caucus Chair."[11] Gray contributed over $139,800 to other candidates during the 1988 election cycle.

Whether fundraising and contributions greatly affect the outcome of party leadership contests is unclear. Certainly campaign finance assistance has become a visible part of candidate strategies. Yet in the four leadership races in which money has played a visible role (for Senate Majority Leader in 1984 and 1988, for House Majority whip in 1986 and for Chairman of the House Democratic Caucus in 1988), the leading candidates all contributed funds, making any effort to "buy" votes difficult. Most Senators up for re-election in 1988 received assistance from all three candidates for Majority Leader.

Certainly other explanations for the victories of Mitchell and Gray in 1988 are available—indeed, these candidates probably did not win because of their fundraising aid. Whether they could have won without raising money for other candidates while their opponents were actively using campaign finance assistance as a strategy is unclear.

The 1986 whip election in the House, however, may be another story. Several members attribute Coelho's victory to his time at the DCCC and to the contributions of his PAC and campaign committee. Indeed, Coelho himself believes that his PAC contributions helped seal his victory.[12] Yet part of Coelho's activity as head of DCCC was not only to channel funds to candidates, but to aid them in other ways as well. Many of the candidates which the DCCC aided during Coelho's tenure there were recruited by him, and he publicly campaigned for many of them. One junior member of the House put it this way "Tony encouraged me to run, and he appeared with me at rallies and at speeches several times throughout the campaign. At times, it seemed that he had more faith in me than I had in myself. Sure, I appreciated the money—but it was the other things that I remember most."

Coelho may have received several votes from those whom he had helped, but many more incumbents had received little from the DCCC or Coelho's PAC. For those incumbents, Coelho's success in raising funds was often seen as averting disaster. Many Democratic incumbents believed in 1982 that the Republicans could actually capture control of the House by raising and spending large sums of money. By substantially increasing the receipts of the DCCC, Coelho earned the support of many members.

Mitchell made a similar point in discussing his support among the 1986 class of Democratic Senators, which he helped elect while serving as chairman of the DSCC. "I did go to all their states and spent time there campaigning and fundraising on their behalf—and yes, I think I'm doing well with the freshmen."[13]

Mitchell did do well with the freshmen, but separating out the impact of his contributions, his campaigning on their behalf, and his promises of a leadership more open to the input of junior members is difficult.[14] Perhaps the best way to conceptualize the role of money in leadership contests is that contributions and fundraising may now be a necessary but not sufficient condition for leadership. Sen. Lautenberg referred to the money raised on his behalf by his three eager colleagues as "a good marketing tool." Another Senator noted that "They help us out to show that they are concerned for us."

Varieties of Financial Activity

The most common method by which members assist their current and potential colleagues is through direct contributions. Although a few members report contributing from their personal funds, most of this activity is through political action committees (PACs) associated with incumbents, or through excess funds in the incumbent's campaign committee treasury.

The number of PACs associated with members of Congress has grown over the years. Figure 9.1 shows the growth of member PACs and Figure 9.2 shows their contributions. By 1988,

45 member PACs were active, contributing $3.7 million to congressional candidates. The largest of these PACs are usually associated with prospective presidential candidates, for whom the PAC serves a number of functions. The PACs of presidential candidates can fund the incumbent's travel, pay the salaries for the campaign's consultants, help to develop and refine direct-mail solicitation lists, and make direct contributions to candidates who may later support the campaign.[15]

Figure 9.1

Number of Member PACs by Election Cycle 1978–1988

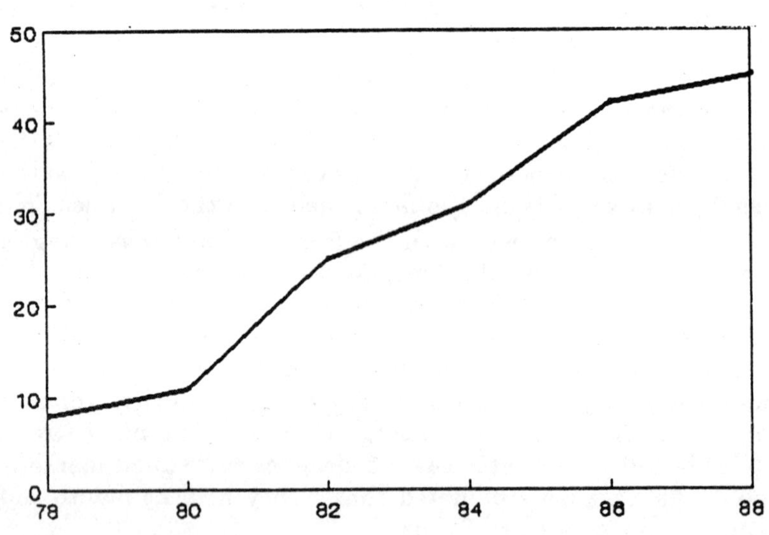

Source: FEC reports.

For members seeking to maximize their influence, PACs offer a clear advantage over merely contributing through their campaign committees. Contributions from a campaign committee are limited to $1,000 per election, but qualified PACs can contribute $5,000. Moreover, it is easier to raise funds for PACs, since they can receive individual contributions five times greater than can the incumbent's campaign committee. These large contributions can come from the same individuals (or PACs) who have contributed to the member's campaign committee.

Figure 9.2

Contributions of Member PACs
1978–1988
(in $ millions)

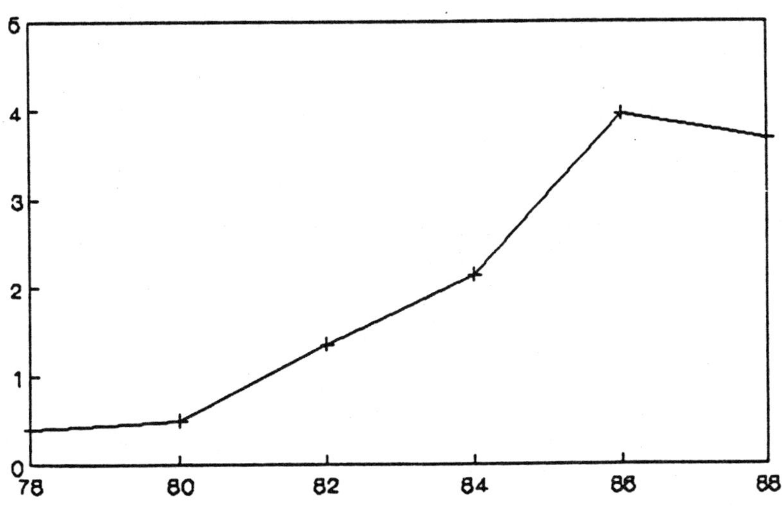

Source: FEC reports.

Member PACs vary in size and contribution strategy. In 1984, fully eight PACs contributed more than $100,000 to other candidates, but an equal number gave less than $10,000. The three largest PACs contributed to over 100 candidates each, while two PACs contributed to only one candidate. Many of these PACs contributed a large proportion of the money to non-incumbents and to incumbents involved in close races, but a few contributed mainly to safe incumbents.

PACs are not a viable mechanism for many members—only members with power or ideological appeal can attract the additional contributions necessary to fund a PAC. Among those member PACs which are not associated with Presidential candidates, the largest are associated with present or potential members of the party leadership, or with the chairmen of important committees or subcommittees. Six of the largest eight member PACs in Congress in 1986 were associated with party leaders or committee chairmen. While Dan Rostenkowski can successfully market a PAC, rank-and-file members of Ways and Means cannot.

For members who have no PAC, contributions can still be made through the campaign committees. Wilcox reported that 238 members of Congress made contributions to other congressional candidates through their campaign committees in 1984, and that these contributions totaled just over a million dollars.[16] In 1988, 249 members contributed approximately $1.4 million. Figure 9.3 details the growth in the numbers of members contributing through their campaign committees, and Figure 9.4 shows the total amounts of these contributions.

Figure 9.3

Number of Members who Contributed through Campaign Committees 1978–1988

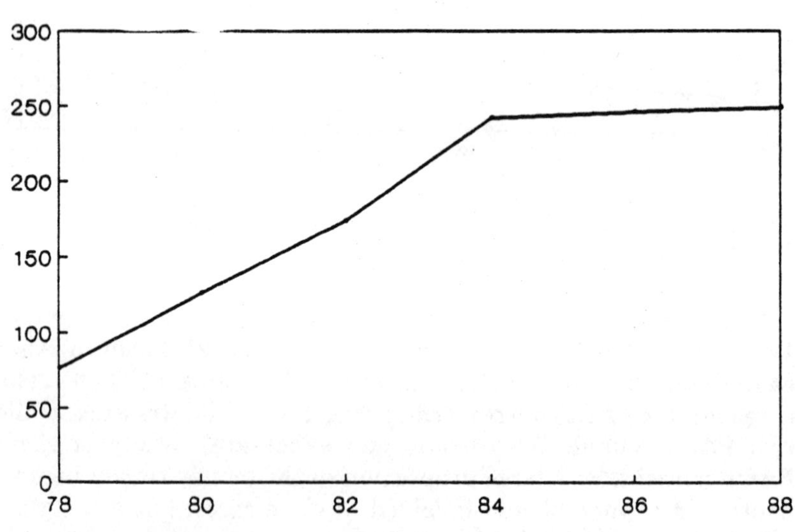

Source: FEC reports.

The majority of these contributors give to only a few candidates: in 1984 the median number of recipients for House contributors was 3, while the median Senate contributor gave to only 1 candidate. A few contributors were quite active however. Fully 28 members contributed to at least 10 candidates through their campaign committees in 1984, and some gave more than

$20,000. By 1986, the top rank of contributors were giving closer to $50,000.

Figure 9.4

Amount of Contributions by Members through Campaign Committees 1978–1988 (in $ thousands)

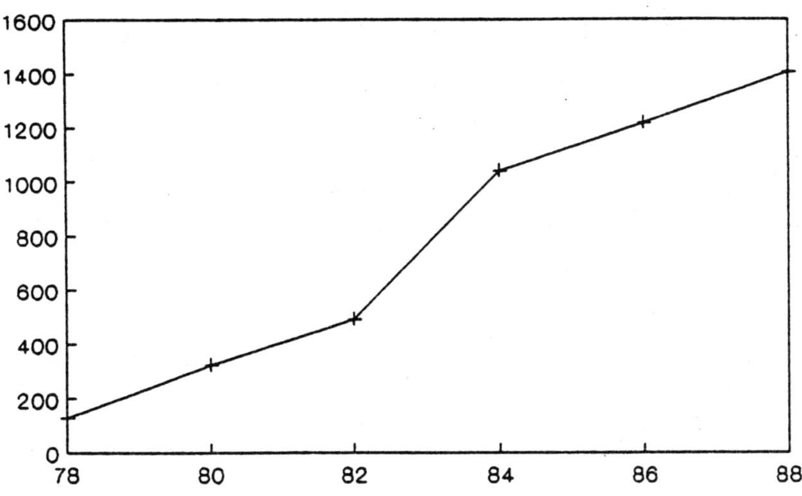

Source: FEC reports.

Some members who sponsored PACs also gave through their campaign committees. This was particularly common among the House leadership, although fully 16 members gave from both types of committees in 1984. Many contributed to the same candidates from both committees. Indeed, Henry Waxman contributed to several candidates through both his PAC and campaign committee, and these candidates also received money from two House incumbents commonly thought of as part of the Waxman machine. In a few cases, however, the contribution behavior of a member's PAC differed substantially from that of his or her campaign committee. Dan Rostenkowski did not contribute to members of the Ways and Means committee through his PAC in 1984, but gave to 13 committee members (most of whom were electorally safe) through his campaign committee.

Although direct contributions are the most common form of financial aid provided by incumbents, there are other ways to fill a colleague's coffers. Party and committee leaders can help more junior members (and non-incumbents) by attending their fundraisers. Dan Rostenkowski was able to substantially increase the take of members of his committee by attending their fundraisers.[17] One junior member of a prominent House committee noted "When the chairman tells me he will attend my fundraiser, I immediately spread the word. This year, I probably raised $30,000 more at the fundraisers that he attended than those where he stayed away."

Sometimes even an unannounced visit to a fundraiser can aid a member. A fundraiser for a liberal Democratic Senator recalled a visit to a Florida fundraiser by Sen. Howard Metzenbaum. "He made a really rousing speech, and asked them all to give the maximum. I'd guess that we took home twice what we would [have received] if he hadn't spoken."

Leaders can go still further, actually sponsoring fundraisers for current and potential members. Often these fundraisers are sponsored by more than one member, and usually draw considerably more money than one sponsored by the candidate him/herself. During the 1988 Senate elections, the three candidates for Majority Leader co-sponsored PAC fundraisers for vulnerable incumbents such as Frank Lautenberg, and for a few promising non-incumbents as well. Two years earlier, Sen. Bennett Johnston held PAC breakfasts for promising non-incumbent candidates, and Sen. Daniel Inouye held fundraisers for a number of candidates as well. Such assistance is potentially more valuable for non-incumbents than for incumbents. One former staff aid in charge of fundraising for a successful Democratic 1986 Senate candidate reported that "the early fundraisers which Johnston and Inouye held for us sent an immediate signal to the PAC community that we were a serious contender. Not only did we raise a lot of money at these events—our flow of receipts also picked up." Fundraisers can also involve more money than could a direct contribution. The fundraiser for one House incumbent reported that the campaign had received direct contributions from the various committees of the Waxman machine, but "the biggest boost was from the fundraiser they held for us. The contributions we received that evening, and those that came in soon afterwards probably made the difference for us."

Funds are often solicited in other ways, as well. During the 1988 elections, George Mitchell did not use a PAC to contribute to candidates. He was quite active, however, in soliciting his strongest supporters to make contributions to vulnerable (and not so vulnerable) incumbents, and to promising non-incumbents as well. For many non-incumbents, Mitchell raised several times the $5,000 limit of PAC contributions.[18]

Other types of assistance are a bit less common. Some incumbents will loan to their colleagues their mailing lists, particularly if they share some common characteristic which would make soliciting from the list successful (e.g. ethnic identity). At other times, candidates who are successful at direct mail will sign the fundraising letter of a candidate.

All of these mechanisms are used by individual members of Congress to aid congressional candidates. Throughout this century, however, the chairmen of the party campaign committees have often benefited from the good will which flows from candidate aid from those committees. The next section will examine the implications of contributions and fundraising by party campaign committees.

The Party Campaign Committees

Although the party campaign committees in each chamber are long-time Washington fixtures, their function has changed significantly over the past few years.[19] Party committees can contribute money directly to a candidate and spend money in coordination with the candidate's campaign. The volume of money which these committees control has risen dramatically. For details on the growing resources of the parties, see Larry Sabato's chapter in this volume.

In the past decade party committees have become more active as vendors of services as well.[20] In addition to media consulting, polling, and candidate training, party committees assist candidates in fundraising. These committees often sponsor PAC and other fundraisers on behalf of a candidate or set of candidates, and solicit funds from PACs and individuals on behalf of particular candidates.[21] The Republican party committees have held "bundling parties," where contributions aimed at influencing party leaders are bundled to candidates. The same held true for the Democrats; Rep. Tony Coelho targeted soft money to aid candidates in close elections.[22]

Although technically the decisions of party committees are made by the committee (comprised of a number of incumbent members) and staff, in practice the head of each party's committee usually gets the credit for contributions. The DCCC in 1986 required formal approval of the list of recipients by the committee members and Democratic party leadership, but members usually credit Tony Coelho with providing the aid.[23] Several junior members told me that they felt that, as one member stated "without Tony's help [in this member's initial bid for the House], I wouldn't be here today. He came through again and again when I needed money."

What Does The Money Buy?

Assessing the impact of money on leadership races, contests for committee or subcommittee chairman, or on public policy is not a straightforward task. Votes for leadership and committee chairs are by secret ballot, and although a number of members announce their votes, many do not.

The majority of members who contribute through their campaign committees seem to do so out of a sense of party obligation. Nearly all are solicited for their contributions by needy colleagues or by the party leadership. Nearly all of their money goes to candidates involved in close elections, and often there are clear ties of friendship involved. While such contributions may involve a small chit in congressional logrolling, it is unlikely to be a big one. As one small contributor put it, "I give to my friends if they need it in a close race. I expect that they will do the same for me if I am ever in a tight one. Beyond that, we never mention it again."

For the major players, however—those with large PACs, who contribute large sums through their campaign committees, or who engage in fundraising on behalf of colleagues—financial assistance is clearly intended to help the incumbent meet some goal: to maximize their prospects of re-election, to enhance their power, in Washington, and/or to make good public policy.[24]

Election

Members do not seek to enhance their re-election by contributing money to other candidates. Indeed, in the 1984 election, some losing incumbents contributed funds early in the election cycle, and at least one regretted that choice. Members do use

PACs as part of their strategies for election to higher office, however. PACs have long been a tool of presidential hopefuls (dating to Reagan in 1976), but their use in the 1988 campaign exceeded all previous election cycles.[25]

Presidential PACs generally contribute to large numbers of candidates from all regions of the country, and from all wings of the party. They are more likely than other member PACs to contribute to non-incumbents, in part because failed congressional candidates can still provide significant electoral support in their districts. As the director of one presidential candidate PAC put it, "We give to liberals and conservatives, incumbents and non-incumbents, winners and losers. We hope that they [the recipients] will support us, and they can do that in Congress or out of it."

PACs have not yet become a common way to run for a Senate seat, although they have been used for that purpose. Rep. Ed Markey used his two PACs to help hone his direct-mail solicitation lists in anticipation of his abortive bid for the Senate.[26]

Power in Washington

More commonly, fundraising and contributions are used to enhance the influence of members in Congress. The PAC director for one influential member of the House put it this way: "The Congressman formed the PAC because he wanted to be a major player in the House. There is no question that he gets more respect because [of it]." Similar remarks come from PAC directors and members in both bodies. As Rep. David Obey noted, "You don't play touch football while the other guy is playing tackle."[27]

In short, many members and staff believe that money is useful in gaining power in Washington, and behave in a manner consistent with these beliefs, but rigorous analysis is precluded by secret balloting for party leaders and committee and subcommittee chairmen.

There have been four contests for committee and subcommittee chairmanship in which money has been mentioned as a factor in the outcome. Many observers attribute Rep. Henry Waxman's rise to the chairmanship of a subcommittee of the Energy and Commerce committee in 1979 to his contributions of $24,000 to committee members.[28] Rep. Gray contributed over $25,000 to House incumbents in 1984, the year he sought the Budget committee chairmanship. In 1986, Reps. Leath and Aspin contributed over $100,000 to members of the House before their contest for the chairmanship of the House Armed Services Committee.[29] Both Sen. Helms and Sen. Lugar contributed to party members prior to their contest for ranking minority member of the Foreign Relations committee.

Most members and staff discount the role of money in the selection of Gray for Budget committee chair (he won a unanimous vote after competing candidates dropped from the race), and in the Helms-Lugar contest, where Helm's victory is best seen as a reaffirmation of the seniority system. They accept the conventional wisdom that Waxman's contributions led to his election as subcommittee chairman, however. One former staff member for the committee argued "There is no doubt that Henry [Waxman] was elected because of his contributions. This was before contributions [by other members] were very common, and the committee members felt that they owed him something." Yet at the time that Waxman was elected, two other liberal, junior members were elevated to subcommittee chairmanships in the House ahead of more conservative, and more senior members. Moreover, the candidate that Waxman beat for the post, Rep. Pryor, was criticized at the time for potential conflict of interest (he held stock in two pharmaceutical companies), and for criticizing the Surgeon General's statements on smoking (Pryor was from a tobacco-growing district). Pryor himself attributed his defeat to the prevailing mood for generational and ideological change.

There is also room for doubt that the large sums contributed by Rep. Aspin and Rep. Leath determined the outcome of their contest for chairman of the House Armed Services Committee. When Aspin lost the no-confidence vote on January 7, those members who publicly commented emphasized his deviations from liberal orthodoxy on the MX missile and contra aid in explaining the vote. When he defeated Leath a few weeks later, he beat a candidate who deviated even further from the liberal position on these issues.

Rep. Charles Bennett, the third (and most senior) candidate for the chairmanship, however, attributes his defeat to the contributions of his rivals. He reported that "When I went around and talked to members, asking them to support me, they would tell me that they had been helped financially by Mr. Aspin or Mr. Leath. One implied that it would all be rectified if I contributed to him too."[30]

It is unclear whether the statements of these members represented their actual motives or an excuse to a colleague that they would not support. It is clear, however, that both Aspin and Leath used campaign contributions as part of their strategies; neither contributed large amounts in earlier election cycles.

Committee and subcommittee chairman may also give to stave off potential challenges. It is probably no accident that several subcommittee chairman on the House Energy and Commerce committee (where Waxman made his successful challenge in 1979) gave to members of their subcommittees.

The role of money in leadership contests has already been described. Once elected, party leaders generally continue to engage in contributions and fundraising activity. Party leaders have long been expected to be party fundraisers. Throughout the 20th century, party leaders have spoken at fundraisers on behalf of their party, and have had some say over the distribution of party resources. In recent years, however, expectations for leadership activity in fundraising and contributions have increased. In 1984, all nine party leaders contributed to congressional candidates, and party leaders were among the list of leading contributors.

Money contributed by the leadership seems targeted to increase the party's strength in Congress, and not explicitly to build legislative coalitions. No contributions by party leaders in 1984 went to committee chairmen, and over half of party leader contributions went to candidates involved in close contests. This does not mean that contributions by party leaders do not aid in coalition building, however. By contributing to candidates in close races and aiding in their fundraising, leaders can build a store of legislative chits to be called in when needed.

Public Policy

The final goal attributed to members of Congress is making good public policy. Contributions and fundraising by incumbents for other candidates could contribute to public policy formation in two ways. First, by contributing to candidates who share the ideology of the giver, a member could attempt to build an ideological bloc which would favor his or her preferred policies. Second, by giving to incumbents (and likely non- incumbent winners), a member could build up political IOUs which could be called in when the members assembles a coalition to back legislation.

Although Wilcox reported a significant correlation between the ideology of contributing members and the average ideology of the recipients of those gifts, he also found that most members gave to candidates with widely ranging ideological viewpoints. A few incumbents seem to give to increase the size of a particular ideological bloc in their chamber, but most give to party candidates regardless of ideology.[31]

There is more evidence that contributions and fundraising help to build legislative coalitions to support the public policy goals of incumbent contributors. Committee and subcommittee chairmen may engage in fundraising and contributing in an effort to build coalitions in committee. Rostenkowski built a list of political IOUs by attending the fundraisers of members. On several occasions Rostenkowski called in IOUs to build consensus for various portions of the tax reform bill.[32] The director of a PAC for one powerful House committee chairman argued "Our contributions and fundraising assistance help [the chairman] build coalitions in committee and on the floor. We sometimes give to guys in the Senate for the same reason—we want their support when our bill comes up for a vote over there."

Other members appear to contribute for similar reasons. A staffer who raised funds for one House Democratic incumbent who gave a sizable amount through his campaign committee described the Congressman's motives: "He gives small amounts to those who ask him, or to those who[m] the party leaders ask [for], but he feels that he gets something for his money. He never explicitly mentions his contributions when asking for support for one of his bills, but they usually feel grateful." Sen. Paul Simon, who shut down his PAC after his unsuccessful Presidential bid, notes that "All gifts create the feeling of indebtedness."

Assessing the Impact of Contributions and Fundraising

What impact does all of this have on the policymaking process? With more than 250 members contributing to their current and prospective colleagues, and with 45 member PACs making contributions to candidates, one inevitable consequence is to further contribute to the decentralization of Congress. Earlier in this century, the party committees controlled what little funds which were forthcoming from members of Congress, but now many different entrepreneurs control a portion of the money. This decentralizing effect should not be exaggerated, however.

Although 250 or more members may make contributions, there are only a couple of dozen major players. Party leaders and committee and subcommittee chairmen are best able to mobilize money to enhance their power in Congress, along with ideological figures who can raise money through direct mail. Contributions and fundraising therefore serve to concentrate power in the hands of those who already have it.

The role of party leaders in soliciting and distributing funds is, to a certain extent, a centralizing influence. That the selection by the party campaign committee as a critical contest affects the flow of resources from members, PACs and other actors is not lost on candidates. While many credit the head of the party campaign committee, others feel an obligation to the party leadership. One junior House Republican stated "I owe Bob [Michel] a lot. He raised a lot of money for my first campaign, and gave me money [through both his PAC and campaign committee]. When Bob tells me he needs my vote, I listen very carefully."

Contributions, Fundraising, and Democratic Values

Contributions and fundraising by incumbents on behalf of other candidates promote the values of competition and political liberty, but may undermine accountability and legitimacy. Probably the most positive aspect of the phenomenon is the channeling of funds to candidates involved in close contests. The majority of contributions made in 1984 by Republicans, particularly those in the House, went to non-incumbents. The biggest recipients of Democratic money were vulnerable freshmen Congressmen, along with a few promising non-incumbents. Over 40% of contributions by incumbents in 1984 went to non-incumbents, and over 40% went to candidates who received between 45% and 55% of the vote. Thus contributions and fundraising by incumbents helps promote the vigorous contesting of those few elections which are competitive.

Such activity also involves political liberty. One member of the House, in discussing a proposed bill which would outlaw contributions by members to other candidates, expressed his outrage. "If I want to contribute to my friend Bob —, I should be able to do it. If I want to call my friends and encourage them to contribute, that is my right. If I want to form a PAC and get contributions and then give to him, again that is my right."

Such activity poses some problems for other values, however. One problem is the inadequate accountability to those who gave the original individual contributions—a problem particularly relevant to those who contribute through their campaign committees. Prior to the 1986 campaign, Senator Packwood solicited the membership lists of feminist organizations, appealing for contributions by stressing his strong pro-choice record in Congress. When Packwood's opponent (a pro-life spokesman) withdrew, Packwood channeled some of his funds to other Republicans, including Rep. Denny Smith (an ardent right-to-life advocate) and to the Oregon state Republican committee, which consequently passed on even more of the money to right-to- life candidates. Such channeling of funds destroys the rationality of campaign contributions, since it is impossible to determine who the ultimate recipient of the funds will be.[33] Although contributors to party committees and PACs want and expect their funds to reach other candidates, contributors to members' campaign committees do not. Clearly, the incumbents who transfer their contributions to other members are not accountable to their contributors.

A different sort of accountability problem is associated with many member PACs. Many member PACs contribute an extremely low percentage of their receipts to other candidates. This is particularly true for the PACs of presidential candidates, (where it is less troublesome, since most contributors are giving to help the candidate's presidential bid), but is also true of several other PACs as well. In 1986, Newt Gingrich's PAC contributed only $3,901 out of over $220,000 raised.[34] Two PACs associated with Rep. Ed Markey contributed less than 3% of their receipts to candidates. The PAC instead served to develop direct-mail solicitation lists which aided Markey's Senate race in 1984.[35]

Markey and Gingrich are extreme cases, but they are also indicative of a common practice in member PACs. Many of these PACs are funded by direct mail, and direct mail is an expensive business. The average proportion of receipts which are contributed to candidates for direct-mail PACs is 15%. Contributors are generally not aware of this fact. The average contributor to these PACs is elderly, and not always well off. Waldman contacted some of the contributors to Markey's PAC and found them "appalled" at the proportion of funds which were contributed to candidates.[36]

Those PACs which are not funded by direct mail raise another problem—they avoid the limits which FECA imposed to limit contributor influence. PACs not funded by direct mail are generally funded by other PACs, which usually also contribute to the member's campaign committee. These PACs can contribute

$5,000 per election to the incumbent's campaign, and an additional $5,000 to his or her PAC. The PAC director for a small trade association told me "We give to the Chairman's campaign and again to his PAC. We don't like doing it, but we feel that it is our only way of getting access."

A related concern arises from the way many member PACs are organized. Some are run, not by members of the incumbent's staff, but by lobbyists and lawyers. The Pelican PAC, sponsored by Sen. Bennett Johnston, has as its inner circle a set of lawyers and lobbyists whose clients frequently lobby the Energy and Natural Resources Committee. Inouye's PAC is also managed by a group of lobbyists, including Tommy Boggs, one of the more prominent lobbyists and fundraisers in Washington.[37] This practice again avoids the spirit of the FECA: lobbyists for organizations whose direct contributions to an incumbent are limited can gain additional influence by organizing and running that incumbent's personal PAC.

A final problem with fundraising and contributions has to do with the legitimacy of Congress as an institution. While few members of the public are aware of the use of money in leadership and committee elections, those who know of this behavior are likely to perceive it as corrupting. Several members of Congress express public displeasure at the sight of members currying favor with their colleagues by contributing money. One said "its just embarrassing." Another added, "it looks like we are all being bought."

Prospects for Reform

During the past few sessions of Congress, a number of reform proposals have included bans on member PACs. There is a fair degree of support for such a ban, especially in the House. Even Rep. Coelho, whose PAC gave more money than any other member PAC in the 1986 election cycle, endorsed such a ban. One manager of a PAC associated with a House Republican said "As long as PACs are legal, we [the member] will have one. We certainly wouldn't fight a ban, though, and would really welcome it. These things create the wrong impression, and are getting too important in leadership races." The strongest opposition to such a ban comes predictably from members with presidential ambitions.

Legislation introduced in the last session of Congress by Rep.

Bennett (who was passed over for chairmanship of the House Armed Services Committee by Rep. Aspin) would ban all member contributions. This legislation has less support. One staff member of the House Administration Committee predicted that the 101st Congress will act on the ban on member PACs, but not on member contributions. Another staff member explained the rationale: "Members may not like these large PACs and the influence which they give their sponsors. But all of them want to be able to give to their friends if asked, and to give it from their campaign committees, not from their own pocket."

What is the likely impact of a ban on contributions and/or PACs? A bill banning PACs would surely lead to more contributions through campaign committees, although few campaign committees could raise and distribute money to match the larger member PACs. A ban on both PACs and contributions through campaign committees would lead to more of the bundled contributions which characterized Sen. Mitchell's behavior in the Senate leadership race. Although the FECA requires individuals who collect and pass along more than $1,000 to report as a conduit, Mitchell did not report his activity, arguing that he was acting as an extension of the recipients' campaigns. Yet such fundraising and bundling activities are difficult to follow and understand, resulting in less complete disclosure—a result which runs counter to the needs for a functioning democracy.

Notes

1. This and any other statistics are from the Federal Election Commission, unless otherwise noted.

2. Peter Bragdon, "In 'Permanent Campaign' Era, Members' Funds Find Many Uses," *Congressional Quarterly Weekly Report* (Sept. 12):2185–2187.

3. This and any other quotations are from personal interviews conducted by the author, unless otherwise noted.

4. Alexander Heard, *The Costs of Democracy* (Chapel Hill: The University of North Carolina Press, 1960).

5. Robert Caro, *The Path to Power* (New York: Alfred Knopf, 1982).

6. Ibid., 656–57.

7. Robert Peabody, *Leadership in Congress* (Boston: Little Brown, 1976), 155.

8. Ibid.

9. Bruce Oppenheimer and Robert Peabody, "How the Race for Majority Leader was Won—By One Vote," *Washington Monthly* no. 9 (1977):51–53.

10. As cited in Stephen Gettinger, "Potential Senate Leaders Flex Money Muscles," *Congressional Quarterly Weekly Report* (October 8, 1988):2776.

11. Shannon Bradley, "Member's Own PACs Face a Ban," *Roll Call* vol. 34, no. 3:26.

12. Brooks Jackson. *Honest Graft* (New York: Alfred Knopf, 1988), 288.

13. Gettinger, "Potential Senate Leaders...,."

14. Ibid.

15. Clyde Wilcox, "Financing the 1988 Pre-Nomination Campaigns," in Emmitt Buell and Lee Sigelman, eds., *Nominating a President in 1988* (Knoxville, TN: University of Tennessee Press, forthcoming).

16. Clyde Wilcox, "Share the Wealth: Contributions by Congressional Incumbents to the Campaigns of Other Candidates," *American Politics Quarterly*, no. 17 (1989):389.

17. Jeffrey Birnbaum and Alan Murray, *Showdown at Gucci Gulch* (New York: Vintage, 1987), 106.

18. Gettinger, "Potential Senate Leaders...," 3.

19. Paul Herrnson, *Party Campaigning in the 1980s* (Cambridge: Harvard University Press, 1988).

20. David Adamany, "Political Parties in the 1980s," in Michael J. Malbin, ed., *Money and Politics in the United States* (Chatham, NJ: Chatham House, 1984), 70–121.

21. Herrnson, *Party Campaigning in the 1980s*, 69–77.

22. Jackson, *Honest Graft*, 145–56.

23. Herrnson, *Party Campaigning in the 1980s*, 40.

24. Richard Fenno, *Congressmen in Committees* (Boston: Little Brown, 1973), 1–15.

25. Wilcox, "Financing the 1988 Pre-Nomination Campaigns," needs page.

26. Steven Waldman, "The Hiroshima Hustle," *The Washington Monthly* (October, 1986):35–36.

27. Cited in Bob Berenson, "In the Struggle for Influence, Members' PACs Gain Ground," *Congressional Quarterly Weekly Report* (August 2, 1986):1753.

28. Frank Sorauf, *Money in American Elections* (Washington, D.C.: CQ Press, 1988), 176–177; Maxwell Glen, "Elite

Group of Members of Congress are Doling Out Political Contributions," *The National Journal* 16 (1984):1567–68.

29. Wilcox, "Share the Wealth," 398.

30. Cited in Viveca Novak, "Mutual Funding," *Common Cause Magazine* vol. 14, no. 5 (1988), 36.

31. Wilcox, "Share the Wealth," 401–404.

32. Birnbaum and Murray, *Showdown at Gucci Gulch*, 126–151.

33. Novak described a chain of contributions from one member of Congress to another, in which money was transferred through many hands before ultimately reaching its destination. She also quotes several contributors who objected to their contributions being passed along to candidates whom they may not personally support. Novak, "Mutual Funding."

34. Ibid., 39.

35. Waldman, "The Hiroshima Hustle," 35–36.

36. Ibid., 38.

37. Gettinger, "Potential Senate Leaders...," 2782–2783.

10

PACs and Parties

Larry J. Sabato

Values at Stake

The relationships between political action committees and political parties are at once symbiotic and parasitic. Both parties work hard to cultivate PACs and secure their money, and most PACs energetically endeavor to be of use bipartisanly (at least to *incumbents* of both parties). At the same time, PACs and parties are rivals for the attentions of candidates, the favors of officeholders, and the devotions of voters. More important, the success of narrow-based PACs necessarily comes partly at the expense of broad-based parties. As parties decline, PACs gain, and in some ways PACs have greased the skids of party decline.

This decline of parties and the pre-eminence of PACs comes at the expense of important democratic values, for PACs and parties perform very different functions in our electoral and governmental system. PACs provide avenues for participation and political liberty, but have questionable effects on competition, accountability, governmental legitimacy, and effectiveness. Parties allow for the expression of more broad-based interests, provide channels for representation and accountability, legitimacy and effectiveness. Given the symbiotic relationship of parties and PACs, both have a valuable role in our campaign finance system, but democratic values could be better served by increasing the significance of the parties and diminishing that of PACs. In other words, I am partial to parties, but not anti-PAC, so this paper will simultaneously *defend* both types of political organization while arguing the case for tilting the electoral system's *balance* in favor of the parties.[1]

Assessing Criticisms Against PACs

It is easy to conclude that political action committees are the root of all campaign financing evils—if one's sources are restricted to news media coverage of politics. Journalists' obsession with PACs, reinforced by the predilections of various public interest groups, has focused attention on PAC excesses to the near exclusion of other concerns in the area of political money. Why is there such an obsession with PACs, and what charges against them generate such emotion?

While a good number of PACs of all political persuasions existed prior to the 1970s, it was during this decade—the decade of campaign reform—that the modern PAC era began. Spawned by the Watergate-inspired revisions of the campaign finance laws, PACs grew in number from 113 in 1972 to 4,268 by the end of 1988, and their contributions to congressional candidates multiplied almost eighteen-fold, from $8.5 million in 1971–1972 to $151.3 million in 1987–1988 (See Table 10.1). This rapid rise of PACs has inevitably proven controversial, yet many of the changes made against political action committees are exaggerated and dubious.

Table 10.1

Growth in PAC Numbers and Congressional Contributions 1972–1988
(in $ millions)

Year	Number of PACs[a]	Contributions to Candidates[b]
1972	113	8.5
1974	608	11.6
1976	1,146	20.5
1978	1,653	34.1
1980	2,551	55.2
1982	3,371	83.6
1984	4,009	105.3
1986	4,157	132.7
1988	4,268	151.3

[a] As of December 31 of each year.
[b] For the two-year election cycles ending in years shown.
Source: Federal Election Commission.

It is said that PACs are dangerously novel and have flooded the political system with money, mainly from business. While the widespread use of the PAC structure is new, the fact remains that special-interest money of all types has *always* found its way into politics, and before the 1970s it did so in less traceable and far more disturbing and unsavory ways. And yes, in absolute terms PACs contribute a massive sum to candidates, but it is not clear that there is *proportionately* more interest-group money in the system than before. The proportion of House and Senate campaign funds provided by PACs has certainly increased since the early 1970s, but *individuals*, most of whom are unaffiliated with PACs together with the political parties, still supply about three-fifths of all the money spent by or on behalf of House candidates and three-quarters of the campaign expenditures for Senate contenders. So while the importance of PAC spending has grown, PACs clearly remain secondary as a source of election funding and therefore pose no overwhelming threat to our system's legitimacy.

Apart from the argument over the relative weight of PAC funds, PAC critics claim that political action committees are making it more expensive to run for office. There is some validity to this assertion. Money provided to one side funds the purchase of campaign tools which the other side must then match in order to stay competitive. In the aggregate, American campaign expenditures seem huge. All 1988 U.S. House of Representatives candidates taken together spent about $256 million, and the campaign of the average winning House nominee cost over $392,000. Will Rogers' 1931 remark has never been more true: "Politics has got so expensive that it take lots of money to even get beat with." Yet $256 million is far less than the annual advertising budgets of many individual commercial enterprises. These days it is expensive to communicate, whether the message is political or commercial. Television time, polling costs, consultants' fees, direct-mail investment, and other standard campaign expenditures have been soaring in price, over and above inflation.[2] PACs have been fueling the use of new campaign techniques, but a reasonable case can be made that such expenses are necessary, and that *more*, and better, communication is required between candidates and an electorate that often appears woefully uninformed about politics. PACs therefore may be making a positive contribution by providing the means to increase the flow of information during elections, and thus enhancing political liberty.

PACs are also charged with reducing competition, and except for the ideological ones, PACs do display a clear, overwhelming preference for incumbents. But the same bias is apparent in contributions from individuals. On the other hand, the best challengers are usually generously funded by PACs. Well-targeted

PAC challenger money clearly helped the GOP win a majority in the U.S. Senate in 1980, for instance, and in turn aided the Democrats in their 1986 Senate takeover. I share Maisel's belief that PACs limit the number of strong challengers by giving so much early money to incumbents, money that helps to deter potential opponents from declaring their candidacies. But the money that PACs channel to competitive challengers late in the election season may then increase the turnover of officeholders on election day. PAC money also normally invigorates competitiveness in open seat congressional races—races without an incumbent candidate.

The fourth major criticism of PACs concerns their influence on legislature behavior—or "vote buying." As Grenzke notes, there is the potential for influence under certain circumstances, but the magnitude of the problem is greatly exaggerated. Furthermore, PACs are influenced in those cases where traditional lobbies—many of whom have merely supplemented their arsenals with PACs—also succeed.

One last line of attack on PACs is more justified. As David Adamany has noted, many PACs are inadequately accountable to donors or voters—a condition most apparent in many of the ideological non-connected PACs, which lack a parent body and whose free-style organization makes them accountable to no one and responsive mainly to their own whims.[3] Many corporate PACs can hardly be considered showcases of democracy either. In few PACs the chief executive officers completely rule the roost, and in many the CEOs have inordinate influence on PAC decisions.

As this brief examination of the charges made about political action committees has suggested, PACs are misrepresented and unfairly maligned as the embodiment of corrupt special interests. Contemporary political action committees are another manifestation of what James Madison called factions. Through the flourishing of competing interest groups or factions, said Madison in his *Federalist No. 10*, liberty would be preserved.

In any democracy, and particularly in one as pluralistic as the United States, it is essential that groups be relatively unrestricted in advocating their interests and positions. Not only is unrestricted political activity by interest groups a mark of a free society, but it provides a safety valve for the competitive pressures that build on all fronts in a capitalistic democracy. It also provides a means to keep representatives responsive to legitimate needs.

The Benefits of Parties

The PACs have stolen the media spotlight, but the parties, an important check on the abuses of PAC power, are holding their own in the long-term battle for political supremacy. This is a surprise, since the party system in the United States has declined and deteriorated in major ways in the last several decades.

Prematurely counted out by many political observers, the parties have surprised many critics by regenerating themselves at the national level through the use of direct mail and other tools of the new campaign technology.[4] The Republican party has led the way, spurred by the hope of breaking out of its minority status, and the Democrats have lately followed, prompted by the party's 1980 election disasters and the need to catch up with the GOP. Despite the press's focus on political action committees, the parties are about as healthy as the PACs. When all national party spending is taken together, the two parties raised $391 million in 1987–88, compared to about $370 million for all PACs.

The Democrats are clearly the junior partner in the arena of campaign finance. Of the $391 million total in 1988, the Republicans raised two-thirds. The GOP has traditionally been more successful at fundraising, but the gap began to grow after 1968 and to accelerate rapidly in the mid-1970s. During this time the Republicans made an enormous success of their direct-mail program while the Democrats continued to rely just on large donors to whittle away at accumulated campaign debts.[5]

The contemporary Republican party has organizational strength unparalleled in American history and unrivaled by the Democrats. As Table 10.2 shows, the Republicans have outraised the Democrats by enormous margins in all recent election cycles, never by less than 2 to 1 and usually by a considerably higher ratio. This GOP fundraising edge inevitably enhances the aid provided party nominees, as Table 10.2 also demonstrates. The Republicans have been able to give nearly the legal maximum gift (both in direct contributions and coordinated expenditures) to every reasonably competitive Senate and House candidate, and frequently the money is given "up front," immediately after a primary when a nominee's war-chest is depleted and the need is greatest.

In the House of Representatives' contests, parties are limited to direct gifts of $5,000 per candidate per election (with the primary and general election counted separately).[6] But in House races these party contributions are being multiplied, since the national party committee, the state party committee, and the national party's congressional campaign committee are usually each eligible to give the $5,000 maximum. Thus, as much as $30,000 ($5,000 x 2 elections [primary and general] x 3 separate party committees) can be directly contributed to every party nominee for the United States House. In Senate elections, the national party committee and the senatorial campaign committee may give a combined maximum of $17,500 to each candidate, and another $10,000 can be added from the state party committee for a total of $27,500 in direct gifts.

Table 10.2

Political Party Finances, 1976–1988[a]
(in $ millions)

	Total Receipts		Total Contributions	
Year	Democrats	Republicans	Democrats	Republicans
1976	18.2	45.7	3.9	6.3
1978	26.4	84.5	2.3	8.9
1980	37.2	169.5	6.6	17.0
1982	39.3	215.0	5.1	19.9
1984	98.5	297.9	11.6	25.0
1986	64.8	255.2	10.7	17.7
1988	127.9	263.3	19.6	26.1

[a]Includes total for the national senatorial and congressional committees as well as all other reported national and state/local spending.
[b]All presidential, Senate, and House candidates are included.
Source: Federal Election Commission

The parties' direct contributions can be significantly augmented with coordinated expenditures—party-paid general election campaign expenditures (for television advertising, polling, etc.) made in consultation and coordination with the candidate.[7] The coordinated expenditure limits are set surprisingly high. For House candidates the national and state parties may each spend $10,000 plus an inflation adjustment; the party committees together could thereby spend $46,100 in 1988 on behalf of each House nominee. Senate candidates are the beneficiaries of even higher limits on coordinated expenditures. The national and state parties can each spend $20,000 (plus inflation), or two cents per voter, whichever is greater. In 1988 the party expenditure limits amounted to $92,200 in the eight smallest states to over

$1.9 million in California—or a national total maximum of about $12.8 million for each party in the thirty-three Senate contests. Importantly, the national party committee is permitted to act as the state party committee's spending agent; that is, with the state party's agreement, the national committee can assume the state party's permitted portion of the coordinated expenditures. This privilege centralizes power in the national committees, and unburdens weaker state party committees that otherwise might not be able to contribute the maximum.

The candidate contribution totals presented in Table 10.2 actually understate by a considerable margin the Republican party's lead. Because the GOP so frequently bumps up against the allowable ceiling on contributions and expenditures, it sends additional aid through back channels: soft money, individuals' donations solicited and collected for specific candidates by the party (and thus counted as individual gifts despite the party's role), and cut-rate party in-kind services for media, polling, and consultants. One journalist estimated that the GOP had at least a $30 million advantage just in the closest 1986 Senate races when money from all sources was taken into account.[8]

The Democratic Party lagged far behind Republicans until massive Democratic defeats in 1980 forced the party to modernize its approach to raising and contributing funds. Even after the better part of a decade, Democrats still trail their competitors by virtually every significant measure of party activity. While the GOP has consistently maintained a large edge, however, the Democrats have considerably increased their total receipts. That is no small achievement.

Why Parties Over PACs?

While individuals and PACs represent particular interests and further the atomization of public policy, the parties encompass more general concerns and push the system toward consensus. There are no more unappreciated institutions in American life than the two major political parties. Often maligned by average citizens and many politicians alike as the repositories of corrupt bosses and smoke-filled rooms, the parties nonetheless perform essential electoral functions for our society. The enormous good that parties do for American society can be suggested by a brief discussion of several purposes served by the parties.

Voting and Issue Cues

The political parties provide a useful cue for voters, particularly the least informed and interested, who can use their party affiliation as a shortcut or substitute for interpreting issues and events they may little comprehend. But even better educated and more involved voters find party identification an assist. After all, no one has the time to study every issue carefully or to become fully knowledgeable about every candidate seeking public office. The result may be increased participation in elections.

Mobilizing Support and Aggregating Power

The effect of the party cue is exceptionally helpful to elected leaders. They can count on disproportionate support among their partisans in time of trouble, and in close judgment calls they have a home court advantage. And because there are only two major parties, pragmatic citizens who are interested in politics or public policy are mainly attracted to one or the other standard, creating natural majorities or near-majorities for party officeholders to command. The party creates a community of interest that bonds disparate groups together over time—eliminating the necessity of creating a coalition anew for every campaign or every issue. More effective government that is broadly accepted as legitimate is the consequence.

Forces for Stability

As mechanisms for organizing and containing political change, the parties are a potent force for stability. They represent continuity in the wake of changing issues and personalities, anchoring the electorate as the storms that are churned by new political people and policies swirl around. Because of its unyielding, pragmatic desire to win elections (not just contest them), each party in a sense acts not only to promote competition but also to moderate public opinion. The party tames its own extreme elements by pulling them toward an ideological center in order to attract a majority of votes on election day.

Unity, Linkage, Accountability

Parties provide the glue to hold together the diverse parts of the fragmented American governmental apparatus. The Founding Fathers designed a system that divides and subdivides power, making it possible to preserve individual liberty but difficult to coordinate and produce timely action. Parties help to compensate for this drawback by linking all the institutions and loci of power one to another, enhancing governmental effectiveness. While rivalry between the executive and legislative branches of American government is inevitable, the partisan affiliations of leaders of each branch constitute a common basis for cooperation, as any president and his fellow party members in Congress frequently demonstrate. Similarly, the federalist division of national, state, and local governments, while always an invitation to conflict, is made more workable and easily coordinated by the intersecting party relationships that exist among officeholders at all office levels. Party affiliation, in other words, is a sanctioned and universally recognized basis for mediation and negotiation laterally among the branches and vertically among the layers. The party's linkage function does not end there, of course. The party connection is one means to ensure or increase accountability in election campaigns and in government. Candidates on the campaign trail and elected party leaders in office are required from time to time to account for their performance at party-sponsored forums and in party nominating primaries and conventions.

The increased money and services from both Democratic and Republican organizations may be drawing candidates much closer to their parties, since the parties are contributing in tangible ways to their nominees' election. Whether or not any gratitude or obligation to the party is created in this fashion, such services as training schools, party issue papers, and institutional advertising put officeholders through a "homogenizing" process that may predispose them more favorably to the "party line" in government. Party leaders and political observers differ about whether such a development is really taking place, but all are agreed on one point: the parties remain less influential than they would be otherwise because alternative sources of funding are available to candidates. And the most available "alternative source" for incumbents is PACs.

Promotion of Civic Virtue and Patriotism

Because identification with a party is at the core of most Americans' political lives, the prism through which they see the world, many voters accept and adopt the parties' values and view of responsible citizenship. These values include involvement and participation; work for the "public good" in the "national interest" (as conceived in partisan terms, naturally); and patriotism and respect for American society's fundamental institutions and processes.

The Symbiotic Relationship of PACs and Parties

On paper one can make a strong case that PACs and the political parties are bound to be competitors. They both raise money from the same limited universe of political givers, large and small. They both try to elect candidates, but in doing so they adopt very different perspectives: most PACs act on the basis of relatively narrow or even single-interest viewpoints, while the parties operate from a fisheye, broad-based, overarching vantage point. And they both vie for the attention, affection and loyalty of candidates and officeholders.

While there is in fact evidence of considerable competition between PACs and parties, what is more surprising is that despite their natural tensions the two have learned to coexist symbiotically: they use one another quite well. PACs need the information about candidates, intelligence about congressional contests, and access to political leaders that parties can provide. The parties seek PAC money for their candidates and their own organizations, which of late have modernized and expanded at a rate that matches the growth of PACs.

The still-developing relationship between PACs and the political parties can be characterized in many ways, for the diversity of the PAC world makes sweeping generalizations difficult. For example, most PACs are determinedly bipartisan, as befits their primary goal of access to officeholders. Business and trade PACs are commonly believed to be Republican-oriented, yet since 1978 more than a third of corporate PAC gifts and well over 40 percent of all trade PAC donations in congressional races have gone to Democratic candidates. In very recent election cycles, business and trade PACs have been even more closely divided between the two parties, causing great consternation among Republican party officials.[9] In some years business committees alone have supplied as much or more money to Democrats than have the traditionally heavily Democratic labor PACs. Unlike the business and trade PACs, labor union committees make no pretense of bipartisanship; an average of 94 percent of all labor PAC money has flowed to the Democrats since 1978. In return, fifteen seats on the DNC Executive Committee are reserved for labor officials.

Democrats have also worked hand-in-hand with many liberal

non-connected PACs such as Pamela Harriman's Democrats for the '80s. While there is no set of PACs as closely tied to the GOP as labor is to the Democrats, the Republicans have had very smooth working relationships with many of the corporate, trade and coordinating business PACs over the years. The independent oil PACs for example have been very supportive of many GOP candidates and party needs since the mid-1970s.

But the parties' relationships with some other PACs are more difficult. The ideological PACs lead the list of party antagonists and there is concern about them in both parties. The rhetoric and actions of many New Right PACs have been anti-Republican party. The GOP has been termed a "fraud" and "a social club where rich people go to pick their noses" by one New Right leader, while others have called for the party's disbanding and the establishment of a new "conservative party."[10] In some cases the conservative PACs have attempted to usurp the functions of the party and establish themselves as substitutes by recruiting and training candidates and creating pseudo-party organizations of their own.[11] Sen. Jesse Helms' Congressional Club has tried to supplant the regular Republican party organization in North Carolina, to the consternation of some GOP officials in the state.[12] NCPAC, which has been accused of stealing contributors' names from Republican party finance report lists,[13] seriously considered declaring itself to be a political party in 1982.[14]

Even though the New Right groups usually end up supporting Republican candidates (or opposing Democratic ones), their antagonism has caused some GOP leaders to take a critical view of their activities.[15] So, too, have Democrats looked askew at the efforts of NCPAC's liberal counterparts. As one Democratic National Committee officer put it:

> I believe the independent PACs are a problem for two reasons. There's a finite pool of political money, and we simply can't afford this drain to them, gambling that they'll spend it wisely... Second, unlike the parties, many of the independent PACs are essentially computer-driven mail-order operations that have no membership and are accountable to nobody.[16]

Fortunately for both parties, the independent, non-connected ideological PACs have fallen on hard financial times, and many (including NCPAC) are mere shadows of their former selves. The parties have easily withstood the assaults of the anti-party PACs and the latter's heyday may well be over.

Most PACs fall between the pro-party and anti-party poles; in fact most could perhaps best be described as indifferent to parties. That does not mean the effects PACs have on party organization and development are neutral, of course. Overall, there is little evidence for the widespread claim that PACs have contributed greatly to the long-term decline of the political party system in the United States. Rather, PACs may be one more manifestation of the atomizing forces which have made the parties less appealing to Americans.[17]

Nonetheless, PACs provide an alternative source of funding and support services for a candidate, weakening his ties with the party and lessening his fear of severe electoral consequences if he is disloyal to his party. But at the same time the competition from PACs is one of many factors stimulating a dramatic surge in party organization, technology, programs, and fundraising that has drawn candidates much closer to the national parties. Parties can now do—or refuse to do—much more to elect their nominees than they could in the past. These party advances were occurring during the same years the PAC movement was maturing, and just as PACs have in some ways limited the parties' influence, so too have the invigorated parties acted as a check on PACs.

Finally, since candidates want campaign cash and PACs have it, there is inevitably a mating dance between the two groups, and the political parties act as matchmakers and, occasionally, chaperons. A multi-candidate PAC is permitted to give $15,000 each year to all national-party political committees combined, and while few contribute that large an amount, about a third of all multi-candidate PACs donated some amount to the parties in recent years. PACs swelled the parties' treasuries by a total of nearly $7 million in 1985–86 for instance. While this sum comprised a modest 5 percent of all PAC contributions, the money was not insubstantial, and was welcomed especially by the financially hard-pressed Democrats. The Democrats received $5.74 million to the Republicans' $1.11 million, an edge attributable in part to the GOP's desire to steer all available PAC money to its candidates.

Most PACs secure some of their information about candidates and elections at regular party briefings and through party newsletters, but PACs are naturally somewhat wary of the slant they receive at briefings. The party's built-in bias is apparent to seasoned PAC managers, and most PACs have learned the hard way after "bum steers" from the parties resulted in the committees' backing losers. The GOP, for example, received a great deal of criticism from the PAC community after the 1986 elections, when many of the Senate and House candidates they claimed were on the verge of victory in fact were defeated.

As PACs have become more sophisticated, they have begun to demand more precise and accurate information from the parties, and both parties are attempting to provide it. The RNC and associated committees have established numerous programs and channels of communication with the PACs. For example, any PAC contributing $5,000 or more to the RNC each year gains a PAC 40 membership, entitling it to meet with Republican congressional leaders for off-the-record breakfasts once a month at the Capitol Hill Club in Washington.

Also, briefings for the PACs are provided by both the Congressional and Senatorial Committees on a quarterly basis in Washington and in major cities around the country. And the GOP usually pays attention to the needs of its candidates, particularly unknown challengers. When a challenger comes to Washington, the appropriate Republican committee will help to set up appointments with PAC mangers in the capital and to design a PAC solicitation program tailor-made to the candidate's strengths.

The Democrats have also recently devoted greater efforts to securing corporate and trade PAC money. From 1981–1986 then Rep. Tony Coelho (D-Calif.), chairman of the Democratic Congressional Campaign Committee (DCCC), made a concerted appeal to business to "not let your ideology get in the way of your business judgment."[18] Coelho's approach, using access to a Democratically controlled House (and now Senate) has clearly worked, as demonstrated by figures on business/trade PAC gifts to Democratic candidates (cited earlier).

Democrats have also followed the Republican lead in using exclusive clubs and offering special access to attract the PACs. For instance, the DNC has a Business Council which PACs can join with a $15,000 annual contribution, and a $2,500-per-year PAC Council which is the rough equivalent of the RNC's PAC 40 Club. Like its GOP counterpart, the PAC Council gathers together legislators and PAC officials for monthly breakfasts. Reflecting labor's prominent role in the Democratic party, there is a separate DNC Labor Council whose price is $15,000 per year for a PAC and a whopping $50,000 for a labor union proper. Democratic services to PACs and party candidates have improved, too.

The party committees have expanded the size of their PAC liaison staffs, conduct regular briefing sessions for PACs, and distribute informational newsletters about key races.

In essence, the role of ice breaker is the fundamental one played by both parties with the PACs. The parties' uneasy alliance with PACs is formed and maintained of necessity—to elect party candidates. Republican and Democratic leaders alike may understand the competing nature of PACs and parties, but they also realize that under the current system of campaign finance, PAC money gives congressional contenders an often crucial competitive edge. So PACs and parties learn to support each other.

Reforms to Strengthen Parties and Diminish PACs

Despite how well the symbiotic relationship between PACs and parties works for them, concerns about the welfare of our representative democracy suggest that some changes might enhance the promotion of important values, including governmental effectiveness, legitimacy, and accountability. Because PACs and parties are so interrelated, giving preferential treatment to the parties will indirectly lessen the influence of PACs and the adverse consequences they have. The current limits of contributions to party committees ($20,000 a year for an individual and $15,000 for a multi-candidate PAC) should be substantially increased. Additionally, individuals as well as corporations, labor unions, and trade associations should be permitted to underwrite without limit the administrative, legal, and accounting costs parties incur, with full disclosure of all donations.

Another way to lessen the importance of PACs is to increase the pool of alternative money. To begin with, the $1,000 limit on an individual's contribution to each candidate per election should be raised to recover its loss to inflation since 1974. (A $1,000 gift in 1974 is worth less than half that today.) Both the $1,000 cap and the companion limit of $25,000 that an individual is permitted to donate to *all* candidates taken together in a calendar year should also be permanently indexed to the inflation rate. Restoring the value of individual contributions will offset somewhat the financial clout of the PACs.

Even more important would be the enactment of a tax credit to benefit the parties. Before landmark tax reform legislation was passed in 1986, federal taxpayers were granted a 50 percent tax credit for all contributions to candidates, PACs, parties, and political committees of up to $50 for an individual and $100 on a joint return. Unfortunately this credit was one of those eliminated in the tax revision, and currently there is no credit for political gifts. The credit ought to be re-established not only to the 50 percent level, but all the way to 100 percent, at least for candidate and party gifts. Such a move would clearly encourage small donations that have few if any real strings attached; the parties not only would remain unencumbered by the perceived debts that come with large contributions, but both parties would have an exceptionally valuable tool to use in expanding their donor and membership base.[19] This would be all the more so if income-taxing states agreed to offer a similar 50 percent credit if the federal government refused to give more than 50 percent; taxpayers in these 43 states[20] would, in effect, get a 100 percent credit.[21]

Realistically, in an era when gigantic budget deficits threaten even essential existing programs, the prospects of securing either a 50 percent or 100 percent credit at the federal level do not appear promising. In one survey, when respondents were asked whether they would favor or oppose "giving people a full tax credit for contributing money to a political party," a solid majority of 55 percent to 39 percent disapproved (five percent had no opinion.)[22] This is somewhat surprising since the public is usually inclined to approve tax credits that might provide some benefit to it. Respondents' negative reactions might signify concern about the budget deficit or, more likely, estrangement from political parties.

Luckily, there is another option that could win both public and legislative favor: a tax "add-on" that permits a citizen to channel a few dollars of his income tax refund to the party of his or her choice. Both parties would clearly gain funds but the budget deficit would be none the worse for it. The voluntary nature of this self-imposed tax will appeal to conservatives and Republicans, while the ready cash will draw the assent of money-starved Democrats and liberals. In its ideal form, the federal 1040 (short and long form) and every annual income tax form on the state level should include an add-on provision that gives a taxpayer the opportunity to check off a gift of $2, $5, $10, $25, $50, or $100 to the party he or she designates.

Will any significant number of taxpayers give money using this device? Several states (including Maine, Massachusetts, Montana, and Virginia) currently have some form of add-on. The

Virginia experience is somewhat typical, with only about 2.2 percent of all eligible taxpayers contributing in recent years, though even this tiny portion has provided several hundred thousand dollars cumulatively to the parties (actually, Virginia is a little on the low side compared to other states; participation rates in all add-on plans combined have averaged about 4 percent.)[23] While giving even small amounts to the political parties will doubtless never become the rage among beleaguered taxpayers anticipating a refund, it is likely that the present minuscule percentage of participation could be substantially augmented by a joint two-party educational advertising campaign undertaken at tax time. The campaign might profitably be keyed to patriotic themes, urging citizens to demonstrate their civic commitment in this small but crucial way. If afforded the add-on's superb opportunity for financial advancement by the federal and state governments, the parties certainly must take full advantage and capitalize on this golden entry on the tax forms. Such a cost-free reform should be among the highest priorities of both national parties and all state parties where an add-on does not now exist.

Fortunately for those who see the compelling need for stronger parties, the political parties are progressing on many fronts already. There are winds at the parties' backs today, forces that are helping to reverse decades of decline. None may be more important than the growing realization of the worth of political parties by many journalists and officeholders, as well as the continued advocacy of party-building reforms by many academics and political practitioners. The resolve of recent national party leaders, such as Republican National Committee Chairmen William Brock and Frank Fahrenkopf and Democratic party leaders Paul Kirk (Democratic National Committee chairman) and Tony Coelho (chairman until 1987 of the Democratic Congressional Campaign Committee), has been of paramount significance to the ongoing revival of political party organizational and financial might.

These suggested reforms in campaign finance are certainly not enough to cure all the ills of the American party system. A separate agenda—which I have elaborated elsewhere—is necessary to revive partisan affiliation in the electorate and to increase volunteer strength in the party organizations.[24] But at least these pro-party changes in campaign finance can enhance the role of the parties while tilting the structure's balance somewhat more to parties and somewhat less to PACs. In society's interests, for sustained health of our representative democracy, these are modest changes worth making.

NOTES

1. This paper will draw information and arguments from three of my other works in the subject area: *PAC Power: Inside the World of Political Action Committees* (New York: W.W. Norton, 1984); *The Party's Just Begun: Shaping Political Parties for America's Future* (Boston: Little, Brown/Scott, Foresman, 1988); and *Paying for Elections: The Campaign Finance Thicket* (New York: The Twentieth Century Fund, 1989).

2. See Larry Sabato, *The Rise of Political Consultants: New Ways of Winning Elections* (New York: Basic Books, 1981); see also *National Journal* 15 (April 16, 1983): 780–81.

3. David Adamany, "The New Faces of American Politics," The Annals, *AAPSS* 486 (July 1986): 31–32.

4. See Sabato, *The Party's Just begun*, Chapter 3.

5. Rhodes Cook, "Democrats Develop Tactics: Laying Groundwork for 1984," *Congressional Quarterly Weekly* 40 (July 3, 1982): 1595.

6. This assumes that the party committee or PAC is a multi-candidate committee. See Sabato, *PAC Power*, 7–8. If the committee or PAC has not qualified a a multi-candidate committee, then a gift of only $1,000 maximum is permitted.

7. Under 2 U.S.C. 441a(d).

8. Thomas B. Edsall, writing in the *Washington Post*, October 17, 1986, A1.

9. See, for example, David S. Cloud, "Feud Between GOP PACs Stings Candidates," *Congressional Quarterly Weekly* 46 (September 3, 1988): 2447–2450.

10. Sabato, *PAC Power*, 150–151.

11. See Margaret Ann Latus, "Assessing Ideological PACs: From Outrage to Understanding," in *Money and Politics in the United States: Financing Elections in the 1980's*, edited by Michael J. Malbin (Washington, D.C.: American Enterprise Institute/Chatham House, 1984), 157–9.

12. See *Congressional Quarterly Weekly* 40 (March 6, 1982): 499–505.

13. See *Political Finance/Lobby Reporter* 3 (July 21, 1982): 188. In response to the GOP charges, the FEC forbade NCPAC from soliciting Republican donors NCPAC had copied from fi-

nancial disclosure reports. NCPAC had not yet solicited them, though the FEC agreed with the GOP that NCPAC's intent to solicit eventually was clear.

14. See *Political Finance/Lobby Reporter* 3 (September 22, 1983): 252.

15. Sabato, *PAC Power*, 151.

16. Ann Lewis, as quoted in Sabato, *PAC Power*, 151.

17. See, for example, Frank J. Sorauf, "Political Parties and Political Action Committees: Two Life Cycles," *Arizona Law Review* 22, no. 2 (1980): 449–50.

18. As quoted in Paul Taylor, "For Business PACs this Year, Suitable Targets are in Short Supply," *Washington Post*, July 27, 1982, A6. See also *National Journal* 14 (August 7, 1982): 1368–73.

19. A 100 percent tax credit would almost certainly increase party giving. The California Commission on Campaign Financing found that 35 percent of state residents would either increase their political gifts or give for the first time if there were a 100 percent credit. See California Commission on Campaign Financing, "The New Gold Rush: Financing California's Legislative Campaigns" (Sacramento: State of California, 1985), 15.

20. Only the states of Alaska, Florida, Nevada, South Dakota, Texas, Washington, and Wyoming have no income tax.

21. Minnesota and the District of Columbia already provide a 50 percent tax credit for political contributions.

22. Cited in Sabato, *The Party's Just Begun*, 213–214.

23. See Holly Wagner, "Costly Campaigns Attract Special Interest Dollars," *State Government News* 29 (October 1986): 20.

24. See Sabato, *The Party's Just Begun*, Chapter 6.

Part III: Problems with Reform

Most of the preceding chapters have called for various reforms of the campaign finance system. The prospects for having any reforms implemented are complicated by the constraints discussed in this section. First, is public opinion on the need for reform strong and clear enough to provide the impetus and direction for reform? Second, is the Federal Election Commission up to the task of enforcing current or reformed laws? Finally, are the political conditions within Congress conducive to reform?

Is the mass public as supportive of campaign finance reform as Common Cause would have us believe? Frank Sorauf's review of poll data indicates that there is non-partisan support for limits on contributions and expenditures but no mandate for public funding. Much of this opinion is congruent with the Progressive bias of the media which are attempting to mobilize public concern on this matter, according to Sorauf. In reality, the importance of campaign finance issues to voters is not likely great enough to affect the outcome of elections or legislative activity. Therefore, those for whom the contours of campaign finance reform are most salient—the political parties and incumbents—will promote reforms to suit their own interests.

Before turning to David Magleby's analysis of what such reforms might look like, given the political interests of the parties and Members of Congress, we consider two perspectives on another constraint upon the effectiveness of reforms. Reforms will only be meaningful if enforced. Both in day to day enforcement activities and at the highest level decisions of its commissioners, however, the Federal Election Commission (FEC) itself is in need of reform.

Kenneth Gross, former Associate General Council to the FEC in charge of enforcement, calls for more timely and certain enforcement of the FECA in routine cases. Decisions delayed until after an election deny voters their channel of accountability. He also sees a need for means to protect the procedural due process of respondents in FEC actions. The reforms he advocates include a tracking system to streamline the processing of routine complaints; better protections for due process to those investigated, including the use of administrative law judges for adjudicating major investigations of violations; random audits; and stiffer, well publicized penalties. These reforms would not only enhance the effectiveness and legitimacy of the FEC, they would increase the accountability of potential violators.

Based on his personal experiences as a commissioner, Frank Reiche shares these concerns about the effectiveness and legitimacy of the Federal Election Commission, focusing on the activities of the commissioners. According to Reiche, the increasing partisanship of the Commission itself has stymied its efforts at enforcement, undermining its credibility. The weakness of the FEC reflects the intentions of Congress but does not serve the public good. Reiche prescribes an appointment process less tied to Congress: presidents willing to look beyond partisan politics in their selections of commissioners; limiting commissioners to a single six year term; and strengthening the FEC chairmanship. Commissioners need to develop some independence from allegiance to party and Congress so that they can effectively serve the public in enforcing campaign finance laws.

The final obstacles to campaign finance reform come from those who must enact the changes: Members of Congress. David Magleby clarifies the politics of reform by offering a schema for understanding institutional and political differences in the House and Senate which, together with partisan differences, diminish the prospects for reform. His schema spells out the different obstacles to reform generated by the different constraints of self-interest, philosophy, and personality faced by House and Senate members of the different parties. The politics of reform point towards the likely acceptance of incremental "face-saving" reforms such as the elimination of honoraria and the grandfather clause, raising the contribution limits for individuals while lowering them for PACs, and requiring the disclosure of soft money. Major disagreements over spending limitations, public financing, increasing party contribution limits, and imposing aggregate PAC limits will likely block these comprehensive reforms. Finally, reformers must beware of the unintended consequences of their changes and the unpredictable response of the Supreme Court.

Our concluding chapter suggests campaign finance reforms to promote a balance of effectiveness, legitimacy, accountability, representation, participation, liberty, equality, and competition. Recognizing that all reforms confront the realities of conflicting values, difficult implementation, illusions and misconceptions, or loopholes and abuses, we nonetheless illustrate how reforms can and should be designed to address three of the values most threatened today: competition, accountability, and legitimacy.

11

Public Opinion on Campaign Finance

Frank J. Sorauf

We have not lacked proposals for reforming the American system of campaign finance in the 1980s. Enacting those proposals has been another matter; indeed there have been no changes in Congress's regulation of campaign finance in the 1980s. The failure, thus, has not been one of ingenuity in formulating proposals but in the politics of mobilizing support for them.

If the last great wave of campaign finance reform is any indication, the politics of reforming campaign money depends heavily on two fundamental influences: the parties' definitions of their own interests, and the deeply felt concerns of the mass public. That reform movement began in the late 1960s with Democratic party and public outcries against Republican spending in 1968 and ended in 1974 after the post-1972 revelations of illegalities in the re-election campaign of Richard Nixon. Embarrassed by all the events at and after Watergate, Republicans could do little to resist the massive reforms of 1974 promoted both by the Democratic party and a mass opinion organized by the emerging Common Cause. The result was the rewriting of the Federal Election Campaign Act (FECA) that is today's regulation of congressional campaign finance.[1]

Parties continue to guard their interests and positions in campaign finance in the 1980s, and their care and concern is not hard to track. On virtually every vote taken in the Congress on campaign finance reform proposals since 1974, Republicans and Democrats have divided sharply. The opinions of the mass public are far more elusive and far less well organized. Indeed, it is not even *clear* which public attitudes bear on the problems of funding campaigns.

The Dimensions of Mass Opinion

Informed members of the mass public form their attitudes and opinions in hierarchies. More specific opinions are nested in greater, more inclusive outlooks; how one views a proposal for government-provided medical care depends on one's broader views about individual responsibility and the role and effectiveness of government. In the case of campaign finance, the individual's opinions about the funding of candidate campaigns undoubtedly reflects wider beliefs about the nature of influence, the political power of money, and the probity and responsiveness of governmental institutions and their elected officials. It is, however, easier to stipulate than to prove those relationships, and attitudes about campaign finance are a very strong case in point.

It seems clear by the 1980s that the mass public sees and evaluates campaign finance in a broader context of distrust of the institutions and processes of American politics. Large numbers of Americans think government responds primarily to organized, special interests and that public officials are not concerned about the ordinary citizen. Pride in American political institutions has declined as alienation from them has increased. Those trends reached bottom in the 1970s, but rises in the 1980s have by no means recaptured the levels of the confident '60s. For example, the CBS/New York Times poll has tracked responses since the late '50s to the question: How much of the time do you think you can trust the government in Washington to do what is right—just about always, most of the time, or only some of the time? More than 60 percent of the sample responded "most of the time" in the early 1960s; that percentage dropped to 22 in 1980 and rose to the high 30s and low 40s in the 1980s.

While the decline of confidence in government and popular support for it is a relatively recent phenomenon,[2] there is another relevant part of the American political culture that dates back almost a century. It is that cluster of attitudes viewing money and wealth as overridingly powerful sources of political influence which we associate with the turn-of-the-century Progressives. From the imperatives of that Progressive worldview flow popular beliefs about political influence and about the ability of the monied "special interests" to thwart the general or public interests we are all said to share.

The connection between the broader, contextual outlooks and specific opinion about campaign finance is most apparent in contemporary reaction to political action committees (PACs). A Harris poll in 1984 showed that Americans respond positively or negatively to PACs depending on the nature of the interests they promote. In May of that year 58 percent of the sample thought environmental PACs a good influence on government and politics in the United States; 34 percent so valued labor union PACs, however, and only 22 percent responded positively to "big company" PACs.[3] Apparently the fear of PACs is driven by more fundamental fears about "big money" and monied institutions in American politics. Moreover, the pattern of that underlying opinion appears to be very close to the classic Progressive view of the dominance and influence of money and moneyed interests in American politics.

Not surprisingly in view of all the notoriety they have won in the last decade, PACs are the only actors in the campaign finance system to win the attention of the pollsters. Questions about them without messages about the interests they represent reveal other aspects of opinion on campaign finance. Popular responses about it are often sharply divided. In November of 1982 the Los Angeles Times Poll found that 38 percent of a national sample was in some degree satisfied with the role of PACs in the campaign that had just ended; 38 percent was dissatisfied, and 23 percent "not sure." Moreover, differently worded questions elicit greatly different patterns of response about campaign finance. In contrast to this 1982 poll, a 1980 Harris poll found that 71 percent of its sample agreed with the statement—one that certainly suggested a conclusion—that "PACs are pouring too much money into the whole political process." Only 19 percent disagreed.

If one shifts to opinion about possible regulations of campaign funding, mass opinion seems easier to grasp. The basic policy choice in dealing with campaign finance is the choice between private, voluntary funding of campaigns and funding that in whole or in part comes from public treasuries. All of the poll data we have indicates that on this basic issue the American people are and have been sharply divided. Indeed, their cumulative opinions appear to depend on how the survey poses the issue. Opinion on public funding, that is, appears to be caught up with other regulatory issues in the public's mind.

Four times in the last decade the Gallup organization has asked a sample of American adults its opinion about public funding. Moreover, the question has been virtually identical over the four samplings; the last one (in 1987) read:

> It has been suggested that the federal government provide a fixed amount of money for election campaigns of candidates for Congress and that all private contribu-

tions be prohibited. Do you think this is a good idea or a poor idea?[4]

The responses to the Gallup questions have all favored public funding: 57 percent to 30 percent in 1979, 55 to 31 in 1982, 52 to 36 in 1984, and 50 to 42 in 1987. In short, as Gallup measures it, support for public funding is consistent but dwindling slowly.

That series of Gallup questions featured two themes: a "neutral" element about public funding and the theme of prohibiting private contributions. If one alters those elements, one seems to get different results about public funding. The Harris organization in 1983 asked a somewhat different question:

> If it came to it, would you favor having *all* Federal elections financed out of public funds, with strictly enforced limits on how much each candidate for President, U.S. Senator, or Congressman could spend, or would you oppose using public funds for this purpose?

The respondents were only 43 percent in favor and 53 percent opposed.[5] Sampling differences may account for some of the difference from the Gallup results of a year earlier (55 to 31). But the difference in questions probably does, too. The Harris question substitutes expenditure limits for the Gallup prohibition of "all private contributions", and it also proposes funding "*all* Federal elections." Perhaps even more importantly—it is less neutral in tone. There is exasperation in the first five words, and the isolation of the negative alternative at the end of a longish question may suggest a negative response.

If one introduces even greater differences in the framing of the question, the results vary further. A Harris poll of 1980 asked a national sample to "strongly agree, somewhat agree, somewhat disagree, or strongly disagree" with the following statement: "All federal elections should be financed out of public funds contributed by the taxpayers." The results were not surprising: 39 percent agreed (only 19 percent "strongly") and 58 percent disagreed (39 percent "strongly"). In the same manner, Civic Service found in a 1985 poll a 65 percent rejection of public funding when the issue was framed this way:

> It has been proposed in Congress that the federal government provide public financing for congressional campaigns for the U.S. House of Representatives and Senate. Would you approve or disapprove of the proposal to use public funds, federal money, to pay the costs of congressional campaigns and how strongly do you feel?

Polls, in other words, find greater opposition to public funding when there is no mention of either limits on private contributions or limits on candidate spending.

Those polls on public funding, then, suggest that the mass public favors limits on campaign contributions and expenditures more than it favors the idea of public funding. Indeed, it appears that large numbers of Americans want statutory limits on congressional campaign finance like the ones that Congress passed in 1974. For instance, polls indicate popular acceptance of present statutory restrictions on contributions. In a 1980 Harris poll 54 percent of the respondents found the $5,000 limit on PACs "just about right," with 8 percent favoring a higher limit, 9 percent a lower one, and 15 percent no limit at all. Similar percentages (57 percent) thought the limits on individual contributions "just about right," and 60 percent opposed doing away with those limits. More generally, a Harris poll in November of 1982 found that 84 percent of the respondents agreed that "those who contribute large sums of money have too much influence over the government," and that 62 percent found "the excessive campaign spending in national elections" to be a "very serious problem." In a move beyond the status quo, however, 68 percent supported unspecified limits on the sums a candidate could accept from all PACs.[6]

The Demographics of Opinion on Campaign Finance

Even less clear than the outlines of mass opinion about campaign finance is the distribution of the opinion in various groups and segments of the national population. The major national survey organizations report no breakdowns of the aggregate responses to their questions. For that more detailed understanding one must turn to statewide polls and the results of referenda in several states.

An instructive example is the poll taken by the Michigan Chamber of Commerce in May of 1986. The central question was one that asked whether the respondents thought PACs should be "allowed to contribute financially to political candidates."[7] A total of 52 percent responded positively, 39 percent negatively. The breakdown of that statewide response reveals an unusual consistency across geographical, partisan, educational, and occupational lines. Republicans responded positively 54 percent of the time, Democrats 51 percent, and Independents 50 percent; union members were 54 percent in favor and white collar workers 57 percent (retirees were at only 39 percent, though). The major differences were demographic. Support for PACs was greater among well-educated respondents, with those who had done "post- graduate" work registering 66 percent support. The relationship between opinion and age was the most dramatic: ages 18–24, 64 percent favorable; ages 25–34, 59 percent; ages 35–44, 57 percent; ages 45–54, 59 percent; ages 55–64, 46 percent; and over 65, 36 percent.[8]

Recent votes on initiative measures in Arizona and California offer useful, but less direct, evidence for exploring the demographic structure of opinions about campaign finance. In November of 1986 the voters of Arizona approved by a 65 to 35 percent vote an initiative that put limits on campaign contributions in that state. The yes vote was fairly evenly spread among the 15 counties of the state; there was in fact a standard deviation of only 4.8 around the statewide mean. Within those limited county-to-county differences, however, there were some very tentative signs of a relationship between "yes" voting and Republican strength.[9]

The California electorate's acceptance of two more complicated initiatives in June of 1988 is more instructive. That was the date of the state's primary election, ordinarily a low turnout election. The first of the initiatives, Proposition 68, proposed contribution limits and then a package of limited public funding and expenditure limits. The other, Proposition 73, prohibited public funding, but proposed limits on contributions and transfers of money from one candidate to another. That latter provision, of course, struck deeply at the California tradition of legislative leaders (such as Assembly Speaker Willie Brown) raising large sums and giving them to legislative candidates of their party. Proposition 68 passed with 53 percent of the vote, Proposition 73 with 58 percent.

In both of the California initiatives voter support was fairly evenly spread across the state's 58 counties; standard deviations from the statewide mean were 5.0 for #68 and 4.8 for #73. Moreover, the correlations with the Democratic percentages of registered voters in the counties were weak; there is, therefore, little evidence that partisanship affected voting.[10] In short, the California votes in 1988 appear to have cut across party lines and loyalties.

What evidence we have about mass opinion supports three

major conclusions about the shape of mass opinion on American campaign finance. First, on the matter of public policy, there is obvious support for legislated limits on the flow of campaign money, but the public is divided over public funding options. Second, opinion about campaign funding appears to be caught up in more basic, underlying belief structures, most notably fundamental distrust about the role of money and monied interests in American politics. And third, those attitudes and opinions we can measure seem to be unusually "non-partisan"—especially for a cluster of questions that the parties themselves see affecting their separate interests in so many ways.

Finally, how intensely held, how effectively organized are the public's opinions about campaign finance? Is the public's opinion about campaign finance deep and intense enough, is it held confidently enough, to provide the demand for legislated reform? There is reason to wonder. Just two years ago the Congress legislated the end of tax credits for individual political contributions in its massive reworking of the income tax code. A number of states, anxious to follow federal practice and to use the federal figure for taxable income, followed suit. Scarcely a peep, much less a protest, was heard from the public or the media, even though the action reduced incentives for the public's preferred source for funding campaigns. To be sure, a number of states have begun in the late 1980s to put limits on contributions to candidates for the first time, but the march of reform in the states comes a decade after federal legislation, and it still leaves more than a third of the states without any substantial limits on campaign contributions.

The political truth is that opinion on campaign finance is largely unorganized and unmobilized. One can hardly count the hortatory efforts of the nation's editorial writers as mobilization, and that leaves largely the efforts of Common Cause. That organization provides its members with pre-printed petitions for their Members of Congress, but although congressional offices receive some of them, they tend to receive comparatively little else on issues of campaign finance.[11]

For millions of Americans, therefore, campaign finance is a low priority interest on their scale of political priorities. It is, moreover, an interest they find difficult to define, difficult even to understand in all of its complexity. Since they do not perceive it in terms of Democratic/Republican or liberal-conservative polarities, it eludes their most common political cues and structures of meaning. It is one of those issues on which judgment comes quickly, usually in response to potent symbols, but on which most citizens will be loathe to spend much of their political currency. It is far removed from their group and organizational lives, far distant from the events of their daily lives and the "gut issues" of American politics.

To the extent that there is an "issue public" for campaign finance, it is very largely the members of Congress and their political parties. In a sense, campaign finance is one of those issues in which the salient interests of the political producers outweigh the far less central interests of the vastly greater numbers of political consumers. The interests of producers touch livelihoods, those of consumers do not.

The Sources of Opinion

Ordinary Americans are distant from the working realities of campaign finance. "Reality" for them are the images and messages of the mass media. Unfortunately, those messages often present a picture of American campaign finance that is simplistic and moralistic, reflecting the deep-seated Progressive distrust of money and the moneyed in American politics.

Two kinds of systematic bias haunt the reporting of American politics in the media. One arises out of media needs to tailor the journalistic agenda and presentation to attract an audience—the search for drama and conflict and a touch of scandal, the need to avoid complexity (especially statistical complexity), the need to personalize the story and draw on the emotions and experience of the reader. As it relates to campaign finance, these imperatives lead the media away, *inter alia*, from extensive data and extended attempts at providing background or defining terms. On the other hand, they encourage reports of increased totals of money, stories about negative, "targeted" spending and "hit lists", and easy judgments about the motives and propriety of participants in the campaign finance system.

A second bias springs from the Progressive worldview about the influence of money in American government and politics:

> ...great enemies of society are the big political machines, the business "trusts," and the other special interests that try to advance their selfish goals at the public's expense by buying elections and corrupting public officials.[12]

It has, moreover, long dominated a good deal of public affairs reporting in the American media, and it continues to do so today.[13] That the very subject of campaign finance, the political uses of money itself, would activate the Progressive outlook in the media ought not to surprise. Nor should we be surprised that it animates the intermediate sources on which the media so often rely—the membership organizations such as Common Cause, public interest organizations such as the Nader group, and the think tanks such as the Center for Responsive Politics. It would indeed be hard to imagine a political subject that would fit more comfortably into the assumptions of the Progressive understanding than campaign finance.

Systematic evidence for characterizations such as these is not easy to develop, but I have tried to do so elsewhere at some length.[14] The journalistic treatment of the "soft money" controversy since middle or late 1987 offers another illustration. The story about the recruitment of large contributions by the national committees of the parties, even the re-emergence of the "fat cats," was a legitimate story. It is less clear that its constant repetition, especially in the *New York Times* was justified; and how does one square the repeated use of the phrase "sewer money" in editorial headings with the usually sober ways of the *Times*?[15] Moreover, coverage of soft money in the national press—the *Los Angeles Times*, the *New York Times*, and the *Washington Post*—hinted at illegality or impropriety without really specifying the charges. Various stories suggested the problem was in the act of national solicitation, in the favors the contributors sought, in the spending of the money directly on the presidential campaign, or in the coordination of presidential and state party activities. Very few stories tried to explain the issues of federalism and the indivisibility of local, state, and national campaigns to the readers.[16] Even fewer noted that Congress in 1979 authorized contributions to state parties and gave its reasons for doing do. Only rarely, indeed, did reporting in the elite newspapers accurately define just what "soft money" is.

The result of all this reporting is something verging on total confusion. It was reporting that better served advocacy than it served the public's need to know. There are real policy questions here—the role of brokers and intermediaries in campaign finance, and the wisdom and administrability of the "party-building" exception, for instance—but I doubt that this reporting clarified them.

So, the sources of information about American campaign finance exhibit the same systematic bias toward Progressive interpretations of political events that the mass public does in its opinions about campaign finance. We will perhaps never know whether the chick has preceded the egg or the egg the chicken. It suffices that there is so great a congruence between effective sources of information and the structure of mass opinion, between the pictures of reality and what millions of people want to believe or have decided to believe. Those reinforcing relationships probably guarantee that neither the source nor the public will change very soon.

The Impact of Public Opinion on Campaign Finance Reform

The link between mass opinion and political action in a democracy always depends on information or knowledge as the spur to action. Certainly those members of Congress who mandated extensive reporting of the movements of money in campaigns—and then the making public of those reports—expected an informed public to act to change or punish practices of which it disapproved. In a general sense, of course, political opinion always works in two main ways: by affecting the outcomes of elections and by spurring government to new controls or limits. In the particular case of campaign finance, opinion appears also to have a third role in expanding legislative powers with which to reform the system.

One searches in vain, however, for evidence that campaign finance has become a major issue in the campaigns themselves. Perhaps there is a perverse logic to the issue—it is incumbent candidates who raise large sums of money so easily, and yet it is those very incumbents who are invulnerable to issues made of it by reason of advantages that include but extend far beyond campaign finance. "Money" more generally can easily emerge as a campaign issue; journalistic accounts find it in five of the six instances in which incumbents seeking re-election to the House in 1988 were defeated.[17] Only in the losing campaign of Rep. Joseph DioGuardi (Republican of New York), however, were issues of money in campaign finance important; in his case there were news reports of improprieties in his campaign fundraising.[18] Allegations of direct personal enrichment in the other losses apparently cut more deeply than issues of campaign funding.[19]

It is, of course, hard to say how often the issues of "legal" campaign finance are raised around the country in any given November. Perhaps the issue is most commonly raised in a candidate's rejection of PAC money and a challenge to the opponent to join the rejection. That rejection, though, tends to come most frequently from challengers whose prospects for PAC money are unpromising at best. Far more common, common knowledge tells us, are issues of "dirty" or negative campaigning. As a private committee of Californians observed:

> Although most voters decry the large amounts spent on campaigns, they have not translated their disapproval into votes against high-spending candidates.... In California, voters react more negatively to "dirty campaigns" than to expensive ones.[20]

In short, voters do not look to the reports of the Federal Election Commission to help them evaluate candidates.

If mass opinion is not strong enough to affect the outcomes of elections, what are its prospects for affecting the work of legislatures on issues of campaign finance? The structure of public opinion in the country appears to favor federal legislation just about as Congress wrote it in 1971 and 1974: in favor of reporting and full information, in favor of limits on all contributions and expenditures, and ambivalent or divided about public funding. Thus, the Court's decision in *Buckley* frustrates the public, just as it frustrates the Congress, by removing the legislative option of free-standing and mandatory limits on campaign spending.[21]

Certainly, there appears to be no public support for "deregulation" of any part of the system of campaign finance. Scholars and legislators may play with the possibilities of reducing or removing the contribution limits on individuals and/or lowering the restrictions on political parties. I know of no poll data on the party question, but reducing limits on individuals has not found favor. The wave of questions Harris asked in early 1980 included this one: "Generally speaking, would you favor or oppose doing away with the limits on contributions made by individual citizens?" Only 34 percent favored the proposal, and 60 percent opposed it.

As the Congress faces proposals for reform of the campaign finance system, it is worth recalling that while it has been divided along party lines about American campaign finance, differences in the public at large do not reflect party differences. Nor does newspaper opinion break along party lines; periodic collections of editorials reprinted in the *Congressional Record* contain zealous reform arguments by daily papers of all partisan stripes. All of that means, therefore, that partisan differences in congressional positions on reform will not necessarily be supported in the broader public. That lack of congruity, however, is possible largely because opinions about campaign finance and its reform are less salient and less organized in the mass public than they are for the people and parties in the Congress. Reform, much more likely, will be driven by those party concerns than by citizen opinion or preferences.

Congressional freedom to legislate reform is in another, less obvious way dependent on public opinion. In its *Buckley* decision the U.S. Supreme Court held, for the first time, that the major actors in the system of campaign finance were exercising First Amendment rights to freedom of speech, association, and political activity. The old saw that "money talks" was elevated to a constitutional principle. It followed, then, that the power of Congress (and state legislatures, via the Fourteenth Amendment) to restrict those First Amendment rights would be subjected to the Court's strictest scrutiny. Moreover, the Court narrowly circumscribed the interests on which legislatures could justify any restrictions on the new constitutional rights. They could act, said the Court, only to prevent "corruption" or "the appearance of corruption."

Why the Court chose to define the legitimate interests of legislatures so specifically and what it meant by corruption need not detain us here.[22] For an assessment of the force of opinion on legislative discretion the operative word is appearance—the *appearance* of corruption. The word and any meaning the justices may have had for it went unexplained in the long majority opinion in *Buckley*. Appearances to whom?—to all adults, to voters, to specialists, to "informed" opinion, or just to the justices? And what if appearances are deceiving, what if mass perceptions (or judicial perceptions) diverge from the "real" reality? Is the Court prepared to permit restrictions on First Amendment freedoms if they are legislated on the mistaken belief that genuine corruption is widespread in American legislatures?

There is little in the jurisprudence on campaign finance to answer those questions. In a deferred challenge to the FECA's limits on independent expenditures in publicly funded presidential campaigns, a federal district court dismissed an array of poll data from the Roper and Harris organizations. The polls dealt too generally with campaign finance, the trial court ruled; only evidence of negative public attitudes created specifically by the statutory section under question would apply.[23] But public opinion is general and diffuse; it is not structured by statutory section or specific component of the system of campaign finance. Only under the most unusual circumstances would the mass public be informed enough about the consequences of one particular statutory clause to be able to offer an opinion about it. How then does one demonstrate the "appearance of corruption"?

To the best of my knowledge, no federal or state regulation of campaign finance has ever been upheld in an American court on the basis of "appearances." In the Supreme Court the question is no clearer now than it was in 1976. The best analogous precedents are those of the 1970s in several cases on capital punishment. At that time the Court faced the issue of the contemporary meaning of the "cruel and inhuman punishment" clause of the Eighth Amendment. In the second of the cases, *Gregg v. Georgia*,[24] one three- man opinion (there being no majority opinion) faced the question head-on, relying primarily on evidence of state legislative action to restore capital punishment, the decisions of juries to impose it, and one statewide decision in a referendum. That same opinion—signed by Justices Stewart, Powell, and Stevens—also cited poll data in a footnote.[25] It is very probably the closest the Court has come to embracing the national sample survey.[26]

If indeed a great majority of Americans were to conclude that the system of campaign finance promoted massive, quid-pro-quo corruption, just how might that mass opinion be demonstrated to a Court eager to protect a newly fashioned First Amendment freedom? A record of legislative action, such as the justices referred to in capital punishment, is out of the question, for legislatures have been prevented from acting by the very *Buckley* decision to which they might seek an exception. Alternatively, the Congress might simply build a legislative record in hearings and floor debate that such appearances exist and then proceed to act on that record. Otherwise, American courts would seem to have to depend on poll data—or on statewide initiative or referendum votes. The problem, of course, is that legislatures have no clear idea what data or what rhetoric will convince the Court.

If survey data do not convince the Court to broaden its grant of legislative authority, the public has two remaining avenues to reform. It is always possible that the electorate of some state will pass an initiative that the Supreme Court might consider an intolerable restriction on First Amendment freedoms were it to be passed by the state legislature. Would the Court defer to a popular majority? Would the majority itself be evidence of the "appearances" of corruption that justified its action? Would the successful initiative thus be its own self-fulfilling constitutional prophesy? The way of the initiative or referendum is not open nationally, but the second solution to restricted legislative power is: the constitutional amendment. Several have been introduced in recent years, but they have garnered little support.[27] The conversion of public perceptions into constitutional amendments is a very problematic route for constitutional change.

Any assessment of the power of public opinion concerns both its direction and its importance for those who hold it. The direction of mass opinion about campaign finance inclines to limited reform. There is a general unhappiness about the flow of campaign money, a part perhaps of more general opinions about the influence of money, the ethics of public officials, and the accountability of government. On the more complex matters of campaign finance specifically, there is support both for the present regulation of campaign money and for the addition of spending limits. There is, however, no compelling mandate for the public funding of campaigns.

The salience or political importance of those opinions is another matter. Not many Americans seem to have made them high priority interests, and so they remain poorly understood and largely unorganized in the American public. On the other hand, these issues are highly salient and easily organized by the political parties. The interests of the parties, especially the office-holding *legislative* parties, will probably remain the dominant ones in the politics of reform.

Only a dramatic mobilization of opinion—an elevation of concern about campaign finance—might alter that situation. Visible scandal might work such a result, and so, possibly, might continued media mobilizations. Either would draw on the reinforcement of the old populist and Progressive worldview. Conceivably, either of the political parties might also mobilize substantial mass support around a reform program. That possibility—the joining of party interests and mass opinion—would indeed replay the reform scenario of 1974.

NOTES

1. A good part of the Congress's 1974 reform package, especially the limitations on expenditures, was declared unconstitutional by the Supreme Court in *Buckley v. Valeo*, 424 U.S. 1 (1976).

2. See Gabriel Almond and Sidney Verba, *The Civic Culture* (Princeton, N.J.: Princeton University Press, 1963) for data on the earlier, more confident time.

3. The Harris questions a year earlier (April, 1983) were different:

> Many business, labor, and other groups have formed political action committees, or PAC's, that support and give money to candidates for office. How much would you trust [the type of PAC] if that group were to support and give money to a candidate for President in 1984—a great deal, somewhat, not very much, or not at all?

Consumer PACs won 61 positive responses, pro-environment PACs 51 percent, pro-ERA PACs 43 percent, a labor union PAC 35 percent, a business corporation PAC 40 percent, and an oil industry PAC 31 percent.

4. The three preceding questions (asked in 1979, 1982, and 1984) inserted the words "from other sources" after the words "all private contributions."

5. William Schneider, "Opinion Outlook," *The National Journal* (December 21, 1985).

6. I am very indebted to Joseph Cantor of the Congressional Research Service of the Library of Congress for making available the CRS file of public opinion polls about campaign finance.

7. The entire question is worth noting as an example of survey questions that evoke positive images in respondents, in this case the image of concerned individual political action. "As you know, a political action committee or PAC is composed of individuals who contribute funds, as a committee, to support candidates and may be composed, for example, of employees, union members or citizens concerned about a particular cause or issue. Generally speaking, do you think political action committees should or should not be allowed to contribute financially to political candidates?"

8. The Michigan Chamber also asked a question about public funding of state legislative elections; its terms, however, focused heavily on taxpayer dollars and taking money away from

other programs, and only 21 percent responded positively. Democratic respondents gave 27 percent support, Republicans 17 percent, and only one percentage point separated union and white collar workers.

9. The percentage of yes votes for that initiative (Proposition 200) and the vote for the Democratic candidate for Superintendent of Public Instruction in each of the 15 Arizona counties correlates at a rho coefficient of -.75. In addition to the problems of small number of cases and limited extent of variation in one series, however, two of the Arizona counties, Maricopa (Phoenix) and Pima (Tucson), account for 77.3 percent of the entire statewide vote for Proposition 200.

10. The correlations with the Democratic percentages of registered voters in the counties were weak: rho coefficients of .12 with #68 and -.22 with #73. That latter coefficient may reflect Republican support for a proposal that renounced public funding.

11. Common Cause was a major organizer of support for the crucial 1974 amendments to the FECA. See Andrew S. McFarland, *Common Cause: Lobbying in the Public Interest* (Chatham, N.J.: Chatham House, 1984). Since then campaign finance reform has been high on its legislative agenda; it has also used that reform issue as a prominent fundraising and membership-boosting appeal.

12. Austin Ranney, *Channels of Power* (New York: Basic Books, 1983), 53.

13. I have set out this argument fully in an article "Campaign Money and the Press: Three Soundings," *Political Science Quarterly*, vol. 102 (Spring 1987), 25–42.

14. Sorauf, "Campaign Money and the Press."

15. See the *New York Times* editorials of October 21, 1988, and January 4, 1989; the editorial of December 12, 1988, contains the phrase "Smell No Evil" in the headline and then makes it clear in the text that the source is the "sewer." Referring to Congressional leadership, the editorial concludes: "Will they shut down the sewer or will the stench continue?"

16. I should mention one conspicuous exception despite its tendentious headline: an article by Charles R. Babcock, "$100 Million in Campaign Donations Belie Notion of Federal Limits," *Washington Post* (November 8, 1988).

17. In addition, one more was defeated in his party's primary, and an eighth, Rep. Mario Biaggi, having resigned too

late to remove his name from the ballot, did not campaign for reelection. "St Germain Out, but Incumbents Still Strong," *Congressional Quarterly* (Nov. 12, 1988), 3266–3270.

18. "An Election Lesson: Money Can Be Dangerous," *Congressional Quarterly* (Nov. 19, 1988), 3366–3367.

19. The conclusion of this sentence comports with the heat of popular opposition to a substantial pay raise for Congress in 1989; it also suggests that the issue of ending honoraria would be more potent with the public than campaign finance reform.

20. California Commission on Campaign Financing, *The New Gold Rush: Financing California's Legislative Campaigns* (Los Angeles: Center for Responsive Government, 1985), 51.

21. *Buckley v. Valeo*, 426 U.S. 1 (1976). The Supreme Court struck down all limits on spending, whether by the candidates themselves or by independent spenders. And by considering the contributions of candidates to their own campaigns to be expenditures, it struck down legislative limits on them, too.

22. I have dealt more fully with those questions and the jurisprudence of *Buckley* in "Caught in a Political Thicket: The Supreme Court and Campaign Finance," *Constitutional Commentary*, vol. 3 (winter 1986), 97–121. For a comprehensive review of the Court's jurisprudence on campaign finance, see Marlene Arnold Nicholson, "Basic Principles or Theoretical Tangles: Analyzing the Constitutionality of Government Regulation of Campaign Finance," *Case Western Reserve Law Review*, vol. 38 (1987–88), 589–607.

23. *FEC v. NCPAC*, 578 F. Supp. 797 (E.D. Pa 1983). On review the U.S. Supreme Court simply agreed with the three-judge panel below that "the evidence falls far short of being adequate for this purpose." *FEC v. NCPAC*, 105 S. Ct. at 1470 (1985). In the trial court the plaintiffs had introduced results of a specially commissioned Roper poll, the most relevant question of which asked:

> Since 1971 [sic] nearly every presidential candidate has chosen to receive Federal funds rather than raise his money from outside sources. But in recent elections some private interest groups have spent very large sums of money on television advertising to support a particular candidate. Some people say this is quite all right and very different from giving the same amount of money directly to the candidate. Others say it is a purely technical way of getting around the 1971 law and should

> be stopped. Do you think it is all right or should be stopped?

Although 65 percent thought it should be stopped, the court thought their views "suggestive" but "fatally" incomplete. The poll does not follow up on the question and ask why those so responding believe independent expenditures should be stopped (p. 827).

24. 428 U.S. 153 (1976).

25. *Gregg v. George*, footnote 25, 181.

26. In the earlier of the capital punishment cases, *Furman v. Georgia*, 408 U.S. 238 (1972), 385–86, Chief Justice Burger, in a dissenting opinion, cited a 1966 poll but covered his jurisprudential tracks completely:

> Without assessing the reliability of such polls, or intimating that any judicial reliance could ever be placed on them, it need only be noted that the reported results have shown nothing approximating the universal condemnation of capital punishment that might lead us to suspect that the legislatures in general have lost touch with current social values.

There is also an interesting periodical literature on the issue of opinion and capital punishment. See Neil Vidmar and Phoebe Ellsworth, "Public Opinion and the Death Penalty," *Stanford Law Review*, vol. 26 (June 1974), 1245–1270; and Austin Sarat and Neil Vidmar, "Public Opinion, the Death Penalty, and the Eighth Amendment: Testing the Marshall Hypothesis," *Wisconsin Law Review*, vol. 1976 (1976), 171–206.

27. See, for example, H. J. Res. 628, 97th Congress, 2d Session (December 8, 1982), introduced by Rep. Jonathan Bingham for himself and 12 other members of the House. It stated:

> Section 1. The Congress may enact laws regulating the amounts of contributions and expenditures intended to affect elections to Federal offices.
>
> Section 2. The several States may enact laws regulating the amounts of contributions and expenditures intended to affect elections to State and local offices.

12

Enhancing Enforcement

Kenneth A. Gross

The history of regulating campaign financing in the United States has been fraught with abuses, disappointments, and failures. Often problems have stemmed from inadequate or nonexistent enforcement. Prior to 1974, federal campaign finance laws were largely ignored.[1] When the 1974 Amendments to Federal Election Campaign Act ("FECA") sought to toughen the laws and create a civil enforcement agency, the Federal Election Commission ("FEC" or "Commission"), some criticized the changes as too little and too late.[2] In response to the landmark Supreme Court ruling in *Buckley v. Valeo*, the 1976 amendments to the law reconstituted the FEC as an independent executive branch agency with exclusive jurisdiction over civil enforcement of the FECA.[3] The Department of Justice continued to have jurisdiction over criminal enforcement of the FECA. Thus, under the present structure, the effectiveness of any campaign finance reforms depends upon the ability of the FEC and the Department of Justice to assure their enforcement.

The FECA's enforcement procedures have been criticized since the creation of the FEC. Congress and the FEC have implemented substantial revisions to the original enforcement procedures, however, these reforms have not quelled the tide of criticism. Most of the recent criticisms directed at the FECA relate to two problems: lack of respondent's due process and lack of deterrence.

Aspects of the enforcement process impinge upon the due process rights of respondents, the political committees and individuals who are subject to investigation. Respondents are not able to address the Commission in person and the Office of General Counsel ("OGC"), the Commission's lawyers, summarize the respondent's written responses to the Commission. Respondents are also unable to see much of the evidence against them or to challenge OGC's final recommendations to the Commission.

Lack of deterrence is another problem. Some participants

in the political process believe that the campaign laws need be given little regard because the chance is slim that noncompliance will be detected and any penalty will probably be small and will come long after the election.

The two problems, lack of due process and lack of deterrence, are addressed below, with recommendations for revisions to the process that will hopefully build on the steps already taken by the Commission. Other recommendations will require legislative action. Before turning to the recommendations, however, it is necessary to consider briefly the present make-up of the FEC and its enforcement process.

The Federal Election Commission

The FEC is composed of six voting members, each serving a six-year term. Each member is appointed by the President and is confirmed by the Senate. In addition to the six voting members, the Secretary of the Senate and the Clerk of the House of Representatives serve on the Commission as nonvoting *ex officio* members. Of the six voting members, no more than three members may be affiliated with the same political party. The voting membership is currently composed of three Democrats and three Republicans. All substantive decisions of the FEC require at least four affirmative votes. Each year the Commission elects a new chairman and vice chairman from among its voting members. The chairman and the vice chairman may not be affiliated with the same political party, and a member may serve as chairman only once during any term of office. The chairman has no more power than the other Commissioners. This maintains the political balance of the Commission.[4]

FEC Enforcement Process

The FEC's enforcement process is multi-stepped, with several unique provisions. An enforcement proceeding or a Matter Under Review ("MUR") may be initiated in two ways, either on the basis of (1) a complaint filed with the Commission ("complaint-generated") or (2) information found by the Commission in the normal course of its business ("internally-generated").

In either case the OGC prepares an analysis and recommendation as to whether or not there is reason to believe a violation has occurred or is about to occur. The Commission votes on the recommendations in a closed meeting. If four of the six Commissioners vote to find reason to believe a violation has occurred, an investigation ensues. If the Commission adopts OGC's recommendation to find no reason to believe a violation has occurred or is about to occur, the matter is dismissed.[5] If the OGC recommends reason to believe but the Commission finds no reason to believe, then the Commission must prepare a statement of reasons in support of its action. If the Commission deadlocks, then it must prepare a statement of reasons explaining its action. The Commission's actions are subject to judicial review.

Once the Commission has found reason to believe a violation may have occurred or is about to occur, it has broad investigative powers. Upon completion of its investigation, the OGC makes its recommendation to the Commission, the investigated party can respond in writing and the Commission makes its decision. The FEC then attempts to settle the matter through a conciliation agreement, which routinely includes a detailed recitation of the facts, conclusions of law, an admission of a violation, and a civil penalty. If the respondent does not voluntarily enter into a conciliation agreement with the FEC, the Commission must bring an action on a *trial de novo* basis in a United States district court.

After the 1979 enactment of amendments to the FECA, the Commission supported a short-cut procedure referred to as preprobable cause conciliation. This is frequently used to reach an early agreement. A request for preprobable cause conciliation must be made prior to the mailing of the OGC's probable cause brief. After that point, as a matter of internal policy, the Commission will not enter into preprobable cause conciliation. If the respondent makes a timely request for preprobable cause conciliation, upon completion of the OGC's investigation, the Commission will offer the respondent a draft conciliation agreement as a basis for settlement. If an agreement is reached, it has the same effect as an agreement reached after probable cause has been found. If an agreement is not reached, the investigation proceeds as previously described.

Although the conciliation process is limited to ninety days by statute, the Commission will enter into a conciliation agreement beyond that time period if necessary to avoid litigation. Once suit is filed, however, a settlement must come in the form of a consent order signed by the court. The FEC will not voluntarily dismiss its lawsuit and enter into a conciliation agreement.

Regardless of the penalty amount in the Commission's offer to settle in the conciliation process, the Commission will sue for the statutory maximum, which is 100 percent of the amount in violation or $5,000, whichever is higher. If the Commission alleges that the violation is knowing and willful, it will ask the court to impose a penalty of 200 percent of the amount in violation or $10,000, whichever is higher. Once the matter is in litigation, there is a substantial risk that the court will impose a higher penalty than the Commission's offer to settle during the administrative conciliation process. Nonetheless most respondents before the FEC are more concerned with the glare of publicity than with the prospect of a penalty, which is usually low compared with the penalties that may be imposed in other types of cases by other federal agencies. The highest amount a respondent has ever agreed to pay the U.S. Treasury in a conciliation agreement was $398,140. That amount, agreed to by the Mondale for President Committee, included a civil penalty of $18,500, a repayment of $29,640, and an additional payment of $350,000, representing the amount of funds the committee received from improper sources. Public scrutiny and the concern of most respondents is heightened by litigating a matter rather than quietly settling through the MUR process. That is why the Commission is generally successful in getting respondents to admit to violations in conciliation agreements. Furthermore, because the risk and cost of litigation are great, an overwhelming majority of the cases are resolved during the conciliation process. Generally, the Commission files suit on less than 10 percent of the MURs and in some years, on less than 5 percent of the cases.[6]

Problems with the Enforcement Process

Several problems arising from the current enforcement process need to be redressed. First, the multi-staged enforcement process of the FEC is cumbersome. As a result, matters may not be resolved in as timely a manner as desired. Some violations that are not halted in time may affect the outcome of an election. (A civil penalty after the fact is a small price to pay for winning the race.) Others, if publicized before the election, might provide voters with important information to consider in their electoral decisions.

Another problem with the enforcement process is its use by political opponents as a weapon in their campaign arsenal.

Ideally, opposing political forces enhance the enforcement of the FECA by monitoring each other's activities and bringing abuses to the attention of the Commission by filing a complaint. In some cases, however, candidates and political organizations are badgered about minor oversights and forced to expend valuable resources responding to complaints that ultimately result in no offense. Underfunded candidates or organizations may be forced to spend valuable resources defending frivolous complaints filed by opponents.[7]

In addition, the present enforcement structure does not lend itself to the effective administration of cases involving factual and legal disputes. The procedural problems the Commission encounters in handling difficult factually disputed cases undermine the Commission's ability to effectively and expeditiously enforce sophisticated violations of the FECA. The investigations are open ended and the respondent's rights to be heard are muted by inaccessibility to the decision-makers. In cases involving such disputes, the relationship between the OGC and the respondent becomes adversarial and would more appropriately be handled under adjudicative rather than investigative procedures.[8]

In complex and difficult cases, the limitations of the current process impair the due process rights of respondents. Much of the inquiry occurs without their ability to appear before the Commission in person. Often their own side of the story is primarily presented to the Commission in a summary prepared by their "adversary," the Office of General Counsel.

Finally, in cases where the FEC and the respondent are not able to agree to a conciliation, the subsequent trial cannot rely upon findings of fact from the previous investigation during the MUR. Scarce Commission resources are expended twice to establish the same violations.

Reforms to Enhance Enforcement

Four reforms could help alleviate many of these problems and facilitate the effectiveness of the campaign finance laws, as well as their ability to promote accountability. Many of these reforms do not require statutory revisions.

The Two-Track System

The Commission's enforcement cases tend to fall into two broad categories: (1) matters involving little or no investigation—"routine cases" and (2) matters involving difficult legal issues and/or requiring a thorough factual investigation—"complex cases." Although the Commission presently has a tracking system to distinguish the complexity of cases, the procedure for handling these matters is essentially the same regardless of their track assignment. This lack of differentiation tends to unnecessarily protract routine cases and deprive the respondent of due process rights in complex cases. Thus, it is suggested that the cases be divided into routine cases, "Track I MURs," and complex cases, "Track II MURs." There are cases that do not fall neatly into either category. Thus, the suggested procedures are not rigid and allow a respondent to settle a matter at any point in the proceeding and avoid the Track II formalities.

In complaint-generated MURs, the FECA prescribes that the respondent be given an opportunity to respond to the complaint before the Commission considers whether a violation has occurred or is about to occur. There is no comparable notice prior to a reason to believe finding in internally-generated MURs. The Commission should amend its procedures so that the OGC provides notice to the respondent of possible violations in internally-generated MURs before reason to believe is found. If the respondent is provided an opportunity to be heard before the reason to believe finding is made, it may be able to provide the Commission with an acceptable explanation of the apparent violation and avert a reason to believe finding.[9]

The processing of many cases could also be accelerated if the Commission revised its procedures to expand the use of preprobable cause conciliation. If the Commission finds reason to believe a violation has occurred in a case involving an apparent violation found in a review of the public record or on the face of a document, it should offer a proposed conciliation agreement along with the reason to believe notice. Examples of cases that would be suitable for this expedited process are matters related to: (1) late-filers; (2) the failure to include the proper disclaimer in campaign materials; and (3) excessive and corporate contributions which do not raise factual disputes.[10]

Routine MURs meeting the Track I requirements could be settled within thirty days of a reason to believe finding if a conciliation agreement is offered simultaneously with the reason to believe finding. In most of these cases, the respondent's only defense would be to attempt to mitigate the violation. If a respondent were unwilling to settle on this expedited basis, then the matter would be retracked as a Track II case and resolved under the procedures below.

In 1987, more than half of the cases which ended in a conciliation agreement involved routine reporting or disclaimer violations. In the first four months of 1988, approximately 75 percent of the cases resolved through conciliation were routine in nature, requiring little or no investigation. In virtually all of those matters the respondents merely argued mitigating factors and did not contest the Commission's finding of a violation. Resolving routine cases in this fashion will substantially alleviate limited staff resources to focus on more complex cases. For cases requiring an investigation and those cases that cannot be resolved under Track I, the OGC would give the MUR a Track II designation. In Track II cases, upon the Commission's finding of reason to believe, the matter would be assigned to an administrative law judge ("ALJ") and would be handled under adjudicative procedures rather than investigative procedures. It is not likely that a large number of cases would require an adjudication. If the number of cases was small, the FEC could use ALJs from other agencies on a temporary basis.

Use of Administrative Law Judges

Enforcement agencies adjudicate facts in several ways, but the most common method is in accordance with the Administrative Procedure Act ("APA") with ALJs presiding over the investigation and briefing process.[11] There are numerous successful models for the functioning of ALJs throughout the executive branch.[12] An ALJ would oversee the development of an accurate and complete record of the facts relevant to the proceeding and render a fair and equitable decision on the merits and record. The OGC would conduct the investigation and bring the evidence adduced before the ALJ, but the complainant could provide additional evidence during the course of the investigation. ALJs cannot make final agency determinations; all decisions would be appealable to the Commission. Because the ALJ proceeding would create a record for review by the Commission and the court, if necessary, such cases should be directly appealed to the United States Court of Appeals for the District of Columbia Circuit. *De novo* review by a trial court would be unnecessary. Nothing in this procedure would prevent the respondent from seeking a settlement of the matter through the conciliation process.

The use of Administrative Law Judges would benefit the system in many ways:

(a) The enforcement process would be structured in a trial-like fashion with deadlines for the investigative period. An ALJ would determine deadlines on a case-by-case basis.

(b) The respondent would have an opportunity to present oral argument and witnesses before the ALJ.

(c) In appropriate cases an ALJ could evaluate a matter on an expedited basis, similar to an application for a temporary restraining order, develop a file for Commission review, and recommend relief.

(d) The respondent could request documents from the Commission once the investigation is complete, and disagreements between the OGC and the respondent over investigative documents could be resolved quickly.

These two reforms address many of the problems under the current system. The two-track system will provide for timely resolution of minor infractions, with benefits for citizens and political practitioners alike. Electoral outcomes will not be able to be distorted because of uncorrected violations. Political actors will not waste resources using a cumbersome process to respond to trivial complaints. The second part of the two-track system will help to overcome some of the weaknesses of the FEC as it attempts to resolve serious infractions. Deadlines will be set for the investigations. Matters that require review by the court will not require a new trial before consideration by the appeals court. The due process rights of respondents will be better protected and the resources of the FEC can be concentrated on complex cases and appeals rather than minor violations and redundant investigations.

The following proposals are directed to the problem of lack of deterrence. Too many participants in the system believe the chances of getting caught are slim and, if caught, the penalty is worth the benefit of non-compliance. When Congress removed the FEC's random audit authority in the 1979 amendments to the FECA, it removed an effective enforcement tool.

Random Audits

Congress should reinstate random audits. The present "for cause" audit provision implemented by Congress in the 1979 amendments to the FECA does not necessarily result in audits of the committees that are most likely to have serious compliance problems. As long as a political committee's FEC filings are in order, a committee could be engaging in serious misconduct and never be audited. The less sophisticated committees that lack the resources to ensure that their reports do not have factual errors are the committees that are likely to be audited.

Penalties

Random audits will only provide part of the incentive needed to assure compliance with the law. Increasing the likelihood of being caught must be coupled with more severe penalties for the offense. But the Commission could be criticized for unfairly departing from past practices if it dramatically increased its civil penalties without proper notice and justification. Therefore, in raising penalties, the FEC should publish civil penalty guidelines for most violations as well as the criteria for determining the penalties. Parameters could be set for violations such as excessive and corporate contributions. The schedules could allow for adjustments depending on aggravating and mitigating factors. Establishing and publicizing more severe penalties may increase deterrence as well as promote consistent expediency in reaching conciliation agreements.

Taken together, these four reforms would help correct many problems that arise from the current enforcement process. They would facilitate effective enforcement which is essential to prevent corruption in the campaign finance system. They would enhance the legitimacy of the FEC and the accountability of violators. Strengthening and expediting the enforcement procedures would also allow the Commissioners to focus their efforts on policy decisions, rather than enmesh them in the administration of complex and disputed cases. Finally, staff and monetary resources would be preserved to allow for the enhanced enforcement necessary for implementing current laws and many of the reforms proposed for the campaign finance system.

Notes

1. *See* The Tillman Act of Jan. 26, 1907, ch. 420, 34 Stat. 864 (1907); Federal Corrupt Practices Act of 1925, ch. 368, tit. III, 307, 43 Stat. 1070, 1072 (1925) (codified in scattered sections of Titles 2, 18 U.S.C.); Smith-Connally War Labor Disputes Act

of 1943, ch. 144, 57 Stat. 163 (1943); and Labor Management Relations Act of 1947 (Taft-Hartley Act) ch. 120, 304, 61 Stat. 136, 159 (1948).

In 1971, Congress enacted the Federal Election Campaign Act to require fuller disclosure of political campaign contributions with the Department of Justice enforcing the law. Federal Election Campaign Act of 1971, Pub. L. No.92-225, 201, 301(a), 86 Stat. 3, 8, 11 (1973) (amending 18 U.S.C. 591 (1970) (repealed 1980), reprinted in [1972] U.S. Code Cong. & Ad. News 3.

2. A statement from the General Accounting Office Comptroller General to the Congress in his *Report to the Office of Federal Elections of the General Accounting Office in Administering the FECA of 1971*, at 22.

3. One final outcome of an FEC enforcement action may be a referral to the Justice department for possible criminal indictment.

4. Other commentators have blamed inadequacy of the FEC enforcement process on the structure of the six-member Commission. For example, Commissioner Reiche's analysis cites the structure of the Commission as a debilitating factor in the Commission's attempts to enforce the law.

5. The complainant may file a petition to review the dismissal in the United States District Court for the District of Columbia. In reviewing the Commission's action, the court will review the factual and legal analysis set forth in the OGC's report to the Commission.

6. For example, in Fiscal Year 1987 the Commission opened 222 internally-generated MURs and 148 complaint-generated MURs. The Commission voted to institute suit on only ten matters. Some of the ten matters related to MURs opened in previous years.

7. FEC compliance matters are confidential. The confidentiality provision was intended to protect against the use of unwarranted complaints designed to unfairly generate negative publicity about a candidate. A recent article in *Congressional Quarterly's Campaign Practices Report* provides several examples of this occurring. Consideration should be given to lifting the confidentiality requirements, at least at the end of the investigative phase of the MUR. "Complaints File to Generate Adverse Publicity Are A Growing Problem for FEC and State Commissions," *Congressional Quarterly's Campaign Practice Reports*, Volume

16, (March 20, 1989): 2.

8. The discussion accompanying the recommendations of the American Bar Association (ABA) points out that "[a]t the point where the General Counsel has recommended in his brief that the Commission find probable cause to believe a violation has occurred, the position of the General Counsel and that of the respondent are clearly adversarial. In deciding whether the arguments should be given more weight, the Commission is in effect exercising a judicial function." ABA Report at p. 5.

9. ABA made the same recommendation in its proposals. The ABA also stated that it believed the Commission may implement this procedure without a statutory amendment. ABA Report at p. 4.

10. The Commission amended its procedures to provide for the offering of a conciliation agreement simultaneously with the reason to believe notice in late-file matters. The Commission adopted this new procedure on an experimental basis. This constructive new procedure should be made a permanent part of the process and expanded to other routine type violations.

11. A statutory change would be necessary to provide for adjudications and ALJs.

12. Examples of federal agencies using ALJs are the National Labor Relations Board, Social Security Administration, Department of Agriculture, Interstate Commerce Commission, Federal Communications Commission, Federal Trade Commission, Federal Energy Regulatory Commission, National Transportation Safety Board, Maritime Administration, Securities and Exchange Commission, Environmental Protection Agency, Occupational Safety and Health Administration and Nuclear Regulatory Commission.

13

Weakness of the FEC

Frank P. Reiche

The Federal Election Commission (FEC) has generally been praised for its role in collecting, collating and disseminating detailed information concerning the financing of federal elections. While operating with limited resources, the Public Records Office and the Commission's Division of Information have provided a wealth of detail concerning the finances of candidates, political parties and political committees.

Equally universal as the praise received by the Commission for its disclosure activities is the criticism directed at it for allegedly lax enforcement of the Federal Election Campaign Act (FECA). "Toothless Tiger", "Ineffectual Watchdog" and "Pussycat" are but three of the descriptive phrases applied to the Commission's enforcement efforts.[1]

Congressional sources have frequently urged the Commission to concentrate its limited enforcement resources on major violations of the FECA where there appears to have been intentional wrongdoing. What Congress has consistently failed to acknowledge is that achieving a reasonable level of disclosure requires effective enforcement, both with respect to intentional and unintentional violations of the Act, since serious political damage can be inflicted by the unintentional as well as the intentional acts of individuals, parties and committees.

Of even greater concern, however, is the widespread public perception that a number of major enforcement decisions have been affected by partisan considerations, which bears directly on the credibility of the FEC as an effective watchdog. The importance of *public* credibility to an agency such as the FEC is not sufficiently appreciated in Washington, although it is a broadly accepted concept on the state level. Unfortunately, the Commission's lackluster enforcement record has diverted attention from its fine disclosure performance.

The FEC has regularly appeared on the endangered species list of many Congressmen and Senators. Indeed, there have been attempts to scuttle the Commission by a variety of means, including the withdrawal of sufficient budgetary support. During my term on the FEC, particularly during the first two or three years, rarely a month, or perhaps even a week, went by without some frontal assault on the Commission in Congress.

The picture before us today is even more distressing. While there have been fewer outward attempts to abolish the Commission during the past two or three years, it commands diminishing respect, particularly in enforcement matters. Commission critics argue that there have been more and more partisan votes on a number of significant issues, some in enforcement cases and others on advisory opinions. The Commission's 1984 refusal to reopen its inquiry into Geraldine Ferraro's 1978 campaign and the Commission's decision with respect to expenditures by President Bush's Michigan committee in 1986, as well as the more recently decided National Republican Senatorial Campaign Committee matter, are but three examples of cases that have contributed toward the perception that Commission decisions are indeed influenced by partisan considerations. To those who doubt the validity of this perception, I would suggest merely that they examine in detail the decisions reached by the Commission over the years in executive sessions and the issues involved.

Some of the matters to which I refer are mere perceptions, but perceptions or not, they are held by sufficiently large numbers of people to warrant the attention of the Commission and Congress. As numerous critics have observed, the perceptions of partisanship and lax enforcement are sufficient by themselves to tarnish the credibility of the FEC. If there is a perception, much less the reality, that the fair enforcement of our campaign finance laws is tainted, then the entire fabric of our democratic society has suffered a damaging blow.

In the FEC's defense, it should be noted that the inability of the Commission to deal promptly with campaign finance abuses and seemingly, in the eyes of many observers, to be subject to partisan pressures, accurately reflects the intention of Congress to establish a weak agency responsive to the political wishes of the existing power base. As Brooks Jackson noted in *Honest Graft*, "Congress designed the Commission to fail, building in the propensity for partisan deadlocks, insisting on the appointment of pliant Commissioners, and creating a morass of procedural defenses for suspected wrongdoers."[2] And yet, it is this same

Congress from which the sharpest criticisms of the Commission emanate.

Since reforms must originate in the Congress, it is important to understand Congress' perception of the Commission. Clearly Congress considers the FEC a partisan body. One need but examine the comments of various Senators with respect to the confirmation of a proposed appointee to the Commission some time ago in order to verify this conclusion. These include the following:

> "Yet we have a partisan Federal Election Commission that everybody understands is partisan..." (Senator Orrin G. Hatch, R-Utah)
>
> "This is a unique position which requires, in addition to basic qualifications, a strong partisanship." (Senator Gordon J. Humphrey, R-New Hampshire)
>
> "Unfortunately, it is a very partisan body [FEC]; and if those of us on this side want our rights to be watched carefully and protected, we must have a strongly partisan representative on that Commission." (Senator Gordon J. Humphrey, R-New Hampshire)
>
> "While it was recognized during the original debate when the FEC was created that it should be an independent agency we did recognize that it would not be non-partisan...." (Senator Robert Dole, R-Kansas)[3]

What is more frightening than the expression of such views is the fact that many Members of Congress have now sincerely convinced themselves that not only is the existence of partisanship an established fact, but it is also a reflection of what the Commission should be. Thus has grown up a tradition of partisanship which is in marked contrast with the less partisan and sometimes non-partisan traditions of many state campaign finance agencies. It is against this backdrop of partisanship that any proposals for the reform of the FEC must be examined.

Reforming the FEC

Turning to a consideration of various proposals that have been advanced for changes in the organization and direction of the FEC, let us first direct our attention to the process by which individuals are appointed to the Commission. Prior to the *Buckley v. Valeo* decision in 1976, the appointment authority lay not only with the president, but also with congressional leaders. As a consequence of that decision, the appointment authority was vested solely in the president, but, by tradition, all succeeding administrations have permitted congressional leaders to submit approved lists to the White House in advance of appointments. This has led inevitably to domination of the process by Congress.

In light of this procedure, combined with the strongly-held view of many senators and congressmen on both sides of the political aisle that those appointed to the Commission serve primarily as representatives of their respective parties, the perceived partisan orientation of many appointees, conscious or subconscious, is readily understandable. Where an appointee's selection is heavily dependent on the participation of legislative leaders, it is only natural that the appointee feel some loyalty toward such leaders and the political party of which he or she is a member.

Every effort should be made to minimize the role of Congress in the appointment process, thereby leaving the responsibility to the president. There is no guaranteeing that such appointments, if left to the president, would result in reducing the partisan inclinations of appointees, but if responsibility for such appointments were centralized in the White House, there would at least be a greater degree of accountability than exists at present. The success of this proposal depends upon a president taking the high political road and seeking people of recognized quality in making appointments to the Commission, as have many governors in various states. Unfortunately, there has been little indication, past or present, that the occupants of the White House would be willing to stand up to Congress in this regard. Furthermore, there is no apparent likelihood of any attitudinal change in Congress' view of the appointment process.

There is also the question of the length of service of a Commissioner; i.e., should their terms continue to run for six years and should they be limited to one or two terms? If an individual Commissioner wishes to be re-appointed for a second or third term, his or her votes will be closely scrutinized by Members of Congress and by the White House as the time for his or her re-appointment approaches. There are those who would suggest that actual decisions have been affected by such considerations. I frankly have not examined any of these allegations in detail and therefore am not in a position to comment on their accuracy, but once again, the mere perception that a Commissioner might, consciously or subconsciously, tailor his or her views as re-appointment time approaches is cause for concern and impacts directly on the credibility of the Commission.

Instead, I would suggest that the terms remain at six years and that Commissioners not be eligible for re-appointment. Not only would this enable individual Commissioners to be their own persons while serving in this capacity, but also, six years is a long enough time to serve in such a politically sensitive post and affords a person ample opportunity to make the contribution of which he or she is capable.

What personal qualifications and attributes should FEC nominees possess? Obviously a judicial temperament is helpful. While the ability to communicate one's views with clarity and succinctness is important, equally important is the willingness to listen and to reflect upon the views expressed by others. If one approaches service on a campaign finance commission such as the FEC with an open mind and intellectual integrity, it can readily become a political graveyard, since you are bound to antagonize people in the process. It therefore helps to minimize potentially divisive partisan tendencies if the people selected do not have any immediate political ambitions. Obviously, practical experience is desirable and it goes without saying that the acknowledged intelligence and integrity of potential appointees are of great importance.

In New Jersey and many other states, we have learned that retired or semi-retired people are frequently good candidates. Unlike many other federal commissions, service on the FEC does not necessarily enhance one's attractiveness to potential employers after you have left the Commission. Hence, it is helpful if appointees have a profession or other job to which they may return or if they are people who are financially established.

As one who has experienced both the weak chairmanship of the FEC and a somewhat stronger chairmanship in New Jersey, I would urge that the FEC chairmanship be strengthened. The required rotation of the chairmanship at the FEC damages the Commission by depriving it of stability and continuity. While there must be limitations on the powers of the chairman of such a sensitive Commission, a rotating chairmanship not only ensures a weak chairmanship, but also contributes toward a weak Commission.

Among the powers of the chairman that should be expanded are the power to supervise the preparation of meeting agendas, more direct involvement in the day-to-day administration of the Commission (working closely with the Staff Director) and responsibility for preparing Commission budgets. To guard against upsetting the delicate political balance on the Commission, a person's term as chair might be established as four years with the president required to appoint someone from the opposing major political party.

Some question the efficacy of an even-numbered Commission and suggest that there should be an odd number so that a tie can be broken under any circumstance. That is frankly not my experience. Instead, I would suggest that it is not the number, but rather the openness, independence and intellectual curiosity of commissioners that matter. In addition, the work of this Commission is so politically sensitive that the unwillingness of either major political party to vest significant authority in a campaign finance commission that might be dominated by representatives of the other party is readily understandable.

Moving to a consideration of various ways in which Congress influences the conduct of Commission business, the Commission should be freed from the pressure of submitting an annual budget to individuals some of whom may have been the subject of Commission investigations. A shift to a two-year budget or even a four-year budget would ease the pressure and permit more long-range financial planning by the Commission, but perhaps a self-adjusting budget such as that used in California would be more feasible.

In *Honest Graft*, Brooks Jackson chronicled an incident involving an FEC Commissioner who was apparently called on the carpet, so to speak, by a congressional leader.[4] Clearly, there must be a shared respect by Commissioners and Members of Congress for the office of Commissioner. Commissioners can do much to alleviate the situation by keeping their distance from those who may have business before the Commission, but Members of Congress have an equal responsibility to refrain from any contact that might be viewed by the public as giving rise to a potential conflict of interest involving a Commissioner. What this really means is limiting the extent to which Commissioners participate in partisan political activities and yes, limiting their social contacts with Members of Congress and political party representatives.

One of the most frustrating restraints on the Commission has been the limitation upon its ability to investigate a matter in advance of finding reason to believe that a violation has occurred. This limitation is partially attributable to a conscious determination by the Commission and is also due to procedural safeguards built into the law by Congress. These safeguards were incorporated into the law on the theory that they would ensure constitutional due process for alleged violators. Instead, the Commission is frequently hamstrung in its efforts to investigate alleged violations. Many state campaign finance commissions and the legislatures of such states have found statutory ways of protecting an individual's constitutional rights while at the same time providing the commissions involved effective procedures by which to investigate and prosecute matters in timely fashion. Indeed, the FEC has much to learn from campaign finance agencies on the state level, just as the latter can profit from the FEC's experience.

In considering the type of Commission the FEC should be, I am not suggesting a vigorously activist Commission, such as the California Fair Political Practices Commission was during its early years. Nor do I favor one that instinctively avoids politically sensitive or politically controversial issues, an accusation frequently leveled at the FEC. While campaign finance commissions should not seek controversy and should try to avoid involvement in ways that directly affect the outcome of elections, neither can they nor should they abdicate their duty to determine issues fairly and legitimately presented to them.

A blue-ribbon study commission should be established by Congress for the purpose of reviewing not only the ways in which we finance our federal elections, but also the impact of this system on the number and quality of candidates seeking elective federal office. Although I believe that Congress should create such a commission, it must not be dominated by Congress if there is to be any reasonable chance for success.

Among those who should be considered for membership on such a panel would be representatives of Congress, the Executive Branch, and the two major political parties, as well as people with experience in the administration and enforcement of campaign finance laws and people having practical campaign experience. It would also be desirable to include representatives of business, labor, academia, the media and public interest groups, but none of these individuals should be appointed to represent a specific constituency.

The existence of such a panel does not guarantee the wisdom of all its recommendations, nor their adoption by Congress, It would, however, ensure that the expertise and collective judgment of an experienced, and yet diverse group of individuals would first be made available to Congress before substantive changes in the law were made.

While I am not optimistic that there will be a significant change in the outlook or operations of the FEC in the near future, I believe we should try to raise the consciousness level of the executive and legislative branches of our federal government until there is a publicly acknowledged awareness that our present campaign finance structure is simply not adequate for the job assigned to it and desperately requires major changes. Furthermore, only if candidates, political parties, political committees, politicians and the public eventually accept the fact that there is no place for hardball partisan politics in campaign finance will the chances for meaningful change be substantially improved. It is fair to say that the Commission is viewed by many as being preoccupied with its perceived congressional and political party constituencies and too little concerned with its primary constituency the general public.

It is frustrating and discouraging to be a proponent of change in our federal campaign finance laws. Crucial though the issues may be, they rarely attract much comment from congressional constituents. In addition, this is a self-defeating process since you are suggesting to a Congress that owes its very existence to the application of current laws that it would be fairer and in everyone's best interest for changes to be made. In essence, this is viewed by the entrenched incumbency on Capitol Hill as a frontal assault on their status and livelihood.

It will take a strong president and a high-minded Congress to accomplish meaningful campaign finance reform. While there has been little evidence of such a will on the part of our recent presidents and Members of Congress, we must maintain unrelenting pressure on both in an effort to bring about the substantial change that is needed if our participatory democracy is to be responsive to an ever-changing electorate.

Notes

1. *The Wall Street Journal*, October 19, 1987.

2. Brooks Jackson, *Honest Graft* (New York: Knopf, 1988), p. 308–09.

3. *Congressional Record*, July 25, 1979, S 10504, S 10519, S 10525, S 10531.

4. Jackson, *Honest Graft*, p. 258.

14

Prospects for Reform

David B. Magleby

Each of the previous chapters has explored problems with our system for financing congressional elections. Numerous reform proposals have been added to those already circulating in Congress. Important values are at stake in reforming the system or maintaining the status quo. Reforms must be carefully selected to balance these sometimes competing values in order to preserve and promote our representative democracy.

Unfortunately, the prospects for the passage of carefully crafted reform are slight, despite some hopeful signs in the late 1980s. Participants in the debate over congressional campaign finance have diverse partisan and institutional perspectives, different philosophical views on the role of government in elections, and they apply different standards in evaluating the need for reform. Previous experiences with the Supreme Court's overhaul of reforms in *Buckley v. Valeo*[1] and with the unintended consequences of the FECA and its amendments also give pause to thoughtful would-be reformers. How are we to assess the potential for successful reform in the context of so many constraints? Explaining why reform efforts succeed or fail and assessing the prospects for reform in the near future are the subjects of this chapter.

Factors Favoring Reform

As the 101st Congress convened in January, 1989, talk of congressional campaign finance reform was widespread. Leaders in both parties and in both houses cited it as an important issue. The early effort by Republicans to positively position themselves on the reform issue stood in stark contrast to their response in 1987 when the issue was largely defined and driven by Senate Democrats.

The Republican interest in reform is a change from their previous position. The behavior of PACs is one reason for the change in Republican attitudes. The 1988 elections again saw increased proportions of corporate PAC money flowing to Democratic incumbents, a source of growing Republican frustration and concern. In the 100th Congress, the Democrats were able to define the issue in their terms, and place Republicans on the defensive. Tired of defending a system which Democrats exploit—including political action committees—Republicans have decided not to leave the campaign finance reform playing field wide open to the Democrats. In short, Republicans have discovered that it is better to advance their own reform agenda than to be caught in a position of only blocking a Democratic bill.

But more seems to be changing than partisan posturing. Ethics in Congress and the executive branch are subjects of increased attention. Early in the 101st Congress, Speaker of the House Jim Wright (D-TX) and Majority Whip Tony Coelho (D-CA) resigned because of charges of violations of the ethics rules of the House. In Wright's case, the charges included acceptance of book royalties in lieu of honoraria, putting the Speaker over the honoraria limit. Ethics charges were also leveled against newly elected Republican Whip Newt Gingrich, who himself had filed the charges against Wright. The preoccupation with ethics issues in the first quarter of the 101st Congress, while not directly involving campaign finance, served to focus public attention on the importance of money in congressional life, especially the large and growing role of PACs.

The change in administration in 1989 also gave new emphasis to reform. The decision of President Bush to propose his own ethics and campaign finance reform package was a departure from the previous administration. Presidential interest in reform of congressional elections and ethics had not been part of the Reagan administration's policy agenda. Indeed, Ronald Reagan would likely have vetoed most reform proposals. In contrast, George Bush unveiled a plan which would dramatically limit political action committees and enhance the role of political parties. While the Bush proposals were quickly labeled by Democrats and the press as partisan, they nonetheless demonstrated that the new president perceived problems with the current system and had devised a plan to deal with them.

An additional factor favoring reform is the growing public and media criticism of honoraria for members of Congress. Honoraria typically come from interest groups and include speaking fees and travel expenses. These stipends are directed at Congressmen or Senators who can help with the interest group's legislative agenda. The Commission on Executive, Legislative and Judicial Salaries recommended that higher salaries for Congress, judges, and high-ranking executive branch officials be coupled with a ban on honoraria and other earned income that "conflicts with or appears to conflict with the performance of official duties."[2] Congressional sentiments appeared to be supportive of banning honoraria and the grandfather clause in the House. This clause permits House members elected before 1980 to convert unused campaign funds to personal use upon leaving office. However, when Congress voted down the salary increase, the ban on honoraria and the grandfather clause was put aside. There appears to be widespread congressional support for banning honoraria but not without a commensurate increase in salary. It is one thing for members to vote against an increase in pay, but quite another for them to vote for what in effect would be a reduction in pay.

Another factor favoring reform is the persistence of pressure from interests such as Common Cause. Perhaps more than any other issue, campaign finance reform has come to epitomize Common Cause in the late 1980s. Its President, Fred Wertheimer, has been identified with the issue for more than a decade. Not only is Common Cause important to the campaign finance issue, the campaign finance issue is important to Common Cause. Congressional campaign spending, especially the role of PACs, figures prominently in the membership drives and fundraising appeals of the lobby. Common Cause and its allied editorial writers can be expected to launch a major offensive again on this issue in the 101st Congress. The results of the 1988 elections will only add to their arguments that the soft money loophole is jeopardizing the presidential campaign finance system, that PACs continue to play too great a role in congressional campaign finance, and that the present system discourages competition and serves to create a permanent majority in the House.

Factors Constraining Reform

Despite developments that enhance the prospects for serious consideration of reforms in the near future, many other factors constrain the likelihood of reform as well as the shape it will take. First, the parameters for acceptable reforms are set by the Supreme Court, especially as expressed in *Buckley v. Valeo*. Campaign finance law, like all law, is subject to judicial interpretation. The court, by striking down part of the law, as it did with the 1974 Federal Election Campaign Act amendments in *Buckley v. Valeo* can powerfully change the law and set the terms of debate for subsequent legislative activity.

Because of *Buckley*, if Congress desires to enact spending limits, it must either make them part of a system of public financing which candidates may refuse, and in so doing avoid spending limits, or amend the Constitution to permit themselves to set spending limits without the *Buckley* strictures. The *Buckley* rejection of limits on independent expenditures is also important and could become even more important under future reform. The Court in *Buckley* retained limits on contributions by individuals and PACs to candidates, but struck the $1,000 independent expenditure limit for any individual or group. Either a reduction in the amount PACs can give a candidate or an aggregate candidate PAC receipts limit would almost certainly lead to an increase in independent expenditures.

A related difficulty may come from judicial review of future reforms. Provisions of carefully crafted laws can be stricken by the court, distorting the consequences of the provisions that remain. One option, included in some recent bills, is a severability clause which says that if part of the law is declared unconstitutional, then the entire provision or entire law is stricken.

Reformers are also aware that even if a law survives the Supreme Court intact (but especially if it does not), the unintended consequences may raise problems as bad as those they correct. Ironically, the FECA's contribution limits for individuals and PACs have made large contributors less dominant but have made fundraising more time-consuming and expensive. At least for House Democrats, one response has been increased dependence on PACs.[3] And the burgeoning number of PACs is itself the result of the FEC's interpretation that the law permits the formation of corporate, labor, and trade association PACs.[4] Bundling, soft money, personal PACs, and the political use of tax-exempt foundations are other examples of how adaptations to reforms can bring undesirable unintended consequences. The important point is that campaign finance reformers must not only attempt to anticipate the ways creative candidates, their advisors, and other campaign finance participants will play the game under the new rules, they must also anticipate which rules will survive court challenge and whether what remains after that court challenge is better or worse than the status quo.

Institutional Differences

Three institutional differences between the House and Senate have been important to reform as well. First, members of each chamber face different electoral risks. House members are in a perpetual campaign[5] and typically represent more homogeneous districts, but once elected, they are unlikely to be defeated. Conversely, the narrow margin of party control in the Senate and its greater prestige mean that far fewer Senate seats go without being seriously contested. House members tend to raise money to pre-empt challengers,[6] while Senate candidates understand that the chances are greater that they will need the money. Also, Senate races cost significantly more than House races, requiring a strong commitment to fundraising.

Second, the two chambers have differed in the levels of cooperation and comity. While the close partisan balance in the Senate adds to the competitiveness of Senate elections, it may also foster a greater spirit of bipartisan cooperation than in the House. For most of the 1980s, Republicans were in charge of the Senate, and they remain within striking distance of a majority. Furthermore, Republican senators feel more fairly treated with their Democratic counterparts in control than do House Republicans.

A third institutional difference also puts a premium on bipartisan cooperation in the Senate—the filibuster. In 1977 the House passed reform legislation, only to see it die in a Senate filibuster after three unsuccessful attempts to invoke cloture. The reform effort of the 100th Congress also encountered a filibuster, with Republicans holding their ground through a record eight cloture votes. It is possible that this exercise served to harden partisan positions rather than identify areas of possible agreement or compromise.

One important result of the different institutional perspectives and structures is that each chamber assumes it will craft the bill for itself. For instance, the 1987 Senate bill was primarily concerned with Senate elections. Had the bill passed, it was assumed that the House would craft its own bill. It is therefore likely, given what we know about the different circumstances and perspectives of the two houses, that the two houses could develop different legislative approaches to campaign finance. Whether one chamber would object to the other's approach is hard to predict.

Partisan Differences

Partisanship has been the major stumbling block to campaign finance reform in the past and remains the major obstacle to reform today. There are three ways partisanship is important to the prospects for congressional campaign finance reform—self interest, philosophy, and personality. As we will see, these three dimensions do not always reinforce each other, and perceptions about each can change. These three dimensions can be briefly defined as follows:

> *Self-interest*—what will campaign finance reform do to me or my party in subsequent elections? It is important to note a possible distinction between party self-interest and incumbent self-interest, a distinction most likely to be found in the minority party. Here the calculus is one of what impact proposed reforms will have on election outcomes.
>
> *Philosophy*—should government be involved in regulating campaign finance? Here the ideology of the participant towards the size and role of government as well as to the possible coercive power of the state in managing elections is the central element.
>
> *Personality*—do the issue leaders from both parties get along well enough to enter into negotiations? Here the central issue is whether personality barriers will make partisan negotiation difficult or impossible.

These three dimensions are not equally important. The work of Mayhew[7] and others would indicate that re-election is more important than philosophy or personality. With respect to personality differences, for instance, it is not uncommon for legislators to ignore previous personal differences when it is in their personal or legislative interest. But personal distrust and dislike can color perceptions about partisan self-interest or partisan philosophy.

Deep partisan differences are found in both houses, though to varying degrees. It is therefore important that we examine all three elements among partisans in both houses. Characterizations like those I am making do not apply to all members of a respective party, but rather reflect the more typical attitude.

House Democrats, in many ways, have the most to lose by reforming the system. If self-interest is defined in terms of securing re-election, the present system is working very well for them. Entrenched in the majority,[8] with increasing success in raising money from pragmatic corporate PACs[9] and strong support from organized labor, they have the ability to direct money to the few truly competitive districts in any given election and continue to hold a comfortable majority in the House. House Democrats are most vulnerable to reforms that deal with PACs, because they are especially dependent on them. Thus, any legislation that lowered PAC contributions or imposed an aggregate PAC limit could seriously damage their ability to raise money, at least in the short run. As a campaign committee staff person summarized, "from my standpoint, I don't need campaign finance reform... I think we're [Democrats] doing quite well with campaign finances."[10]

One caveat for House Democrats is that at some point public perceptions about the propriety of the present system, especially heavy dependence on PAC money, could change. If it were to do so they would have the most to lose. Therefore, one could argue, as many House Democrats do, that candidates must run for office under the present rules but simultaneously work to change those rules.

The idea of governmental involvement in monitoring and regulating the flow of money in congressional elections is not a major problem for many House Democrats. On balance, they see the costs of such governmental activity in tax dollars, loss of candidate autonomy, and a larger bureaucracy as worth bearing if they can achieve the benefits of reform—limit the rising costs of campaigns and the role of interested money, and permit a wider spectrum of persons to run for the House.

House Democrats appear to be caught between their self-interest and their philosophy toward reform. They became attached to reform as an idea when Republicans appeared to have a fundraising advantage. However, they are slowly coming to realize that the system works well for them. Democrats could rationalize their reform impulse with their self-interest by championing campaign finance reform that made them even more secure. They could do this in several ways, but the most apparent would be to impose spending limits that are too low, denying challengers sufficient funds to communicate their message.[11] The possibility that Democrats will succeed in proposing reforms that reinforce their grip on the House is of widespread concern to House Republicans.

The perception among House Democrats that Republicans

are attempting to exploit the ethics issue at the expense of House Speaker Jim Wright is an example of the politics of personality problem. No House Republican has been more outspoken or critical of Wright than Georgia Republican Newt Gingrich. Speaker Wright does not much care for Gingrich either. The reason this dispute is important to campaign finance reform is that Gingrich, with the beginning of the 101st Congress, has become the senior Republican on the Elections Subcommittee of the House Administration Committee, replacing Bill Frenzel (R-MN), who has taken the ranking Republican position on the Budget Committee. Gingrich has asserted himself in his new position, and intends to be a player in whatever campaign finance reform is considered by the House. How Democrats will respond to Gingrich in this new capacity remains to be seen, but his presence in the leadership may impose an interpersonal roadblock that reinforces their partisan self-interest in opposing reform.

House Republicans have the opposite mix of self-interest and philosophical concerns. The present system does not serve their partisan self-interest even though it may serve some individual Republicans very well. Majority Leader Michel's 1988 letter to PACs said that Republicans "find it disturbing to see so many contributions going to members who consistently oppose the interest you and other business leaders advocate."[12] Many of the proposed reforms would help challengers, a group that is disproportionately Republican. Incumbent House Republicans are not yet convinced that change could help their party or themselves. But it is clear that House Republicans are disillusioned with the status quo, and one of the objects of their frustration is current campaign finance practices.

If House Republicans could follow their ideology, they would, in the words of a senior campaign committee professional, "Have a law that said that every dollar given to a candidate must be reported. It must be reported in a timely manner and advertised to the general public so the public and the voter always knows who gave what to whom. That's all I'd do." Republicans are especially opposed to spending limits. Republican opposition to recent comprehensive reform bills also reflect a Republican view that less government is preferred.

The politics of House Democratic personalities on the campaign finance issue also have stood in the way of bipartisan coalition building. Former Majority Whip Tony Coelho (D-CA) and other House Democratic leaders, most notably former Speaker

Jim Wright (D-TX), were anathema to many House Republicans. They personified an arrogance of power best exemplified by the "stealing of the Indiana 8th Congressional district." In the 1984 House election, Republican challenger Richard McIntyre had been certified as the winner by the secretary of state—a reversal of the unofficial vote count which had Democratic incumbent Frank McCloskey leading. Part of the explanation for the difference was the fact that punch-card ballots in two counties had been run through a punch-card reader twice. But in what was interpreted by the Republicans as a purely partisan move, a special task force, comprised mostly of Democrats, counted some absentee and disqualified ballots but refused to count others, declared McCloskey, the Democrat, the winner by four votes.

The effect of the McCloskey/McIntyre dispute is but one manifestation of what House Republicans felt to be the arrogant use of power by Jim Wright and Tony Coelho. The departure of Wright and Coelho may reduce the partisan distrust of Republicans towards Democrats but it may also result in greater hostility towards Democrats. In the days and weeks following the resignations of Wright and Coelho there was open talk among Democrats of settling the score with Gingrich and the Republicans. At the very least, the problems of Wright and Coelho served to heighten Democratic concerns about the electoral consequences for individual members and the Democratic party and gave new hope to the beleaguered Republicans as they entered the 1990s.

Senate Republican individual and partisan self-interest in many ways coincides with House Republicans. Their earlier success in getting corporate PAC money has declined relative to the Democrats as the result of a more aggressive Democratic PAC fundraising effort able to capitalize on the possibility, and then the reality of Democratic control. Republican Senate Leader Robert Dole's chastisement of corporate PACs in 1988 for their support of Democrats was similar in tone and content to the message of House Minority Leader Michel.[13] In sum, it appears that Republicans are uncertain of the extent to which the present system works for them, and are willing to threaten, if not seriously consider, reform.

One obstacle to reform is the Republican opposition to an expanded role for government in election regulation. Senate Republicans share the predisposition of House Republicans that less regulation is almost always better, though they appear less strongly attached to this view. One outspoken critic was Idaho Senator

Symms. He characterized the Boren-Byrd bill as "Changing our electoral system from one based on the principle of voluntary participation to one based on the socialist principle of forced participation."[14]

By most indications, the Senate appears not to suffer from the same interpersonal friction on this issue as exists in the House. The Democrat most identified with recent reform efforts, David Boren (D-OK), is someone Republicans have worked with before. Boren's PAC limitation bill in the 99th Congress was cosponsored by Barry Goldwater, and when considered on the floor won 26 Republican votes. Boren's chief cosponsor in the 100th Congress, Majority Leader Robert Byrd, may have made the bill so high-profile as to scare away Republicans, but it is more likely that the bill's use of public financing and spending limits was what turned off Republicans.[15] Regardless of the greater Senate comity, if reforms do not properly balance partisan interests, the outcome will likely be a filibuster.[16]

Senate Democrats are the least torn by ideological and self-interest inconsistency on the campaign finance issue. Their return to the majority in 1987 will make fundraising among corporate and other business interests easier, but the electoral status quo is not stacked in their favor as it is for their House Democratic counterparts. Senate Democrats are also comfortable with an enlarged governmental role in financing and regulating elections. Finally, there is comparatively little personal friction on this issue in the Senate, making future bipartisan negotiations possible.[17]

Table 14.1 summarizes the perspectives for the party groups in each House on comprehensive campaign finance reform.

Table 14.1

	Barriers to Comprehensive Reform		
	Self-Interest	Philosophy	Personality
House Dems.	*Barrier*	*No Barrier*	*Barrier*
House Reps.	*Uncertain*	*Barrier*	*Barrier*
Senate Reps.	*Uncertain*	*Barrier*	*No Barrier*
Senate Dems.	*No Barrier*	*No Barrier*	*No Barrier*

Given this analysis of the role of perceived self-interest, philosophy towards a larger role for government in financing elections, and the politics of personality on these issues, it is not surprising that the group most predictably in favor of reform is the Senate Democrats. None of these factors are barriers to action by them, and indeed for many the first two factors are reasons to initiate reform. Republicans are uncertain about their self-interest, not knowing whether their traditional advantage in fundraising is more important than attempting to curtail Democratic exploitation of incumbency, especially among corporate PACs. They are philosophically troubled by the expanded role for government mandated by many reform proposals. Senate and House Republicans must choose between a possible partisan advantage resulting from reform and the expanded role for government which would come with public financing, spending limits and the like. Senate Republicans, unlike their House counterparts, do not face a serious problem with personality politics. In the past, however, they have been willing to carry the battle for their House Republican colleagues because of the more favorable rules and procedures in the Senate. Finally, House Democrats are not philosophically opposed to large scale reform, possibly including public financing and spending limits, but they seriously doubt that it is in their self-interest to change a system which has been working so well for them and their party. Moreover, in the wake of the Wright and Coelho bloodletting, they find working with Republicans on this issue to be difficult.

Prospects for Reform

Reform of congressional campaign finance can have many different meanings. Because the campaign finance system is so complex and there are so many different approaches to reform, it is possible for almost everyone to argue for some change in the system, without necessarily agreeing on the specific reforms. Congress has taken two different approaches to reform in the past. *Comprehensive reform* attempts to deal with the entire gamut of campaign finance issues—amounts of money raised and spent, regulatory and administrative concerns, etc. Examples of comprehensive reform efforts include the Federal Election Campaign Act of 1971, the amendments to the FECA of 1974, the Obey-Railsbach, Senate, and Carter administration proposals of 1977, and the Boren-Byrd bill of 1987. *Incremental reforms* do not presume to address the whole range of issues, but rather address a single issue or set of issues, or focus on "housekeeping" or reorganizing concerns. An example of the former would be the

Boren-Goldwater PAC limitation bill of 1986; examples of the latter would be the FECA amendments of 1976 and 1979.

Comprehensive Reform

Comprehensive reform encounters many more obstacles than does incremental reform. It is typically easier to build a legislative majority to change a few things than to revamp the entire system. Comprehensive reform requires a deeper commitment to change and a perception that something is seriously wrong. Scandal has most often created this perception. The Watergate scandal was such a catalyst for the 1974 amendments to the Federal Election Campaign Act—the most important and successful recent comprehensive reform episode.[18]

Reform follows major scandal because it creates pressure on Congress to regulate and restrain itself, and it overcomes the self-interest calculations arising for incumbents under the status quo by making support for change politically expedient. Other factors which are necessary to successful comprehensive reform efforts are bipartisan support, especially in the Senate, and a willing if not supportive president.[19]

There has not been a scandal of the proportions of Watergate concerning congressional campaign finance; and despite President Bush's interest in campaign finance reform, a bipartisan consensus on comprehensive reform appears remote. Nonetheless, many ethics and campaign finance-related controversies may make it difficult for Congress to ignore campaign finance reform. For these reasons only incremental or face-saving, partial reform appears likely in the near future.

Whether members actually would vote for comprehensive reform in Congress depends very much on what is being proposed. If reform means spending limits, with some form of partial public financing, Republicans are opposed and Senate Democrats are in favor. Even when public financing was removed from the 1987–88 Senate bill, and a mix of subsidies or incentives substituted, Senate Republicans still objected.[20] As for House Democrats, their views on spending limits and public financing have not been tested since those members of Congress expanded their fundraising in the 1982 election cycle. A final option to deal with costs and spending levels is the constitutional amendment approach; such an amendment has been repeatedly introduced by Senator Hollings (D-SC).

Political action committees are one of the most frequently

cited problems with the present congressional campaign finance system. Senate Democrats and Republicans supported PAC limitations in the 99th Congress. The rhetoric of Republican leaders in both houses, like that of President Bush, indicates that they would support reduction of the contribution limits of PACs or perhaps eliminating them altogether. Senate Democrats joined forces with Senate Republicans in supporting the Boren- Goldwater bill in 1986, but it is unclear whether they would support a stand-alone PAC limitation bill. House Democrats are almost certain to object to a PAC limitation bill that does not include spending limitations and other topics of concern to them.

The predictable result of a reduction in the PAC contribution limits, or the imposition of an aggregate candidate PAC receipts limit, will be increased use of independent expenditures by PACs. How Congress can respond to this consequence is limited by the *Buckley* decision, but legislation could include a requirement that independently-financed advertisements disclose the source of the sponsor and that the expenditure was independent of the candidates. Previous public financing bills have also included provisions whereby candidates could obtain public funds with which to respond to independent expenditures intended to help their opponents.

In addition to addressing the issues of public funding, PACs, and independent expenditures, comprehensive reform legislation will probably attempt to deal with the millionaire's loophole, and will require disclosure of soft money. Because the parts of the campaign finance system are so interconnected, it is hard to see reform in any one of these areas which would not include the others as well. Court rulings make it necessary to include public financing with spending limits; doing something about PAC contribution limits may also mean doing something about party and individual limits. Lowering PAC contribution limits or imposing an aggregate PAC receipts limit on candidates requires doing something about independent expenditures. But such comprehensive legislation provides something for almost everyone to disagree with and has led to partisan and cross-chamber stalemate in the past.

Incremental Reform Alternatives

Because of the barriers to comprehensive reform, Congress may pursue a more modest reform agenda. One approach that would draw attention away from the impasse over comprehensive congressional reform would be to reform the presidential campaign finance system by adjusting or eliminating the state by state primary election spending limitations and by eliminating or restricting the expenditure of soft money in presidential elections. Both of these issues have been widely discussed; neither touches upon the more proximate personal and partisan concerns of congressional campaign finance.

But there are incremental congressional campaign finance changes which Congress could consider if it chooses to do so. Here the agenda could include disclosure of soft money in congressional elections, changes in the structure and procedures of the Federal Election Commission, imposition of pricing requirements on broadcasters that would limit the costs of broadcast advertising, and adjustment of the individual contribution limits to inflation. None of these incremental reforms generate much excitement among members or external groups, however, and therefore they will more likely arise in the context of other reform bills.

One incremental approach which could become viable is "face- saving" reform. Here the concern is to improve the image of the Congress, and one way to do so would be to limit PACs. Other face-saving reforms include banning honoraria, abolishing the grandfather clause, restricting fundraising to the two year period of the election, not permitting carry-over funds from one election cycle to the next, and banning leadership PACs.

If comprehensive reform appears unlikely, incremental change faces serious obstacles of its own. Many incremental reforms are seen by members as benefiting one party at the other's expense. An aggregate PAC receipts limit for candidates, for instance, would be perceived by House Democrats as an attack on them. Similarly, Democrats in both Houses would resist raising the individual contribution limits because they believe that there are more well-to-do Republicans than Democrats. Restrictions on PACs and modifications of individual contribution limits are the types of incremental reforms which require parties to trade advantages. One party is not going to give up its advantage without the other party giving up something. This is why incremental reforms rarely can be considered separately, and why the consideration of incremental reforms often leads to more comprehensive reform packages. It is also doubtful that advocates of serious reform, in and out of Congress, will want to accept incremental reform, especially if it is designed to take the heat off Congress but not change things very much. Court rulings, the different reform agendas of the two parties and two houses, and the interrelated nature of the issues—all prompt more comprehensive approaches.

Conclusion

The prospects for campaign finance reform are paradoxical because of the politics of such reform. Incremental approaches may be inadequate, but comprehensive reforms are impracticable. There are strong incentives for Congress to change the way congressional campaigns are funded, but there are even stronger reasons to resist change. True, there is bipartisan interest, public and congressional concern about ethics issues, presidential support, and public pressure, exemplified by Common Cause. But would-be reformers also face the constraints of *Buckley*, the prospects of unintended consequences, and the institutional and partisan differences in Congress. Despite all the talk of reform, therefore, the most likely result is continued stalemate, with each party blaming the other for the lack of reform legislation. In the absence of a major scandal and strong public pressure for change, the philosophical and pragmatic objections to changing the campaign finance system make reform unlikely.

Any reform bill that passes is therefore likely to be mostly "face-saving". Such a modest reform could include, but is not limited to, abolishing honoraria, eliminating the grandfather clause, raising individual and party contribution limits while lowering limits for PACs, and requiring the disclosure of soft money receipts and expenditures by political parties. While such changes would in important ways improve the current system, they do not address the more fundamental problems nor are they likely to reduce the pressure for reform in the long run.

Notes

My research on Congressional campaign finance was greatly enriched by a year as an American Political Science Association Congressional Fellow, where I worked with Senator Robert Byrd (D-WV) on this and related issues. Subsequently, research on this topic has been supported by the Brookings Institution and the College of Family, Home and Social Sciences at BYU. I appreciate the granting of interviews by more than twenty participants and observers of congressional campaign finance, some more than once. Research assistance for this paper has been provided by Janna Brown, Kelleen Leishman, David Passey and York Faulkner. I appreciate the comments and suggestions provided by Don Norton.

1. *Buckley v. Valeo* 424 U.S. 1 (1976).
2. Commission on Executive, Legislative, and Judicial Salaries, *Fairness For Our Public Servants* (Washington, D.C., 1988).
3. Richard Conlon, "The Declining Role of Individual Contributions in Financing Congressional Campaigns," *Journal of Law and Politics* (Winter 1987): 467–98.
4. See FEC Advisory Opinion 1975-23 (December 3, 1975).
5. Barbara Hinckley, *Congressional Elections* (Washington, D.C.: Congressional Quarterly Press, 1981).
6. Gary C. Jacobson, *The Politics of Congressional Elections*, 2d ed. (Boston: Little, Brown, and Co., 1987), 53.
7. David R. Mayhew, *Congress: The Electoral Connection* (New Haven: Yale University Press, 1974).
8. Not only have virtually all House incumbents seeking reelection been successful in recent elections, but in 1988, 85% of the successful incumbents won with 60% or more of the vote.
9. Unless otherwise cited, this and any other information is the result of personal interviews conducted by the author.
10. Theodore J. Eismeier and Philip H. Pollock III. *Business, Money, and the Rise of Corporate PACs in American Elections* (New York: Quorum Books, 1988).
11. Gary C. Jacobson, *Money in Congressional Elections* (New Haven: Yale University Press, 1988); Donald Philip Green and Jonathan S. Krasno, *Salvation for the Spendthrift Incumbent: Re-estimating the Effects of Campaign Spending in House Elections.* Paper presented at the Annual Meeting of the American Political Science Association, 1988.
12. Chuck Alston and Janet Hook, "An Election Lesson: Money Can Be Dangerous," *Congressional Quarterly Weekly Report*, November 19, 1988, 3366–67.
13. Carol Matlack, "Lobbying Focus," *National Journal*, November 5, 1988, 2818.
14. Steven Symms, Statement, *Congressional Record*, June 10, 1987, S7914.
15. Byrd's aggressive pursuit of Republican Senator Pack-

wood during one cloture vote briefly raised the issue of personality.

16. Senator Mitch McConnell (R-KY) claimed to have enough votes to maintain a filibuster in the 101st Congress. Chuck Alston, "Campaign Finance Gridlock Likely to Persist," *Congressional Quarterly Weekly Report*, December 17, 1988, 3535–28.

17. Senate Republicans do express frustration with the way they were ignored in the early stages of the process in the 100th Congress.

18. David W. Adamany and George E. Agree, *Political Money: A Strategy for Campaign Financing in America* (Baltimore: Johns Hopkins University Press, 1975).

19. Robert E. Mutch, *Campaigns, Congress, and Courts: The Making of Federal Campaign Finance Law* (New York: Praeger Publishers, 1988); Herbert Alexander and Brian A. Haggerty, *Financing the 1984 Election* (Lexington, Mass.: Lexington Books, 1987).

20. It is unclear whether a system of subsidies and incentives which do not include public funding will withstand judicial challenge.

15

Conclusion: Reforms and Values

John R. Johannes and Margaret Latus Nugent

Clearly, there are serious problems with the congressional campaign finance system. What are we to do about them? The message of this entire volume, and especially in this concluding chapter, is that an explicit and abiding concern for values ought to inform the reform movement. Furthermore, in designing reforms, some values will have to be selected over others. That choice, needless to say, will be controversial.[1]

As our opening essay suggested, the concern for values applies at all levels of the political system. In selecting values and ordering them, it is crucial to bear in mind the hierarchy of levels within the political system and the need to distinguish among them. Congressional campaign finance serves the electoral system which, in turn, yields a Congress that is part of democratic government in the United States. The danger is that, in pursuing a particular value for the campaign financing system, the governmental system will be disrupted. Asserting a value—liberty or equality, for instance—as essential to campaign finance and then building a finance system around it does not necessarily mean that either our system of elections or, indeed, American democracy itself will be more free or equal. As several of the authors point out, for example, any realistic and affordable system of equal campaign funding will assuredly become an incumbent's protection act, thus undermining elections and denying accountability, effectiveness, and legitimacy to the broader institution (Congress) toward which the elections and the finance scheme are directed. Again, an emphasis on personal freedom to donate or spend as much as one wishes is bound to threaten broader values such as the effectiveness of Congress, representation, and legitimacy. Even merely promoting vigorous enforcement of campaign finance laws runs the risk of impinging on political liberty, if the FEC broadens its definition of political speech to allow for increased regulations.[2]

Conversely, minimizing an otherwise desirable value within an election funding scheme does not necessarily mean that that value will be weakened at the broader level of Congress. If a financing system without mass participation—one based, say, primarily on large contributions from wealthy individuals—allowed all candidates to get their messages across to the public and thus produced highly competitive elections, one would anticipate greater voter turnout and thus enhanced electoral participation. As Stephen E. Gottlieb reminded the conference participants:

> It is often necessary in systemic analysis to compromise the purity of subsystems for larger ends. There is good reason to expect that here......Nor will this be the first time that the people have been stripped of power in the name of electoral purity.[3]

In short, one must be careful not only in selecting values but in applying them at various levels. One does not want to miss the forest for the trees.

Obstacles to Ideal Reform

In the ideal world, each of the values we have been discussing would be maximized at the level of congressional activity, in general elections, during the recruitment and nomination process, and in the system of financing campaigns. But ideals are like the stars: we cannot grasp them; we can only use them as guides on our journey. Any attempt to realize each of the eight values in anything approaching a complete fashion—even at any one level of analysis—will fall short for several reasons. Many of these values conflict when put into practice. Implementation of any of them is often difficult. Often reforms that are recommended are based on assumptions and illusions. Finally, enacted policies usually contain loopholes and result in unintended consequences. The real world of reform is far from the ideal.

Conflicting Values

When the Supreme Court issued its ruling in *Buckley v. Valeo*, it implicitly settled the conflict between political equality and political liberty: rich Americans could spend as much as they wanted on their own campaigns or, via independent spending, on those of their favorite candidates. Equality at the level of contributions, by definition, took a back seat. The FECA itself grants a greater ability to contribute to candidates' campaign war-chests to political parties and PACs than to individuals. And all attempts to equalize spending between incumbents and challengers or to restrict the influence of PACs—see Maisel's and Grenzke's proposals for example—run smack into the value of freedom. Indeed, the tension between liberty and equality goes beyond campaign financing, for whenever political liberty allows people to obtain power it promotes inequality, whereas the more equality is extended, the more liberty is impinged upon.[4]

As we have seen, an emphasis on individual freedom can undermine other values as well. Accountability would suffer if large contributions could sway legislators, as Brooks Jackson, Susan Manes, and Ellen S. Miller[5] have argued (but recall Grenzke's rebuttal of these claims). Independent spending by PACs surely testifies to the nation's commitment to liberty, but unless there are provisions for timely and periodic reporting to voters and to those who finance the PACs, accountability is missing.

Accountability, likewise, cannot be an absolute value. David Adamany argued for limitations on out-of-district money as a way of enhancing accountability and, perhaps, legitimacy. Indeed, for many districts, such restrictions might bring about more equality, participation, and local representation. However, not only would such proposals interfere with the value of liberty, they would effectively weaken national representation and participation: Why shouldn't conservatives who have no hope of winning in a liberal district be able to help fund like-minded candidates in competitive districts where they have a chance to win? Do we, in the name of local accountability, deny effective representation to others? Further, limiting contributions primarily to local constituents clearly ties legislators to their districts but in so doing makes it more difficult for voters nationwide to penalize the party responsible for bad policy.

Difficult Implementation

As desirable as each of these values is, achieving them in any complete sense is bound to be frustrated by practical problems of implementation. And, of course, if laws cannot be implemented, they are not effective. When effectiveness is challenged, questions about legitimacy are not far behind. As Ruth Jones suggested, doubts about legitimacy may undercut participation. Finally, dwindling participation raises questions about representation, accountability, equality, and liberty.

Consider the example of participation. Is it possible to force or even entice citizens into participating in the democratic process via campaign finance? How? As Jones showed, reforms to date have had limited success.

Take another example, Professor Maisel's proposal to limit the importance of PACs by restricting their contributions to 25 percent of a congressional candidate's campaign fund. This proposal attempts to balance concerns of legitimacy, equality, liberty, accountability, representation, and competition. Assuming that the 25 percent limit makes sense, how is it to be implemented? Officially, at least, the amount spent by a candidate is not known until the FEC issues its reports months after the election is over.[6] Even candidates themselves do not know precisely how much they have spent until well past the November balloting date. How, then, can anyone know what 25 percent of that total is, and how can anyone know it far enough in advance to plan a funding strategy? Worse, what happens when a winner is caught having taken more than the allowed amount? Giving back several thousand, or even tens of thousands of dollars, is not all that difficult for an incumbent, unless it has to come out of his or her own pocket. Might we vacate someone's seat for a violation of this law?

Similarly, Maisel's proposal for an April 1 starting day for PAC contributions can be rendered useless. PACs could promise their money, but not deliver it, well before that date; and candidates could borrow against the certainty of eventual PAC funding. Within minutes after midnight, the dollars would begin flowing, mostly to incumbents. The provision could therefore be implemented in letter only, but not in reality or spirit.

The most obvious case concerns public funding. Adequate funding of congressional races would cost something on the order of $400,000 per district and perhaps $10,000,000 per Senate race. Can the federal government afford this? And how should such funding be made equal for districts and states with different populations and media market situations?

Assumptions and Illusions

Even before one debates the implementation of reform, one must consider its underlying assumptions. Too often, in debates on campaign finance reform—or almost any political reform, for that matter—certain propositions are accepted as true without having been tested. In the area of campaign finance, several are prominent. One is the proposition that somehow money from individuals is more pure and more democratic than money from groups; another is that money raised in small amounts from a large number of donors is somehow better than that from a few "fat cats." Accordingly, many conclude that reforms should encourage mass participation and constrain large donations from the wealthy and from "special interests." Such assumptions may be false and thus mislead reformers. For example, should not the cost, in terms of a legislator's time and energy, of raising money by means of small gifts from individuals be considered? Or why should we assume purity of motive on the part of individuals who give directly to campaigns but not on the part of those who give via PACs or parties? PAC contributions, after all, merely aggregate individual contributions.[7] Conversely, bundled funds of many smaller contributors, presented by a PAC, can easily exceed the clout of "fat cat" donors, given current restrictions. Nor is it obvious that congressmen would be less attentive to the views of PACs whose donations in fact come from many small individual gifts than to those representing "big money."

A variation on this theme of illusions concerns reform proposals based on faulty or incomplete data or partial analyses. Professor Maisel argued that surplus campaign funds—large "war-chests"—deter challengers. Thus, to increase competition, he concludes that such funds should be given to the FEC. The argument is perfectly logical *if* in fact surpluses deter. As Gary Jacobson pointed out, however, there is no evidence that the surpluses, as opposed to the incumbent's winning margins at the last election, legislative accomplishments, and/or reputation and popularity among constituents (which undoubtedly correlate highly with large surpluses), are the deterrent.[8] Perhaps, as Benjamin Ginsberg reminds us, our attention would be more profitably turned to gerrymandering, which he maintains is a leading cause of incumbency re-election rates.[9]

Unintended Consequences and Loopholes

As John McAdams has written, "a whole army of people who are very clever, quite ingenious, and more than a little devious will work to undermine any reform."[10] No better testimony is needed than the problems in FECA pointed out by Anne Bedlington and Candice Nelson. Closely related to loopholes is the proverbial problem of unintended, and often unforeseen, consequences. Professor Nelson, for example, indicated that lowering PAC contributions to candidates probably would lead to much larger independent expenditures. Almost everyone agrees that capping spending at any reasonable level would serve to weaken challengers and ensconce incumbents further. Linda L. Fowler, in commenting on Dr. Maisel's paper, noted that forbidding PACs to contribute to campaigns before April is especially likely to hurt challengers, who need not only the cash but the "imprimatur" that PACs can bestow. Candidates in open races might find themselves underfunded. She also noted that such a reform would have a particularly harsh impact on women, who have been especially dependent on early PAC donations.[11] Jacobson adds that such a move might enhance the power of PACs, since legislators in need of PAC money would hesitate to offend such groups until they know that they have ample funds. Worse, the rush for PAC funds would occur in late spring and summer of the second session when congressmen ought to be legislating, not chasing campaign money.[12] Congressional effectiveness therefore would suffer.

Other unfavorable consequences might result from the common preference for numerous small donations rather than a few large ones. Already we have seen that direct mail experts have become extremely important in campaign financing; the more emphasis is placed on lots of small donations, the greater the power of direct mail companies. Moreover, the unintended effect of restricting spending directly or indirectly will be that candidates must become more and more dependent on the media for "free" coverage—another transfer of political power.[13]

Finally, even if participation could be sharply increased, more harm than good could accrue to the system. If apathetic and generally uninformed—and perhaps cynical—citizens were stirred into action and contributed, might they become veritable "bulls in a china shop," making unreasonable demands on the system and expecting, by virtue of their contributions, quick and easy answers to problems that are intractable? Or, if extremists are mobilized by passionate direct mail appeals, might Congress become paralyzed by polarization on issues? What then happens if no policies are forthcoming?

These four sets of problems—conflict among values, difficulty of implementation, assumptions and illusions, and loopholes and unintended consequences—make very difficult the task of developing and legislating satisfactory campaign finance schemes. That does not mean, however, that reform efforts necessarily should be set aside in hopelessness. Rather, what is called for is a careful prioritizing and balancing of values, along with a humble and cautious approach to proposing specific reforms. No matter how clever one might be in designing proposals, none will be exempt from the hazards discussed above. Panaceas, in other words, simply do not exist.

An Ordering of Values

In establishing priorities among values and in specifying a sound campaign finance system, two principles must be borne in mind. One concerns the relationship of system to subsystem mentioned above: we are primarily interested in maximizing the basic values at the systemic level. Thus we are concerned that Congress as an institution—and through it American democracy more generally—be legitimate, effective, accountable, and representative, and that American citizens be able to participate in the congressional governing process in a free and reasonably equal fashion. Although other considerations bear on each of these values, we focus here on elections, and more specifically congressional campaign finance, as the proximate means to the end of good congressional government. Therefore, in addition to legitimacy, effectiveness, accountability, representation, liberty, and equality, we must also be concerned about promoting competition. Finally, it is imperative that campaign finance reforms at least not exacerbate existing problems in the congressional electoral process or in Congress itself.

The second principle is practicality: reforms must be reasonable and workable if they are to succeed. Unrealistically perfect proposals probably would not be enacted for several reasons. They might promote one value at the expense of others. They might be unacceptably complex, providing ample opportunities for loopholes, thereby undermining legitimacy. And they might too greatly threaten the existing political status quo. If enacted, they would cause innumerable problems of implementation and enforcement. Failures of implementation could become serious problems themselves.

Given these guidelines, we believe that, *systemically*, the key values are effectiveness, legitimacy, accountability, and, to a somewhat less extent, representation. Congress, above all, must be able to govern, it must be accepted as the legitimate authority, and, if the system is to be democratic, Congress must be accountable to the voters and representative of their needs and wants.

The values of participation, liberty, and equality are secondary in three senses. First, they simply are not as crucial as the core values in that *essentially* good democratic government can exist even if these values are somewhat constrained. The same cannot be said for the core values. Second, they are contributory to the core values: free and reasonably equal participation in government is the mechanism for accountability, representation, and legitimacy. Third, they are, strictly speaking, attributes less of Congress and the electoral process than of the voters. The value of competition falls in the middle. Competitive elections are important mechanisms for accountability, representation, and legitimacy. Unlike participation, liberty, and equality, competition is primarily applicable to the electoral system. The point of distinguishing between core and contributing values is to establish priorities. Corners may need to be cut a bit on the values of equality, liberty, and participation in order to save the core values. We likewise want to avoid reforms that would undermine these core values, even if they would help to realize the contributing values. Inevitably, we are forced to seek prudent trade-offs.

In the *Buckley* decision, the Supreme Court seemed to give privileged status to the value of liberty above all other values—an understandable bias given the First Amendment. Throughout this book, however, we have seen that other fundamental values are being undermined by a campaign finance system that gives primacy to the liberty of political spending. It is our view that the values most in need of support in the 1990s are legitimacy, accountability, and competition.[14]

That legitimacy is dwindling should be evident from the contributions of Susan Manes, Anne Bedlington, Frank Sorauf, Kenneth Gross, and Frank Reiche. Areas where accountability is seriously lacking were highlighted by Candice Nelson, David Adamany, and Clyde Wilcox. Of course, where accountability is absent, legitimacy eventually diminishes. Finally, Sandy Maisel and Janet Grenzke focused specifically on the importance of competition and remedies to foster more contested elections in order to enhance accountability and representation. The twist that Larry Sabato adds, with which we strongly agree, is that a vibrant system of political parties can play a key role in promoting these values. Party recruitment and support of candidates can promote competition. Meaningful party labels allow voters to hold individual Members of Congress as well as the party in power accountable for policies. Legitimacy is fostered in a system where special interest groups must work through the broader agendas of the parties. Even effectiveness is enhanced if greater control over the funding of legislators' campaigns gives party leaders more clout with which to lead.

Proposed Reforms

The reforms we offer (many of them gleaned from our contributors) build the foundation for systemic competition, accountability, and legitimacy from the ground up. Our cornerstone, in agreement with Sabato and Ginsberg, is elevating the political parties to pre-eminence. As long as disclosure is maintained, party spending in federal elections should be unlimited. (If one insists on limits in individual districts, the limits should be much higher than spending by individuals or PACs.) To encourage channeling funds through the parties, individuals should be allowed to give $60,000 per year to all party committees combined, and PACs could give an aggregate of $20,000 per year, with both limits indexed for inflation. As a further incentive, we see no harm in Sabato's suggestion of tax add-ons only for partisan contributions.[15]

While fostering party dominance in financing campaigns will not cure all ills and may fall prey to unintended consequences, we believe it can significantly improve competition, accountability, and legitimacy, as well as effectiveness and representation, without significantly hindering liberty, equality, and participation. Parties take a national perspective and could be expected to target money where it would most affect competition nationally—open seat districts where both parties had a chance and districts where incumbents were vulnerable. Parties are more representative and, usually, more accountable than PACs; if they have greater election finance influence, they could do more than PACs or individuals to enhance effectiveness in Congress. This does not deny either PACs or individuals the right of participation; they are merely encouraged to spend more via the parties. Finally, by channeling funds through an important integrating mechanism (the party), at least some of the danger of "special interest" influence on Members of Congress will be removed, enhancing legitimacy.

Competition

Apart from strengthening the parties and allowing them to

compete vigorously, how shall we foster competition? Let us first explain that we are not purists who insist on competitive elections in each congressional district biennially. Often incumbents are uncontested because they are doing their jobs and pleasing their constituents.[16] What is important is enough competitive elections nationwide to allow for the representation of national trends in public opinion. In addition, since Senate elections are usually hotly contested, our focus is on the House.

A means for funding a strong challenge in at least some House districts and for sustaining competition for open seats is needed. Equality of funding is not the remedy. In a world of independent expenditures, wealthy candidates, soft money, and all the other problems and loopholes, how could *real* equality be guaranteed? Even formal equality is unlikely; the only way incumbents would vote for such a measure would be to set the equal amounts so low that challengers in effect had no chance to win. Nor would schemes like Grenzke's—as clever as it is—be enacted. Indeed, her proposal may not be workable, since it involves continuing and periodic infusions of dollars, returns of dollars to the FEC, reports, and checking. What if one candidate claimed inaccuracy of reporting that led to inappropriately large amounts of funding being given to the other? What happens in the dozen or so states in which primaries are held in September? What if the incumbent holds off most of his or her fundraising and spending until very late in the race? In short, the scheme is cumbersome and fraught with difficulty.

Rather than equality, sufficiency is what reforms should seek. Incumbents, as Maisel and others have shown, have little problem raising as much as they want. The question becomes: how can we assure that there will be enough good challengers, and how can we provide them enough money? In an ideal world, there would be ample public funding, with challengers receiving more than incumbents, but no incumbent would ever vote for such a provision. The best that can be hoped for is that most challengers somehow be guaranteed *enough* money to mount a viable campaign. As long as they can do that, given the diminishing returns on incumbents' spending, we can expect generally competitive races.

We suggest that sufficiency can best be obtained by encouraging a diversity of funding sources—individuals, PACs, parties, and government—with an emphasis on the latter two. Public funding could contribute a flat grant, say $200,000, as a "grubstake" to each candidate, payable the day after the primary election.[17] Granted, this money would flow to those who do not need it as well as to those who do, and it will not be equally efficacious in all districts, but when public funding is at issue, equality must be honored if any legislation is to be enacted. This subsidy might not provide all that a challenger needs to mount a viable campaign, but, together with primary spending and additional general election spending, especially party support, challengers should be guaranteed enough funds to make their views known to a majority of voters. Ideally, one might want public funding for the primaries as well, but here the limits of practicality are reached.[18]

One source for some of this public money could be surplus campaign war-chests, as proposed by Professor Maisel. Although his proposal is predicated on the unproven premise that such large war-chests deter potentially strong challengers, banning carry-over campaign funds probably is harmless and certainly would appeal to those interested in more equality and "fair play."[19] If the already strapped Federal Election Campaign Fund proved inadequate for financing these "grubstakes" in addition to the presidential elections, the public treasury would have to be tapped. Granted, some may object to this burden on the budget while others may fear that this subsidy will fuel further spending in campaigns, but democratic elections are worth the investment.

The political parties would also provide essential support to competitive elections. In addition, if the lid on individual giving to candidates were raised from $1000 per election to $5,000, friends and supporters of the challenger, as well as enemies of the incumbent, could provide a substantial amount. Raising this limit and indexing it for inflation would put individuals on an equal footing with PACs, potentially diminishing the influence of special interests.

Accountability

Competitive elections are a central mechanism for holding representatives and, in the presence of a strong party system, Congress as a whole accountable. But, as David Adamany noted, candidates are not the only ones who need to be accountable. PACs are often inadequately accountable to their donors for how contributions are spent. We believe that requiring PACs to provide every donor with a biennial report on their political activities—candidates funded, amount given to each, and amount spent independently—along with an accounting of the proportion of funds spent on fundraising and administrative costs would disclose information donors can use to assess how well the PAC is serving their interests. Although PACs can manipulate such numbers to their advantage,[20] the reporting requirement might provide an incentive for them to attend more closely to the wishes of supporters. Granted, the cost of this report will only increase the overhead expenses of PACs, further decreasing the proportion of expenses they direct toward political activities. On the other hand, most PACs will simply seek to offset this effect by including another solicitation with their report! Sponsored PACs will also be more concerned about accountability to donors than to their corporate leadership if the practice of using treasury funds to cover administrative costs is ended. Equality among PACs of all types will also be enhanced thereby. In a similar vein, payroll deduction plans should require a renewed contributing decision each year or should be abolished, for they reduce the ability of donors to exercise the right of exit.

In the case of independent spending, the efficacy of schemes to compensate those adversely affected is questionable, but greater accountability to voters might offset the effect of such spending. We share the views of Adamany and Nelson that more prominent disclaimers featuring the actual name of the PAC or individual funding the independent ad should be required. We also believe accountability would be enhanced if the content of any independent expenditure were required to be disclosed by filing a transcript of any broadcast or a copy of any printed material with the FEC.

Soft money and personal PACs also raise accountability problems that deserve consideration. Despite Adamany's perceptive arguments about the technical difficulty of implementing the disclosure of soft money, this loophole has become such a blatant threat to legitimacy that some efforts at disclosure are essential. Imposing limits on soft money might be considered in the future, but, as such limits might be equally difficult to enforce and might lead to unforeseen unintended consequences, why not see whether disclosure alone is adequate to provide the necessary accountability? Like the use of soft money, member to member giving and personal PACs also threaten accountability and legitimacy. In addition, these practices can have a decentralizing influence in Congress and weaken party loyalty.[21] Personal PACs and contributions to other members from one's campaign committee should be banned because of their adverse impact on legitimacy and accountability. Of course, Members will likely continue to assist with fundraisers for each other and may engage in bundling, but the absence of a way to prevent such activities should not preclude addressing those problems which do have a remedy.

Legitimacy

Since competition and accountability both enhance the legitimacy of the electoral system as well as government at large, all of the previous reforms will serve this goal. In addition, some specific issues that directly undermine legitimacy need to be addressed: The ethics issues of honoraria and the grandfather clause are not directly related to campaign finance, but often their abolition is tied to consideration of other election funding reforms. In order to restore congressional credibility, these two questionable practices should be prohibited, and legislative trips should be required to meet the standards applied to executive branch trips, as Bedlington recommended.

To promote the legitimacy of our campaign finance system, we must also increase the effectiveness of the agency that oversees this system. The two- track system, use of Administrative Law Judges, random audits, and more severe and certain penalties that Gross recommends are one side of this coin. Reiche's call for a less partisan FEC should also be heeded. Since creating an odd numbered Commission might be politically impractical as well as unwise, the best way to promote objectivity and independence among Commissioners is to limit their service to one term. If an even numbered Commission is retained, Reiche's reforms to strengthen the Chair as an administrator also make sense. Finally, if a switch is made to biennial budgets, these must certainly be approved in non-election years or sensitivity to congressional pressure will only increase.

The most troubling issue facing those who wish to restore greater legitimacy is bundling. Eliminating all bundling will be practically impossible; however, the largest and most egregious bundling schemes can likely be ended by withdrawing the legitimation found in the Code of Federal Regulations. Furthermore, as the FEC has often undermined its credibility by tie votes on advisory opinions regarding bundling, outlawing it will also enhance the Commission's effectiveness and legitimacy. The inability to stop bundling is a serious concern, for several of the reforms we suggest might provide incentives for more bundling, and bundling weakens accountability and legitimacy.

Conclusion

Since campaign finance reform proposals are legion, generating new proposals or a revised blend of them is not the most significant contribution of this book. Furthermore, we are not so naive as to believe that our reform agenda is any less subject to the vicissitudes of public opinion or the political pressures of Congress than are other proposals. Nor can they totally avoid the realities of conflicting values, difficult implementation, assumptions and illusions, or loopholes and unintended consequences, although we have attempted to take these factors into consideration. Nonetheless, our goal is to illustrate how reforms should be evaluated in light of the most important issues at stake—the fundamental values of our representative democracy—and how a hierarchy of values can inform the design of concrete proposals. If this book challenges any reformers or students of reform to think more explicitly of balancing legitimacy, effectiveness, accountability, representation, participation, liberty, equality, and competition in the changes they recommend or implement, then we shall have succeeded.

Notes

1. The choices we present in this chapter reflect the authors' judgments and are not to be construed as the recommendations of the other contributors or of the Bradley Institute for Democracy and Public Values of Marquette University.

2. Michael J. Malbin, "Comments on the Prospects of Reform," remarks presented at the Conference on Campaign Finance Reform and Representative Democracy, Bradley Institute for Democracy and Public Values, Marquette University, Milwaukee, Wisconsin, February 24–25, 1989.

3. "What's the Point? Commentary on the Nelson, Bedlington and Sorauf Papers." Paper delivered at the Conference on Campaign Finance Reform and Representative Democracy.

4. J. Roland Pennock, *Democratic Political Theory* (Princeton, NJ: Princeton University Press, 1979), 46.

5. Brooks Jackson, "The Sullen Majority: Living on Bribes" and Ellen S. Miller, "Panelist Commentary," delivered at the

Conference on Campaign Finance Reform and Representative Democracy. See also the *Congress Speaks: A Survey of the 100th Congress* (Washington, D.C.: Center for Responsive Politics, 1988).

6. Benjamin L. Ginsberg, "Participation and Competition," presented at the Conference on Campaign Finance Reform and Representative Democracy.

7. Herbert E. Alexander, "The Case for PACs," a Public Affairs Monograph, 13–14.

8. "Comments on L. Sandy Maisel's 'Electoral Competition and the Incumbency Advantage in the U.S. House of Representatives' and Ruth S. Jones's 'Contributing as Participation: Mass or Elite Control?"' paper delivered at the Conference on Campaign Finance Reform and Representative Democracy.

9. "Participation and Competition." See also Richard Born, "Partisan Intentions and Election Day Realities in the Congressional Redistricting Process," *American Political Science Review* 79 (June, 1985), 305–319; Bruce E. Cain, "Assessing the Partisan Effects of Redistricting," *American Political Science Review* 79 (June, 1985), 320–333.

10. "Six Theses on Campaign Finance Reform," *Vox Pop Newsletter of Political Organizations and Parties*, vol. 8, issue 1, 6.

11. "Commentary on Participation and Competition," presented at the Conference on Campaign Finance Reform and Representative Democracy.

12. "Comments on L. Sandy Maisel's..."

13. McAdams, "Six Theses."

14. Although agreement was not unanimous, the priority of these values was also the consensus of the campaign finance scholars and practitioners who attended the Conference on Campaign Finance Reform and Representative Democracy.

15. Because we believe the avenues for soft money have already provided ample opportunities for corporate and labor funds to support the parties, however, we do not endorse Sabato's recommendation to allow disclosed but unlimited underwriting of the administrative, legal, and accounting costs of the parties.

16. John C. McAdams and John R. Johannes, "Determinants of Spending by House Challengers, 1974–84," *American Journal of Political Science* 31 (August, 1987), 457–483; Johannes and McAdams, "The Congressional Incumbency Effect: Is It Casework, Policy Compatibility, or Something Else?" *Amer-*

ican Journal of Political Science 25 (August, 1987), 512–542.

17. Gary C. Jacobson determined the point at which challengers match the recognition level of incumbents to require $150,000 in 1974 and $250,000 in 1984. See his *Money in Congressional Elections* (New Haven, CN: Yale University Press, 1980), 151–157 and *The Politics of Congressional Elections*, 2d ed. (Boston: Little, Brown and Company, 1987), 49–52, 122–124.

18. If one objects that primaries absolutely must be publicly and adequately funded if democracy is to reign, perhaps the solution is to look elsewhere for our nominations—a return to district caucuses and conventions.

19. One harm, however, would be that Members of Congress who have lost the security of war-chests will be preoccupied with fundraising throughout the next election cycle in order to replace these funds.

20. Margaret Latus Nugent, "When is a $1,000 Contribution Not a $1,000 Contribution?" *Election Politics: A Journal of Campaigns and Elections*, Vol. 3 No. 2 (Summer, 1986), 13–16.

21. Although the PACs of party leaders may provide them with incentives for party loyalty, our reforms to boost the coffers of the congressional and senatorial campaign committees should allow these organizations to replace candidate PACs as sources of funds and objects of loyalty.

About the Contributors

Dr. David Adamany is a graduate of Harvard College and the Harvard Law School, in addition to holding an M.S. and Ph.D. in Political Science from the University of Madison, where he served as Professor of Political Science. He served as Dean of the College of Wesleyan University and as Vice President for Academic Affairs at California State University, Long Beach, and at the University of Maryland. He is now President and Professor of Law and Political Science at Wayne State University. His numerous articles and books include *Campaign Finance in America*, and (with George E. Agree) *Political Money: A Strategy for Campaign Financing in America.*

Dr. Anne H. Bedlington, an Adjunct Professor in the Department of Government at American University, is studying the campaign finance behavior of PACs and parties. A graduate of Brown University, she received her Ph.D. from Cornell University in 1974. After serving as an Assistant Professor of Government at Smith College from 1973-1977, she worked at the Federal Election Commission as Supervisory Statistician until 1982. She has written, with Lynda W. Powell, "Money and Elections" in *Research in Micropolitics.*

Dr. Janet Grenzke is currently president of the polling firm, Abacus Associates. She teaches at the Graduate School of Political Management and has also taught at the College of the Holy Cross, Mount Holyoke College, the University of Massachusetts, and Smith College. She received her B.A., M.A., and Ph.D. from the University of Michigan, completing her doctorate in 1977. Since writing *Influence, Change, and the Legislative Process*, she has published several articles on money in congressional elections in scholarly journals.

Mr. Kenneth A. Gross is an attorney with Skadden, Arps, Slate, Meagher & Flom. As Associate General Counsel of the Federal Election Commission from 1980 to 1986, he headed the Enforcement Division in the Office of General Counsel and supervised the legal staff that advises the FEC's Audit Division. Mr. Gross is a co-chair of the Practicing Law Institute's seminar on "Funding Federal Political Campaigns—PACs, Corporate Political Activities and Lobbying Laws," Chair of the Political Campaign and Election Law Division of the Federal Bar Association, and a member of the George Washington University faculty. Since graduating from the University of Bridgeport in 1972 and receiving his J.D. from Emory University School of Law in 1975, he has published articles on campaign finance in the *Federal Bar Journal*, *Business Laws, Inc.*, and others, and authored the 1987–1988 supplement to *Federal Regulation of Campaign Finance and Political Activity.*

Dr. John R. Johannes, Dean of Marquette's College of Arts and Sciences, is the Chairman and original Director of the Bradley Institute for Democracy and Public Values. A graduate of Marquette University in 1966, he earned his Ph.D. in Government from Harvard University in 1970, after which he returned to Marquette to join its Political Science Department, which he chaired from 1980-1988, becoming dean thereafter. Author of *To Serve the People: Congress and Constituency Service* (1985), he has published articles in *The Journal of Politics*, *American Journal of Political Science*, *Polity*, *Western Political Science Quarterly*, *Legislative Studies Quarterly*, *Review of Politics*, and *Public Policy.*

Dr. Ruth S. Jones is Professor and Chair of the Department of Political Science, Arizona State University, Tempe, Arizona. During the 1989–90 academic year, she served as Loaned Executive on the Arizona Board of Regents. Since obtaining her Ph.D. from Georgetown University, she has held faculty positions at Kansas State University and the University of Missouri, St. Louis. Her research and publications focus on political participation, socialization and campaign finance. A frequent consultant to private, legislative and gubernatorial commissions addressing state-level campaign finance reform, her recent scholarly publications and presentations have established her as one of the noted experts on public campaign financing at the state and local levels.

Dr. David B. Magleby, Associate Professor of Political Science at Brigham Young University, has recently turned his attention to campaign finance after concentrating on ballot initiatives and direct democracy. He served as an American Political Science Association Congressional Fellow in 1986–1987. In addition to his numerous publications in scholarly journals he has written, with Candice J. Nelson, *The Money Chase: Financing Congressional Campaign Finance Reform.*

Dr. L. Sandy Maisel, Professor of Government at Colby College, is the Chair of the Legislative Studies Section of the American Political Science Association. A graduate of Harvard University, with a Ph.D. in Public Law and Government from Columbia University, Maisel has taught at Colby for eighteen years, with his years in Maine interrupted by visiting professorships and by a one year appointment as Task Force Director for the House of Representatives Commission on Administrative Review, the Obey Commission. A former candidate for Congress, Maisel is author of *From Obscurity to Oblivion: Running in the Congressional Primary*, and of *Parties and Elections in America: The Electoral Process*; editor and co-author of five other books on electoral politics; and author or co-author of a number of articles on electoral politics and campaign finance which have appeared in scholarly journals and books.

Ms. Susan Manes is the Vice President for Issue Development and also a registered lobbyist for Common Cause, overseeing the development of issue policy positions and investigative research. Manes joined Common Cause in 1985 as Senior Lobbyist specializing in campaign finance and tax reform issues, becoming Director of Issue Development in 1986, and assuming her current position in 1988.

Dr. Candice J. Nelson is a Visiting Fellow at The Brookings Institution. She graduated from Wheaton College in Massachusetts in 1971, received her M.A. from U.C.L.A. in 1974 and her Ph.D. from the University of California at Berkeley in 1982. From 1980 to 1986 she was an Assistant Professor in the Department of Government at Georgetown University. During 1986–1987 she was an American Political Science Association Congressional Fellow. She is co-author, with David Magleby, of *The Money Chase: Financing Congressional Campaign Finance Reform.*

Dr. Margaret Latus Nugent, Assistant Director of the Bradley Institute for Democracy and Public Values, graduated from Marquette University in 1979, receiving her M.A. in 1981 and her Ph.D. in 1984 from the Politics Department of Princeton. In addition to her dissertation on ideological PACs, she has authored several articles on ideological PACs, the New Christian Right, and federal election laws. At the Bradley Institute, she organized its conference on campaign finance reform and congressional elections, featuring most of the leading scholars and practitioners in the field.

Mr. Frank P. Reiche, currently an attorney, was appointed by President Carter to the Federal Election Commission in 1979, serving until 1985. He chaired the FEC in 1982. Prior to his experience at the federal level, he was appointed the first Chair of the New Jersey Election Law Enforcement Commission, a position he filled from 1973 until he joined the FEC.

Dr. Larry J. Sabato is a Professor of Government and Foreign Affairs at the University of Virginia. A former Rhodes Scholar and Danforth Fellow, he received his B.A. from the University of Virginia, and did his graduate work at Princeton and Oxford Universities. Sabato is the author of eleven books and monographs, including *The Rise of Political Consultants: New Ways of Winning Elections*, *PAC Power: Inside the World of Political Action Committees*, and *The Party's Just Begun: Shaping Political Parties for America's Future.*

Dr. Frank J. Sorauf has been in the Department of Political Science at the University of Minnesota since 1961, teaching previously at Penn State and the University of Arizona. He attended the University of Wisconsin in Milwaukee for two years, and after additional study at the University of Wisconsin in Madison and Harvard University, received his Ph.D. at Madison in 1953. At the University of Minnesota, he chaired the Political Science Department from 1966 to 1969 and served as the Dean of the College of Liberal Arts from 1973 to 1978. He is the author of *Party Politics in America*, *The Wall of Separation*, and *Money in American Elections*, as well as other books, essays, and scholarly articles.

Dr. Clyde Wilcox is an Assistant Professor of Government at Georgetown University. He received his B.A. from West Virginia University in 1975 and his Ph.D. from Ohio State in 1984. After a stint as a statistician for the Federal Election Commission, he taught at Union College for a year before moving to Georgetown in 1986. He has published articles in a number of political science, sociology, and history journals.

Index